THEOLOGY AND THE CHURCH

DUMITRU STANILOAE

THEOLOGY AND THE CHURCH

Translated by
ROBERT BARRINGER

Foreword by
JOHN MEYENDORFF

ST. VLADIMIR'S SEMINARY PRESS
CRESTWOOD, NEW YORK 10707
1980

BX
695
.S7

Library of Congress Cataloging in Publication Data

Staniloae, Dumitru.
    Theology and the church.

    Collection of essays from various Romanian journals.
    Includes bibliographical references.
    1. Orthodox Eastern Church, Romanian—Collected
works. 2. Theology—Collected works—20th century.
I. Title.
BX695.S7   230'.19498   80-19313
ISBN 0-913836-69-9

© Copyright 1980

by

ST. VLADIMIR'S SEMINARY PRESS

ISBN 0-913836-69-9

PRINTED IN THE UNITED STATES OF AMERICA
BY
ATHENS PRINTING COMPANY
461 Eighth Avenue
New York, NY 10001

Contents

Foreword

As Orthodox theology gradually discovers its mission and formulates its message in the midst of today's Western society, it is important that its roots be solidly planted. Indeed, there cannot be any tradition without continuity, consistency and also a "catholic" awareness of spiritual unity with those who are "doing theology" in situations different from our own.

In the past years, important works of several Orthodox theologians of Greek and Russian backgrounds were made accessible to English readers. However, with the exception of several minor essays published in periodicals, the writings of the most influential and creative Romanian theologian of our time, Fr. Dumitru Staniloae, have remained largely unknown. The publication of this book thus fills a noticeable gap by reminding Western readers of the dynamic reality of contemporary Romanian Orthodoxy. In a fresh and masterly synthesis, rooted in the tradition of the Greek Fathers and open to the legitimate concerns of contemporary Christian thought, the author gives a dynamic presentation of the Orthodox doctrine of the Trinity as the basis of ecclesiology and anthropology.

Born on November 16, 1903, in Vladeni, Dumitru Staniloae received his secondary education in Brasov. He studied theology in the capital of the then Romanian Bukovina, at the Faculty of Cernauti (1922-1927). As a student, he seems to have been primarily and legitimately preoccupied with the confessional identity of the Orthodox Church, which, in northern Romanian lands was just coming out of a long struggle for survival under Hungarian Roman Catholic or Protestant predominance. In the late 'twenties, Staniloae produced a licentiate thesis on "The Baptism of Children" and a doctoral dissertation on "The Life and Activity of Patriarch

Dositheos of Jerusalem." As is well known, Dositheos, the author of the "Orthodox Confession" of 1675, had formulated an Orthodox reaction to the Calvinistic Confession of Cyril Loukaris. After spending a relatively brief period abroad, where he studied in Athens, Munich, Berlin and Paris, Fr. Dumitru started a long career as professor, then rector, at the Theological Faculty of Sibiu, in Transylvania (1929-1946).

It was during that period that his thought and methodology underwent a substantial and creative change. In 1930, he published a Romanian translation of the then standard Greek textbook of dogmatic theology by Androutsos, an example of the basically Latinizing scholastic approach to theology. But soon he resolutely turned to the study of the Greek Fathers. In 1938, his short but extraordinarily well-documented book on *The Life and Teaching of St. Gregory Palamas* was published in Sibiu. Staniloae's vision of God and of man's destiny abandons Western concepts shaped during the Reformation and Counter-Reformation: he discovered the soteriology of the Greek Fathers, the dimensions of divino-human communion and cosmic transfiguration. His book on *Jesus Christ, or the Restoration of Man* (1943) conveyed this discovery to a wider readership and defined Staniloae as a pioneer of theological and spiritual revival in Romania.

The tragedy of World War II and the radical political changes which followed it could not but have had an influence on the theological activities of Fr. Staniloae. He dedicated most of his time to a silent manifesto about the "one thing necessary," and by 1948 produced the first three volumes of a Romanian (expanded and footnoted) version of the *Philocalia*, the well-known compendium of patristic writings on prayer. Thus his name became inseparably associated with the monastic revival of post-war Romania, although Fr. Dumitru himself was a married, secular priest.

In 1946, he began teaching at the Theological Institute of Bucharest, now separated from the State University. The particular situation of the Romanian Church under the new regime still allowed for the publication not only of several more volumes of the *Philocalia* but also of important theological works: *Orthodox Christian Doctrine* (1952) and the

Textbook of Dogmatic and Symbolic Theology (two volumes, 1958).

The years 1958-1962 present a five-year gap in Fr. Dumitru's biography, something which was not uncommon among many Christian leaders in that period not only in Romania but also in other Balkan countries and in the USSR. After his return to his teaching post at the Institute in 1963, Staniloae resumed his remarkably productive work. His major concern may appear paradoxical on the part of an editor of monastic texts: he strives to assume into a balanced Orthodox theology the totality of creation, the world and human culture. Frequently referring to St. Maximus the Confessor and his doctrine of the creative Logos, Staniloae always envisages the incarnation as the basis of the ultimate and total transfiguration of the cosmos. Occasionally criticized for his ontological optimism and his reluctance to reflect upon the inner brokenness of creation as a result of the Fall, Fr. Staniloae remains, by the example of his life and the perseverance of his witness, a theologian of hope. Applying the same positive approach to the issue of the relationship between Orthodoxy and Western Christianity, he also presents the truth of his convictions — uncompromisingly — as a liberating solution for all rather than as judgment upon others.

For almost half a century in Romania, Staniloae has fought against a routine scholasticism which would replace substance and imagination with empty academic self-sufficiency. He has done so in the name of a truly "catholic" and dynamic Orthodoxy. He is indeed a man of the Church, and deserves to be heard everywhere.

—*John Meyendorff*

CHAPTER I

Trinitarian Relations
and
The Life of The Church*

Ecclesiology is the central theme of the ecumenical movement. The Christian world's quest for unity is one with its quest for the Church; Christian unity means the Church, a Church in which all Christians wish to see themselves united. All who work for Christian unity must ask themselves therefore what kind of unity this is to be, or, in other words, what nature must the Church have so that she may correspond to God's plan for her and yet at the same time be the expression of the broadest and freest but also the closest fraternal union of all Christian men and women.

It is the Protestant world which is searching most assiduously for this unity which is the Church. But the unity and the Church which Catholicism offers do not attract the Protestant world because the unity and the Church which it is seeking cannot be marked by the hindering of personal freedom and diversity.

Protestants are looking for the signs of a Church which is fully satisfying, which transcends their own individualist form of Christianity. Catholics too will do the same when once they come to recognize certain deficiencies in their own ecclesiology.

Whether they are or are not acquainted in any detail with the Orthodox Church, we note with pleasant surprise that

---

* Originally published in Romanian in *Ortodoxia* 16 (1964), 503-525.

as often as some one or other group of these Christians sketch-
es the image of the Church that it is seeking, the result,
in principle, usually resembles Orthodox ecclesiology, and
even at times the concrete form of the present-day Orthodox
Church. Catholics aspire to the "sobornic" liberty of the Orthodox, and Protestants to their communitarian unity, while
both groups consider that what they are seeking resembles
most closely the form of ecclesial life which flourished in the
earliest Church. It is obvious however that both groups also
believe they can reach this true Church by penetrating more
deeply into the very roots of their own form of Christianity.
Nevertheless, as a concrete model to guide them in this
search into the depths of their own Christian experience or
as a confirmation of what they find there, they have before
them the essential characteristics of Orthodox ecclesiology.

In order to encourage the use of Orthodox ecclesiology
by the many Catholic and Protestant theologians who consider
it to be the nearest approximation to the ecclesiology they
are seeking, Orthodox strive to penetrate deeper themselves
into the interpretation of their own ecclesiology, firstly, by
indicating the presence of those dimensions for which the
contemporary ecumenical perspective is searching, and secondly, by pointing out that these dimensions represent potentialities that could in fact be realized in a form adapted to
the Church's contemporary mode of understanding, and thus
become the expression of a united Christianity.

The present study attempts to make a partial contribution
in this direction.

* * *

A unity such as the one we have sketched can exist only
as a gift in Christ, and Christ is present only through the
Spirit. Now it is a common observation of Western theologians that the life of Orthodox Christians bears the seal of a
wholly remarkable feeling for the presence and the activity
of the Holy Spirit. And it is this which gives to the Orthodox
Church a note of unity in liberty that is unknown in either
Catholic or Protestant ecclesiology. In a paper read at the

World Conference of the Commission on Faith and Order of the World Council of Churches held in Montreal in July of 1963, Professor Roger Mehl said: "It seems to us that the refusal of the Orthodox Church [to recognize papal primacy] springs from an original conception of the relations between ecclesiology and pneumatology; that the exemplary seriousness with which Orthodoxy has always considered the doctrine of the Holy Spirit, the action of the Spirit in the Church, has preserved it from the pitfalls of an abstract legalism. In our encounters we must ask ourselves — after elucidating the relations between Christ and the Church — what is the place of the Holy Spirit in ecclesiology as a whole. The Churches of the Reformation must realize the fact that the theology of the 16th century did not devote sufficient consideration to the pneumatological problem . . ." [1]

The lack of understanding of the pneumatological aspect of the Church in Catholicism has been illustrated recently by Pope Paul VI both in his opening address at the second session of the Second Vatican Council (29 September 1963) and in his encyclical *Ecclesiam Suam* of 6 August 1964. In both places it is only in function of Christ that the Pope describes the Church and calls for her renewal. We can see today in this predominant Christologism, which finds its natural expression in a "filioquism" subordinating the Holy Spirit to the Father and the Son, the root cause of the exaggeratedly institutional character of the Roman Catholic Church. [2]

The Orthodox theologian Nikos Nissiotis says: "The Roman neglect of the Holy Spirit is more evident than ever before; the schema *De Ecclesia*, though it begins with a trinitarian basis and by accepting the mystery of the Church, proceeds in its systematic exposition to overlook both things. The Holy Spirit, once mentioned, is entirely forgotten throughout the rest of the text. I do not mean by this remark that he is simply not mentioned, but the spirit that governs the schema and the Vatican Council as a whole shows a lack of consistent teaching about the Holy Spirit. In this way its right christological basis becomes in the end christomonism which is quite inflexible in the discussion of the particular controversial issues of ecclesiology. Thus the concepts of the hierarchy and

the People of God, as well as the royal priesthood, are thought
out on a sociological and juridical rather than a charismatic
basis. The lines of succession Christ — Peter — Pope, and
Christ — the Eleven — bishops become the inflexible *de jure
divino* structure of a hierarchical institution which is obliged
afterwards to set definite limits to the one Church, taking as
criterion, not the wholeness of the sacramental charismatic
life of the Church, but the discipline and order *sub Pontifice
Romano."* [3]

To this institutionalism Protestants oppose an individualist and anarchical experience which some represent as the
fruit of the Holy Spirit (though it surely cannot be this, for
the Spirit is always the Spirit of the community: 1 Cor 12),
and others as an expression of an accentuated but isolated
union with Christ which, inasmuch as it is incompatible with
the restraints of institution or even of community, does away
with all such restraints.

In the Orthodox Church preoccupation with Christ has
not only been kept in balance by a similar preoccupation with
the Holy Spirit, but it has always been the Orthodox judgement that union with Christ can be lived only in the Holy
Spirit, and that the experience of being in the Holy Spirit
is nothing other than union with Christ. The more vividly one
knows Christ and the more one comes to live in him, the more
one knows and lives in the Holy Spirit. The more spiritual a
life one leads the more lovingly is one bound to Christ. By
its own uninterrupted experience Orthodoxy confirms the
words of St. Paul: "No one can say 'Jesus is Lord' except by
the Holy Spirit." (1 Cor 12:3).

In this perspective we might say that from the Orthodox
point of view the exclusive concentration on Christ in Western
Christianity does not in fact suggest the presence of an ever
more intimate union with him, for this union is not affirmed
in the Holy Spirit. The proof is that Catholicism treats Christ
as if he were removed from the Church — hence the need to
have a vicar for him — while in Protestantism Christ is
similarly thought to remain at a distance from the faithful —
however movingly this is expressed — for he has no effect on
the conduct of their lives or on their ecclesial union. In both

traditions Christ is at a distance, because both have for all practical purposes forgotten the Holy Spirit through whom Christ is present. And the Church as the Body of Christ exists effectively where the Holy Spirit is present.

The indissoluble union between Christ and the Holy Spirit who truly constitutes the Church and sustains the life of the Christian within the Church has its profound roots in that indissoluble union which according to Orthodox teaching exists between them within the sphere of their inner trinitarian relations. We shall try to demonstrate this in what follows.

Relations Between The Son And The Holy Spirit

In the patristic period the problem of the relation between the Son and the Holy Spirit was clearly stated, but it found no systematic explanation and assumed a very general form in the proposition used by certain Fathers: "The Holy Spirit is (comes forth, proceeds) from the Father through the Son."

After the ninth century, however, the problem of the procession of the Holy Spirit became one of the polemical themes separating East and West, and the West reproached the East with the fact that they recognized no relationship between the Son and the Spirit, for they did not admit the procession of the Holy Spirit from the Son as well as from the Father while the West recognized a relation of the origin of the one from the other (*oppositionis relatio*). In response Byzantine theologians attempted to show that on the one hand a relationship of origin between Son and Holy Spirit was not necessary, and that on the other hand there *did* exist a certain relationship which distinguished Son and Holy Spirit as persons.

In particular three Byzantine theologians from the period after 1054 tried each in his own fashion to resolve the problem of the direct relationship between the Son and the Holy Spirit by explaining the Fathers' expression "through the Son". These were Gregory of Cyprus (Patriarch of Constantinople 1283-1289), Saint Gregory Palamas (died 1359), and Joseph Bryennios who flourished at the beginning of the 15th century.

The ideas of the first two of these men have been used by a number of Russian theologians in some lectures given in 1950 in the context of a Catholic-Orthodox dialogue on the theme of the procession of the Holy Spirit.[4] In his presentation of these interesting papers, Vladimir Rodzianko, then priest of the Serbian parish in London, says that the purpose was to show that there exists a certain eternal relationship between Son and Holy Spirit, and that this eternal relationship is the basis of the temporal "mission" whereby the Son sends the Spirit into the world. Thus the Orthodox theologians attempted to build a bridge between the two "theological schools" of East and West. Rodzianko claims however that the bridge was not sufficiently well constructed and so he attempts to add his own contribution to buttress it.[5]

We will indicate here how each of the three abovementioned Byzantine theologians views the relationship between the Son and the Holy Spirit, and try to show also what implications these views have in the area of ecclesiology. It is perhaps worth noting here that as far as we know the thought of Joseph Bryennios has not been exploited by any of the more recent theologians.

The Relation Of The Son To The Holy Spirit In The Thought Of Gregory Of Cyprus

Patriarch Gregory of Cyprus saw himself under the obligation of explaining the expression "through the Son" in order to pose a counter-weight to the Catholicising distortion of this phrase which was then being spread abroad by the unionist Patriarch John Bekkos and others among his adherents. These men were eager to achieve the union of the Orthodox and Catholic Churches at the Council of Lyons (1274), and by identifying the preposition "through" (διά) with the preposition "from" (ἐκ), they taught that "the Father is the cause of the Spirit through the Son ... therefore the Son appears as cause together with the Father, contributing with the Father to the existence of the Spirit." [6]

Moreover, because Bekkos and the others in the defence of their thesis referred to the expression of St. John of Damascus, "the Holy Spirit proceeds from the Father through the Son", Gregory of Cyprus declared that the Damascene did not mean by this that the Father gives existence to the Spirit through the Son, but that he clearly wished to represent the manifestation (τὴν φανέρωσιν) of the Spirit through the Son who has his existence from the Father. Otherwise he would not have referred in the very same chapter to God the Father alone as the source of being in the Trinity,[7] and thus, by his use of the word "alone", deprive the other hypostases of any causal character, nor would he have said in another chapter, "We speak of the Holy Spirit as belonging to the Son, but we do not say he is from the Son." [8]

The particular idea of Gregory of Cyprus is that the Holy Spirit is manifested through the Son not only temporally but also eternally: the "manifestation" or "shining forth" of the Spirit through the Son represents the eternal relation between them. According to Gregory, the expression "through the Son" used by some of the Fathers "indicates the irradiation and manifestation of the Spirit through the Son, for, in a manner known to all, the Paraclete shines forth and is manifested eternally through the Son, like light from the sun through a ray. The phrase 'through the Son' points also to the fact that the Spirit is led forth and given and sent down upon us through the Son, but not that the Spirit subsists (ὑφίσταται) through and from the Son or that he receives his existence through and from him." [9]

The movement of the Spirit towards existence (the procession) which is from the Father and the movement towards manifestation or illumination which is from the Son are neither to be confused nor separated. The latter continues the former, or, better, as Gregory says, concurs with the former and is conceived together with it (τὴν διὰ τοῦ Υἱοῦ ἀΐδιον ἔκφανσιν, συντρέχουσαν καὶ συνεπινοουμένην τῇ ἐκ Πατρὸς αὐτοῦ εἰς τὸ εἶναι προόδῳ).[10] According to Gregory, these two acts are so united and the latter (the illumination through the Son) has its cause so much in the former (the procession from the Father) that he even used certain common terms for both of them. Thus he says that the Father is the One who sends forth (προβολεύς) the Spirit in the sense that he causes him to proceed and to shine forth also through the Son. Through this emission (sending forth) or "projection" (προβολή) Gregory understands the double but inseparable act of the procession of the Holy Spirit from the Father and his shining forth through the Son. The possibility of the latter act depends however upon the procession from the Father.[11]

In the same way by the word πρόοδος (progress, movement forward, advance, launching out), which expresses as an act of the Spirit what προβολή indicates as an act of the Father upon the Spirit, Gregory points as much to the motion of the Spirit forward from the Father towards existence as to his progress from the Son towards illumination. Between these two parts of the same act there is a very close connexion, for the outward movement forward to illumination makes present the movement towards existence (τὴν γὰρ εἰς ἔκφανσιν ἐνταῦθα καὶ ἔκλαμψιν ... τὴν εἰς τὸ εἶναι πρόοδον ... παρίστησιν).[12]

This use of common terms (προβολή, πρόοδος) for an act with two parts: procession and illumination, caused the Metropolitan of Ephesus John Cheilas to accuse Gregory of confusing the Spirit's movement towards illumination through the Son with the idea of procession through the Son, and of conceiving this latter as a prolongation of the procession from the Father according to the Catholic model. "The God-bearing Fathers always conceive of and use the term 'progress' (τὴν πρόοδον) with reference only to the most Holy Spirit and only in order to describe his coming into existence, similar to the terms 'procession' and 'projection' (προβολή). Hence any who distort the meaning of this word and write in a dogmatic tone that in some places in the writings of the saints this word describes the coming into existence but in other places the manifestation and illumination [of the Holy Spirit], must be considered falsifiers of the true doctrine."[13]

Gregory rejected this accusation and demonstrated that he was not confusing the illumination of the Spirit through the Son with his procession through the Son. According to Gregory this illumination of the Spirit through the Son does not mean his coming into existence as it does in the procession which, accordingly, he attributes to the Father alone. Nevertheless, if Gregory intended to make a distinction between the eternal shining forth of the Spirit through the Son and his coming into existence through the Father, his choice of certain common terms for both (προβολή, πρόοδος) was not a very happy one, as it made it possible for some to confuse the two. Even less felicitous was his likening of the relation between the Spirit and the Son with the relation between light and a ray. In fact he said: "There coincides with the sending forth into existence of the same Spirit from the Father the manifestation of the same Spirit through the Son, just as in the shining forth of the sun's light the coming forth to the light coincides with the manifestation of the light through a ray." [14] He specifies, it is true, that the Spirit "proceeding and subsisting from the Father from whom the Son also is begotten, comes forward (προέρχεται) and shines forth through the Son, while having his complete subsistence from the Father himself. This occurs in the way in which it is also said of the light that it is from the sun through the ray, having the source and cause of its existence in the sun as its natural principle, but passing through (διϊόν) and coming forward (προϊόν) to the light and shining forth through the ray, from which the light receives neither existence nor being (οὐχ ὕπαρξις, οὐδ' οὐσίωσις), but only comes forward to perception through it, as has been said. In no way does the light have the principle of its existence through or from the ray. This comes clearly and immediately from the sun, and the sun is also the origin of the ray itself through which the light is manifested when it comes into (προϊόν) our perception." [15]

But in fact the ray and the light are one thing, the ray being only a form of light, or the light only the substance of the ray. If, however, we are able to separate the light from the ray, it then becomes difficult to distinguish clearly this separation of light and ray from the light's coming into existence from the substance of the ray as a particular entity.

Of the thought of Gregory of Cyprus we need then retain only the following: firstly, the affirmation of an eternal relation between the Spirit and the Son which is the illumination or shining forth of the Spirit through the Son and, as such, is distinguishable from the procession or coming into existence of the Spirit from the Father; secondly, the assertion of a very close connexion between the begetting of the Son by the Father and, on the one hand, the procession of the Spirit from the Father, together with, on the other hand, the shining forth of the Spirit from the Son; and thirdly, the affirmation of a connexion between the eternal shining forth of the Spirit through the Son and the sending of the Spirit into the world by the Son. New efforts are required however if these points in the thought of Gregory are to be explained satisfactorily.

Before we attempt any such explanation we should not neglect to mention that according to Gregory the shining forth of the Spirit through the Son is not the expression of the identity of essence between Son and Spirit but the expression of a personal relation. If it were true that this relation resulted exclusively from their essential identity, it would no longer distinguish the Spirit from the Son and the Father, because there could then be a shining forth of the Spirit from the Father, or of the Son from the Spirit and the Father, or of the Father from the Spirit and the Son.[16] Gregory is categorical about this, however, and appeals to St. Gregory of Nyssa for support: "Now Gregory of Nyssa adds to the individual personal attributes of the Spirit which distinguish him from Father and Son the fact that he is manifested and shines forth through the Son."[17] He goes on to say: "If, therefore, you never know the Paraclete apart from his individual personal attributes (τῶν ἑαυτοῦ ἰδιωμάτων χωρίς), you will not deny, if you are sensible, that his manifestation through the Son as a proper characteristic of himself as eternal (ὡς ἴδιον αὐτῷ τῷ ἀϊδίῳ προσόν) is itself also eternal."[18] To deny the Holy Spirit his manifestation through the Son means to deprive him not of an attribute common to Father, Son and

Spirit and hence of an essential attribute or relation, but to deprive him of an attribute and relation which is personal and specific. And just as any personal attribute within the Trinity points to a direct bipersonal relation, so the shining forth of the Spirit through the Son also indicates a direct bipersonal relation between these two persons. Not only does the Spirit receive another personal attribute (besides procession from the Father) in his shining forth from the Son, but the Son also receives a new personal attribute besides his generation from the Father. The Spirit shines forth through the Son not simply as a divine essence but precisely as the Holy Spirit; and the Son manifests the Spirit in turn in his character as Son, also differentiating himself as Son in this way. Thus we cannot think of the Holy Spirit without thinking of the Son through whom the Spirit shines forth. Nor can we think of the Son without the Spirit whom the Son manifests. Just as it belongs to the Holy Spirit not only to proceed from the Father but also to be made manifest through the Son, so it belongs to the Son not only to be begotten of the Father but also to manifest the Spirit who shines forth through him. Or as St. Basil the Great says: "The Son is he who makes known (γνωρίζων) through himself and with himself the Spirit who proceeds from the Father." [19] And the Holy Spirit, says Gregory of Cyprus, has as a characteristic sign of his individual hypostatic attribute the fact that he makes himself known with the Son and that together with the Son he has his subsistence from the Father. [20]

Let us now however attempt another explanation of the "shining forth" of the Holy Spirit through the Son. It is our belief that such an explanation must begin with that "coming to rest of the Holy Spirit" upon the Incarnate Son which is spoken of by both the New Testament writings and by the Fathers of the Church. From this starting point we move to the conclusion that the same "resting" of the Spirit upon the eternal Son takes place before his incarnation. For when the Son becomes man, he receives as man what he has as God. "Rest" cannot be explained as the opposite of weariness — for the Spirit cannot grow weary — but as an "end to all further departing", as an "abiding" in the Son. This meaning

is implied also by the word "procession" which does not mean
a simple going forth of someone from another, as for example in the case of one being born; it means rather a setting
forth from somewhere towards a definite goal, a departure
from one person in order to reach another (ἐκπορεύομαι =
I set out on the way in order to arrive somewhere). When the
Spirit proceeds from the Father he sets out towards the Son;
the Son is the goal at which he will stop. "Therefore we must
ask ourselves", says St. Gregory Palamas, "when the Spirit
goes forth from the Father in a movement we neither see nor
understand: can we say that, according to the evidence of
Scripture, he has someone in whom he can rest in a manner
which befits God? If we search the Scriptures we discover
that the Father of the Only Begotten God has seen fit to disclose this very thing to John the Precursor and Baptizer of the
Lord who said: 'I myself did not know him; but he who sent
me to baptise with water said to me, 'He on whom you see
the Spirit descend and remain, this is He who baptizes with
the Holy Spirit.' (Jn 1:33). . . . And that no one may think
that these things were spoken and accomplished by the Father
with reference to the Incarnation of the Son . . . let us listen
to the divine Damascene who writes in the eighth of the Dogmatic Chapters: 'We believe also in the Holy Spirit who proceeds from the Father and rests in the Son.' " [21]

This procession of the Spirit from the Father towards the
Son in whom he "comes to rest", "abides", "remains", has a
profound and double significance. Firstly, it means that the
Spirit does not take his origin also from the Son, for this
would mean that the Spirit goes forth from the Son instead
of coming to rest in him. Were it true that the Spirit goes forth
also from the Son, the Godhead would be capable of an infinite "unwinding", for just as the Son, though himself caused,
would become a cause in his turn, so also there would be
nothing to prevent that the Spirit, caused by the Son, would
himself be able to become a cause and so on indefinitely. But
in the Godhead only the uncaused Person — the Father —
is cause; each of the other Persons who have come forth,
comes forth immediately from the ultimate and absolute
cause, having communion with that cause and partaking of

it. Otherwise we would have a progressive watering-down of the divinity, an endless chain of Persons each further removed from the uncaused cause and hence participating in him to a correspondingly lesser degree.

In the second place, if the procession of the Spirit from the Father were not to have as its goal his "rest" in the Son, but instead a separate existence as Person alongside that of the Son, there would again be no compelling reason why still other Persons might not arise from the Father, having their existence alongside Son and Spirit and so on indefinitely. Is to be three in number a sufficient reason in itself why the divinity should not multiply continuously?

But because the Holy Spirit proceeds from the Father and comes to rest in the Son, and therefore is not begotten like the Son, an endless multiplication of the divinity is avoided, and a certain internal unity is achieved, for not only is the unity between Son and Spirit made manifest in this way, but that between the Father and the Son is also strengthened. The Spirit proceeding from the Father comes to rest in the Son who is begotten of the Father, and, like an arch, unites Father and Son in one embrace. Thus a unity among the three Persons is manifested which is distinct from their unity of essence. If there exists nothing between the two to unite them, the number two represents separation. The duality which appears at the begetting of the Son by the Father is reduced to a unity by the procession of the Spirit. St. Gregory Nazianzen says: "A complete trinity [is formed] from three perfect elements, for the monad is in motion because of its richness, but it transcends the dyad for it is beyond [the distinction of] matter and form from which bodies arise, and defines itself as trinity (for this is the first [stage] of synthesis beyond duality) in order that the divinity be neither too restricted nor overflow to infinity. For the first of these shows a lack of generosity and the latter a lack of order. The first is wholly Jewish, the second pagan and polytheist." [22] The third in the Trinity does not signify a further extension of the Godhead, but rather a bond between the two, and represents the perfection of the unity of the many. The Father causes the Spirit to proceed in order to unite himself with the Son and because

he has begotten the Son. This would be a possible interpretation of the formula of St. John of Damascus: the Father
causes the Spirit to proceed through the Son, that is, because
of the fact of the existence of the Son.

We will not pursue all the consequences of the relation
of Spirit and Son here, but only those which concern soteriology and ecclesiology in general.

The "rest" or "abiding" of the Spirit upon the Son or in
the Son signifies not only the union of the one with the other
in the order of eternity but also their union in the temporal
order. The presence of Christ is always marked by the Spirit
resting upon him, and the presence of the Spirit means the
presence of Christ upon whom he rests. The Spirit is the one
who shines forth, that is, the one who stands out over Christ
like a light, and Christ is he who has led us into the light of
the Spirit. If it was only at Pentecost that the Apostles fully
recognized Christ as God, that was because it was only in
the Ascension of Christ that the Spirit which rests upon him
and shines forth from him as God was poured out upon him
completely as man.

This is why Scripture never speaks of seeing the Spirit
for his own sake, nor even of the vision of the Spirit in general — apart from the times when he showed himself symbolically as a dove, as tongues of fire, or as a cloud — but instead
speaks only of seeing Christ "in the Spirit". Scripture speaks
of "receiving" the Spirit, but not of seeing the Spirit. For the
Spirit is only the spiritual light in which Christ is seen, as
objects are seen in material light. And just as we cannot say
that we see the material light, only other objects in it, in the
same way we do not say that we "see" the Spirit, but Christ
in or through the Spirit. The Spirit is the milieu in which
Christ is "seen", the "means" by which we come to know him
and to lay hold of and experience the presence of Christ.
As such, the Spirit enters the system of our perceptual subjectivity. He is the power which imprints itself upon and
elevates this subjectivity. In this sense the Spirit also "shines
forth" through spiritual men, the saints.

Therefore, although there is no knowledge or experience
of Christ as God apart from the Spirit, neither is there any

experience of the Spirit by himself in isolation for he is only the means of supernatural perception.[23] If the Spirit is the means and the intensity of all knowledge of the transcendent Godhead, Christ as the Logos is the structured content of this knowledge.[24] Where this content is wanting the soul becomes lost in its own structures, in an inconsistent and disordered enthusiasm, and this has indeed happened with so many anarchical "experiences" and so many enthusiastic but destructive currents within Christianity which cannot be said ever to have possessed the Holy Spirit truly if it is true that the Spirit is not present apart from Christ. Moreover where the Spirit is absent as the means by which we come to the living knowledge of Christ, Christ becomes the object of a frigid theoretical science, of definitions put together from memorized citations and formulae.

The Holy Spirit is experienced as a kind of fluid spiritual atmosphere which rises within us and raises us up towards God in an ever greater understanding and love.[25] As such the Spirit can neither stand still nor can we take hold of him. He is like the air, like a fragrance which changes at every moment, like the soul itself for he is the supreme model of the soul. St. Cyril of Alexandria described the whole life of the saints as a perfume ascending to God. Such a life is steeped in the activity of the Holy Spirit. Just as in the Trinity the Spirit subsists in a continuous procession from the loving Father towards the beloved Son, and in a loving "irradiation" from the Son towards the Father, so within us the Spirit exists within a ceaseless flowing of the Son towards us and of ourselves towards the Son from whom we receive the Spirit. He is this flowing current of the love of the Son or, more exactly, of the Father, returning from us also as a current which is united with our loving affection for the Son or, more precisely, for the Father. He moves in us and from us in the way that light or perfume or the air moves, that is, without our being aware of him. "Let us not try to hinder the flight of the Dove towards the Lamb. It would be a temptation to interrupt this flight, to hold the Dove in our hands and feast our eyes as we please, to caress it, to study it carefully, to take our delight in contemplating it." The activity of the Spirit within us is

such as to make us cry out: "O my dove, in the clefts of the
rock, in the covert of the cliff, let me see your face, let me hear
your voice, for your voice is sweet, and your face is comely."
(Song 2:14)[26]

The second consequence which follows upon this "resting"
or "abiding" of the Spirit in the Son (apart from their indissoluble union with us) is that when the faithful receive
the Spirit of Christ they do not receive him apart from Christ;
they are not attached to him at a distance from Christ, but
rather in Christ, because it is "in Christ" that they have been
raised up. This would not be so if the Spirit were to proceed
"and from the Son", or if, proceeding from the Father, he
were not to rest in the Son. In that case the faithful might
possess the Spirit without being in Christ, or they might possess Christ without being in the Spirit. We might better understand this by reference to a similar distinction: although
we are "in Christ", nevertheless, because of the fact that the
Son goes *forth* from the Father by generation, we are not
also in the Father in exactly the same way that, once in the
Spirit, we are consequently also in Christ. That is why the
Western Christian world (Catholic and Protestant) sometimes affirms a presence which is said to be in the Spirit but
not also in Christ, or speaks of one priesthood that is Christ-
ological-institutional and another that is pneumatological,
an idea which can even be found in the works of some Russian
theologians writing in the West (Lossky, Gillet).

According to Orthodox teaching the faithful can possess
the Spirit only "in Christ" and vice-versa.[27] They are united
with Christ through the Spirit who never leaves Christ, who
"shines forth" from him but does not "come forth" from him.
In this way the faithful participate with Christ in the "rest"
of the Holy Spirit who comes upon him. Obviously, since the
faithful, unlike Christ, are not divine hypostases they have
only a partial share in the energy of the Spirit. Because the
human hypostasis is not equal to the divine hypostasis, it
cannot contain the fullness of the hypostasis of the Spirit, but
inasmuch as it is united with Christ it is in a position to receive the abiding of the Spirit when he descends upon Christ,
or better, inasmuch as it does receive the "rest" of the Spirit

coming down upon it, it is therefore only that "rest", that "abiding" which has, in fact, come down upon Christ that the human hypostasis is able to receive. The Spirit never leaves this position of resting upon Christ, for his rest as an hypostasis is in Christ as the incarnate Son of God. But the Spirit can cease to rest upon man for there is no eternal hypostatic relation between men and the Spirit.

Inasmuch as through our union with Christ, with the incarnate hypostasis of the Son, we possess the Spirit, two things follow: on the one hand, we form, in a certain sense, one person with Christ; and on the other hand, because, unlike Christ, we do not possess the Spirit in his hypostatic fullness, but only as much as we can contain and as corresponds to the person of each of us, the Spirit simultaneously accentuates in us what is specific to us as persons. These are not two separate moments as Lossky thinks, but in virtue of the very fact that we are united to Christ through the Spirit, union with Christ also accentuates our growth as persons.

Everything that has been said here about the faithful must be understood to refer to them as members of the Mystical Body of Christ. The Spirit "comes to rest" (alights) upon the Church and in the Church because he comes to rest upon Christ, its head, and because the Church is united with Christ.

Since even the term "irradiation" does not, as we have seen, mean that the one who shines forth also *comes* forth from the one in whom he radiates his light, it does show that when the Spirit communicates himself to us, he does not as a consequence come forth from or leave Christ, and therefore we do not possess him in isolation from Christ. Rather the Spirit unites us in Christ and gathers us together in him. But inasmuch as we are united with Christ, the Spirit who shines forth from Christ also shines forth from us, or from the Church. He does not however shine forth as a complete hypostasis in the manner in which he shines forth from Christ, and this for two reasons: firstly, because unlike Christ the faithful are not divine hypostases, and secondly, because the shining forth of the Spirit from the faithful is in proportion to their respective stages of growth in virtue, and this could scarcely be the case were the Spirit to shine forth from them in the fullness of his Person. In other words the human persons of the faithful are penetrated only by the *activity* of the Spirit who, as Person, is united with Christ the divine Head of the Body and Head of every believer who is a member of his Mystical Body. Hence as human beings the faithful cannot have that same integral personal relation with the divine Persons which these Persons have among themselves on the basis of their common essence: they can have only a relation "through grace", that is, through communion or through the activity, the energy of the Spirit.

For this reason Gregory of Cyprus avoids giving the name "irradiation" to the manifestation of the Spirit through the saints. Nevertheless the tradition of the Church strongly affirms this "irradiation" while obviously distinguishing it from the "shining forth" of the Spirit from Christ. The measure of this irradiation of the Spirit in the saints is proportionate to their growth in Christ and to the presence and effective activity of Christ within them.

St. Symeon the New Theologian, describing the fright which took hold of his soul at the sight of God's glory, and his own attempt to hide from it, continues in these words: "But you my God seized me all the more/Ever more you enfolded me and embraced me/Within the bosom of your Glory, my God,/Within the folds of your garments,/Gathering me in and covering me with your light." [28] And elsewhere he says: "For the mind is lost in your light/And is filled with irradiation and becomes light/Similar to your Glory." [29]

Where the experience of the Spirit in the Church and in the faithful grows weak, there appears a Church which is predominantly juridical and institutional, or a religious life characterized by an exaggerated individualism. It is not because the presence of Christ apart from the Spirit produces these phenomena — as some Western theologians and even some Orthodox authors hold — for Christ does not in fact abide in the Church and in the faithful apart from the Spirit. Rather it is because he is conceived either as a remote figure who has left behind a vicar to guide the Church according to his commands (Catholicism), or else as the one who allows each believer to guide himself according to the reasonings of his own conscience (Protestantism).

The Relation Of Spirit And Son In The Thought Of St. Gregory Palamas

In the passage from St. Gregory Palamas quoted above we saw that he took from the older trinitarian theology the idea that the "abiding" or "resting" of the Holy Spirit in the Son constituted the eternal relation between them. Although Gregory also says that this relation is essential rather than personal, if it is in fact a particular relation between Spirit and Son, it cannot any longer be essential in character. But Palamas knows of a still more special relation between Son and Spirit, or, more accurately, he gives a new and more precise account of the Spirit's relation of "abiding" or "resting" in the Son. And this represents a step forward in comparison with Gregory of Cyprus.

According to Palamas, even the Father and the Son have a new relation between themselves through the Spirit. For the Spirit is the love of the Father for the Son which comes down upon the Son and returns as the Son's love for the Father. This is how Palamas expresses the idea: "No sensible person can conceive of the Word without the Spirit. [Gregory wants to suggest here the indissoluble personal bond between the Son and the Spirit.] The Word of God from the Father therefore also possesses the Holy Spirit who comes forth together with him from the Father. . . . Now this Spirit of the supreme Word is like an ineffable love of the Begetter for the Word which was ineffably begotten. The Word, the beloved Son of the Father, avails himself (χρῆται) of the Spirit in his relationship with the Father, but he possesses the Spirit as the one who has come forth together with him from the Father and who abides in him (the Son) through the unity of nature . . ."[30] The Son has the Spirit from the Father as the Spirit of Truth, of Wisdom, the Spirit of the Word . . . and through the Spirit the Son rejoices together with the Father who has his joy in the Son (ὃς τῷ Πατρὶ ἐπ'αὐτῷ χαίροντι συγχαίρει) ... For this joy of the Father and of the Son from before all ages is the Holy Spirit who is common to both in what concerns their inner association (ὡς κοινὸν μὲν αὐτοῖς κατὰ τὴν χρῆσιν) which also explains why the Spirit is sent forth by both upon those who are worthy, but why he is *of* the Father alone in what concerns his existence, and therefore proceeds from the Father alone with respect to existence." [31]

Two ideas emerge from this text:

A. Through the Holy Spirit the Son returns to the Father in order to love him through the Spirit, just as the Father causes the Spirit to proceed in order to love the Son through him, or because of his love for the Son. The procession of the Spirit is therefore linked to the generation of the Son. The Spirit does not move beyond the Son within the Trinity, nor does he proceed in isolation from the generation of the Son thus remaining alongside the Son, as it were, without any personal relationship to him. Instead the Spirit is from the Father for the Son, together with the Son, towards the Son, through the Son (that is, because of the fact that the Son exists). Within the Trinity the Spirit is the one who brings the Father and the Son into unity (a unity of love, not of being), not the one who unravels this unity still more.

B. But the Son loves the Father through the Spirit as the one who begot him and caused the Spirit to proceed. Thus in this love the Son does not change his character as Son in order to become identical with the Father. The love of the Son for the Father differs from the love of the Father for the Son. Through the Spirit the Son responds with his own joy (συγχαίρει) to the joy which the Father takes in him, that is to say, the Son does not take the initiative in rejoicing. As Son, the Son does not possess the Spirit in the way that the Father does, that is, as causing the Spirit to proceed from himself, but he possesses the Spirit as one who receives him from the Father and, as Son, possesses him. Were the Son to possess the Spirit as one who caused him to proceed, he would no longer be related to the Father through the Spirit as a Son towards his Father. In such a common procession of the Spirit, the hypostatic properties of Father and Son would be identified. It would no longer be the Son's love, as Son, for the Father which was manifested in the Spirit, but rather the hypostatic identity of Father and Son. All that the Son has he has from the Father, and hence together with his own existence he also possesses the Holy Spirit as the manifestation of his filial love.

When we put the ideas of St. Gregory Palamas together with those of Gregory of Cyprus we may rightly consider that the former throw fresh light on the thought of the Cypriot. The irradiation of the Spirit from the Son is nothing other than the response of the Son's love to the loving initiative of the Father who causes the Spirit to proceed. The love of the Father coming to rest in the Son shines forth upon the Father from the Son as the Son's love. It does not have its source in the Son but in the Father. When it falls upon the Son, however, it is shown to the Father; it is reflected back towards the Father, and joins with the loving subjectivity which the Son has for the Father, in the same way that the Spirit of the Father who is communicated to us returns to the Father in conjunction with our own loving filial affection for him. This is so because the Son is not a passive object of the Father's love, as in fact we ourselves are not passive objects when the Holy Spirit is poured out upon us. The fact that it is through the Spirit that the Son loves the Father does not mean however that it is not he himself who loves the Father, and similarly, the fact that it is through the Spirit that we love the Father does not imply that it is not we ourselves who love him. The Spirit of the Father penetrating within us as the paternal love kindles our own loving filial subjectivity in which, at the same time, the Spirit is also made manifest. Here we see illuminated the truth that every time a person is truly aware of someone else, this feeling does not belong to that one person only but is also experienced by the consciousness of the other. There is no purely individualist subjectivity.

Let us turn now to see how the Spirit descends through the Son in the temporal order and thereby manifests his eternal relation with the Son. When the Son becomes incarnate and unites men with himself, the love of the Father which is

upon him and his own response to the Father's love are as-
similated by all who are united with the Son. All are beloved
of the Father in the Son and all respond to the Father in the
Son with the Son's own love. This is the climactic moment of
the condition of salvation: the union of all with Christ in the
Spirit, and through the Spirit, in the consciousness of the
Father's love for them and of their own love for the Father.
Hence salvation is recapitulation in Christ. All are loved in
the Son by the Father and all respond in the Son with the
Son's love, for inasmuch as all are found in the Son, the Spirit
of the Father hovers over all and shines forth from all upon
the Father. "Although man has turned away from God and
grieved him on account of his disobedience and numberless
sins, Christ has once again set him before the face of the Father
in himself as in the first (man)." [32] And "through Christ and
in him we have received a heavenly blessing from the Father,
and have been sealed for adoption through the Holy Spirit." [33]

The Holy Spirit does not leave Christ because he is communicated to us; rather he unites us in Christ that we may
rejoice together with Christ in what is his, and that we may
become co-heirs with Christ in his inheritance from the Father,
that is, the Spirit. (Eph 1:11-14)

If the Spirit proceeded also from the Son, the Son would
not possess the Spirit, nor would we have our own existence
through the Spirit in the consciousness of sonship, and were
this the case we would remain outside of Christ, not united
with him as conscious sons of the Father, nor raised up in the
Son by the Spirit. We do not experience the Spirit as a separate,
definite Person because we are not aware that he stands between ourselves and the Son. We do not possess the Spirit
apart from Christ, but, possessing the Spirit, we have Christ
himself within us together with his own awareness of himself as Son before the Father, a filial consciousness which we
assimilate as our own. Christ's consciousness as Son cannot
exist in us apart from, separated from Christ himself. Its
existence implies Christ's presence in us or the fact that we
have been raised up in him. A Christ without the penetration
of his filial consciousness within us — without the Spirit — is
impossible. At most we could theorize about such a posses-

sion of Christ. Moreover, a presence of the Spirit without Christ, if the Spirit is Christ's consciousness as Son *vis-à-vis* the Father, is also impossible. "For all who are led by the Spirit of God are sons of God." (Rom 8:14) But the Spirit can bestow this quality on us only because he is the "Spirit of adoption", "the Spirit of the Son" (Rom 8:15; Gal 4:6). "And because you are sons, God has sent the Spirit of his Son into our hearts, crying, 'Abba! Father!' So through God you are no longer a slave but a son, and if a son then an heir," (Gal 4:6-7)[34] or a "fellow heir with Christ". (Rom 8:17)

The Son of God became man not only to confer on us a general kind of divinity, but to make us sons of God. This is why the Son and no other Person of the Trinity became man, for, having the Spirit of the Son, he imparts this Spirit to us also so that we might have the Spirit in the Son and with the Son and thus be truly the sons of God and conscious of that fact.

The Relation Of Spirit And Son In The Thought Of Joseph Bryennios

Joseph Bryennios was a Byzantine theologian who in the year 1422 gave a series of twenty three lectures at the imperial palace in Constantinople on the subject of the procession of the Holy Spirit. At the end of the series, having in view a unionist synod which was soon to meet (although in fact it did not finally take place), he delivered a "Word of Counsel Concerning the Union of the Churches" in which he explained a schema of Hierotheos the teacher of Dionysius the Pseudo-Areopagite which touches directly on our theme.[35]

In the thought of Bryennios the relations between the three divine Persons are more complex. He shows first of all that each Person has two names: "The Father is not only called Father but also Cause of Procession, and the Son is not only the Son but also truly the Word, and the Spirit is not only the Spirit but also He Who Proceeds." [36] But the Father does not have his names in the same fashion as do the other two Persons. His names belong to him as cause, and there-

fore each of them in itself indicates the special causal relation with one of the other two Persons alone. "The Father is
not said therefore to have his names, that is, Father and Cause
of Procession, in the same way as this is said of Son and
Spirit. Instead, as the one who alone causes and is not himself
caused, he has each of his names in relation to one aspect of
himself only, for of the Son he is the Father only, not also
the Cause of Procession, and of the Holy Spirit he is the
Cause of Procession only and not also the Father." [37] Inasmuch
as each of the other two Persons is not only himself caused
but also shares the fact of being caused together with the
other, one of his names expresses the relation both with the
other Person as sharer in a common cause and also the relation with the Father who is himself the cause of their shared
causation. "Now to the Son and the Spirit as to those who
alone are caused by the Father but who are not themselves
causes of one another, one of their names belongs with reference (in relation) to the Father alone, and the other with
reference to that aspect of the Person which shares in the fact
of being caused by the Father." [38]

Thus besides the relation which exists between the Father
and each of the other two Persons produced by this dual-
natured causality, there is another relation between these two
Persons and between each of them and the Father. Although
this relationship is not a causal one, it is not on the other hand
a purely essential relation, but, according to Bryennios, derives
from the fact that the two Persons are differently caused by
the Father and so indicates at one and the same time their
common and different character as beings who have their
causation from the same source and hence also their distinct
personal character. "That is to say, the Son, because he is the
one who is Son, alone possesses the name of Son *vis-à-vis* the
Father, for he is the Son of one Father only, not of two; but
the name of Word which belongs to the Son alone within the
Holy Trinity has reference not only to the Father as the one
who is Mind, but also to the Spirit in another way. . . . For
the Word belongs to the Father as one who exists from within
him, but the Word belongs to the Spirit not as one existing
from within the Spirit but as one who has his existence from

without, and in fact from the same source whence the Spirit has his own existence, and as one who is consubstantial with the Spirit. The same is true of the one who proceeds. He truly is He Who Proceeds and is so called only in reference to the one who caused him to proceed, that is to say, to the one who is and who is called Father with reference to that other Person who shares with him the character of being caused, namely, the Son. But the Spirit is not and is not given the name of Spirit with reference to the Father alone, but he is Spirit and is called Spirit correctly and truly with reference also to the Son. However, the Spirit belongs to the Father and is named Spirit as one who exists from within him, while in reference to the Son he is Spirit not as one who has his existence from within the Son, but as one who through the Son, that is, together with him, comes forth from the Father and shares one being and one glory with the Son." [39]

Nevertheless, as Augustine says, the expression "Spirit of the Father" is not generally used, in order to discourage the idea that the Father begets the Spirit. Nor is the expression "Son of the Spirit" used lest the idea arise that the Son is also born of the Spirit. [40]

We will now attempt a brief interpretation of these non-causal relations between Son and Holy Spirit of which Bryennios speaks.

Even among men there exist personal relations which differ from those which depend on the fact that one person has received his existence from another. In the first instance, there clearly does exist a personal relation between those who share an immediate causation, but more or less close relations can certainly be established among all men on the basis of their common origin, and these relations rest ultimately on the basis of a common nature. The relation of one person with every other human person actualizes some new characteristic or virtuality in those who are in relation. We might say that each human being in some measure is born or "comes forth" from every other human being when he enters into relation. Rather than speaking of a "birth" or a "coming forth" properly so called, it is more correct however to speak of an actualization, an enrichment, and of a reciprocal definition based on what men possess in virtue of their origin, which, ultimately, is a common origin. Every person "passes through" the other or others in order to manifest as fully as possible what belongs to him in his very being by virtue of his coming into existence. This "passage" is precisely the relation he has to one or other group of persons, and the result of this passage is the manifestation or the "shining forth" of that person in a new light.

Now these relations between human beings reflect in an obscure fashion the perfect relations which exist between the Persons of the Trinity, with this difference that because the divine Persons are infinite they do not contribute to one another's enrichment.

Between the Son and the Spirit there exists inevitably a relation similar to that between those who originate from the same source. Through this relation each divine Person contributes — in a form proper to each — to the manifestation of the divine fullness. It is impossible for each divine Person to manifest the infinitude of the divine life uniformly or in isolation from the others. If such were possible the *raison d'être* of the trinitarian nature of the divinity would be lost. We have seen in St. Gregory Palamas that as the Spirit "passes through" the Son, "shining forth" from him and joyfully coming to rest upon him, the Son thereby manifests his divine fullness in filial form and actualizes the infinity of the divine life in the form of a perfect filial affection for the Father. But in this "passage" the Spirit also receives his distinctive character as the Son's loving affection for the Father. In this sense the Spirit is called the Spirit of the Son. This is a new aspect of the divine life of the Spirit alongside that which he has through his procession from the Father, or more precisely, the former is a new aspect of the latter, an inseparable consequence of it. For if, in virtue of his coming forth from the Father, the Spirit is the love of the Father for the Son (yet without being called the "Spirit of the Father" in order to avoid any impression that he is begotten by the Father), then by virtue of his manifestation in the Son and of his relation with the Son, the Spirit is also revealed as the love-response of the Son for the Father, thus manifesting the divine love in all its aspects and creating the opportunity for all these different aspects to be revealed.

Joseph Bryennios says that the relation between Son and Spirit also has a meaning which is the converse of that which we have already seen. Not only does the Spirit "pass through" the Son, revealing himself as the Spirit of the Son, and revealing the Son as possessing the Spirit of the Son (although the Son is not called the Son of the Spirit in order to avoid any impression that the Son is begotten by the Spirit), but conversely, the Son also "passes through" the Spirit in some manner, revealing himself as the Word of the Spirit, and at the same time revealing the Spirit as one who possesses the Word, not as one from whom the Word is absent. Clearly, the Son also manifests his character as Word of the Father, but Father is to be understood here specifically as the one from whom the Son originates. If, in the Father, the Word has the cause of his coming into concrete existence, through the Spirit he manifests his penetrating power and affection. The Spirit on "passing through" the Son makes manifest, and is himself revealed as, the filial consciousness of the Father's Only-Begotten Son. But when the Son also "passes through" the Spirit who has already passed through him and whom he also possesses, he reveals himself as the Word of the Spirit and makes the Spirit reveal himself as the Spirit of utterance. At the same time the Son remains the Word of the Father inasmuch as he comes forth from the Father, and the Spirit utters the Word of the Father, or, rather, it is in the Spirit that the Son of the Father speaks. That is to say, the context of the utterance of the Spirit is Christ, while it is in the Spirit that Christ speaks. Moreover, when the Spirit utters the Word of the Father he speaks about the Father, and when it is in the Spirit that the Son speaks, he speaks from the Spirit, that is, from the power of the Father. Every relation between two Persons implies also the third Person.

The union between the Son and the Spirit consists first of all in the fact that the Spirit "shines forth" from the Son, and secondly that the Son as Word echoes back from the Spirit. In general a person first perceives (by virtue of his union with the perception of the other, which in turn has been penetrated by the perception of the first person), and then he speaks from out of this perception (or his own perception is suffused with the *logos* of the other). Consequently, if we do not lay hold of the Holy Spirit in our unexpressed interior and exterior experience, but only of Christ, yet, inasmuch as the Spirit has become the instrument elevating and intensifying our faculties of spiritual perception, once we begin to speak, express, and witness to what we know and experience, we realize that we are speaking from the Spirit or from what the Spirit tells us of Christ. For in speaking we are more active and detached from ourselves than when we "see" or "experience". And those who listen realize this even more than those who speak. The Word spoken by the divine Spirit differs from the natural word; it has a penetrating and conquering force. It is miraculous and reveals depths deeper than those of nature, the very transcendent realities themselves.

As the Church is the Body of Christ upon which the Holy Spirit rests just as he rests upon the Head of the Body (and this is true of the individual members of the Church as well), so through her Head and through the Holy Spirit the Church finds herself in immediate relation with the Father. In this manner we all communicate in the Son and in the Holy Spirit from the ultimate and absolute source of existence which is the Father, not by nature, as Son and Spirit do, but by grace instead. We communicate from this ultimate source through both rays which originate from it and which are united among themselves in order to make us partakers of this source under the double form of the revelation and communication of the Father.

* * *

St. John Damascene spoke of *perichoresis* among the three divine Persons and this has been interpreted as meaning a reciprocal interiority for it cannot be understood only as the motion of each Person "around" the others, if, as we have seen, even among men where unity is so much weaker, more is involved in personal relations than the mere motion of one person around the other, for there is in fact a certain interior presence of the one within the other as a prerequisite for any "coming to rest" of the one in the other or of any "passage" of the one through the other. Thus with respect to the Holy Trinity, *perichoresis* must mean *a fortiori* a passage of the Spirit through the Son and of the Son through the Spirit. The Father is also included in *perichoresis* inasmuch as the Spirit passes through the Son as one who is proceeding from the Father and returning to him. Similarly the Son passes through the Spirit as one begotten by the Father and returning to him. It should also be observed that each divine Person manifests the divine fullness in a form which shows the effects of this passage through the others and of his interior relation with the others. Consequently, on account of these interior relations with the others no divine Person is ever, either in the Church as a whole or in the individual believer, without the other divine Persons or without the particular characteristics of the others. "The Church is filled with Trinity", said Origen,[41] and the faithful too, for according to St. Maximus the Confessor the purpose of the saints is "to express the very unity of the Holy Trinity." [42] Christ and the Spirit work together to make us sons of the Father. It is inadmissible to say that the faithful lack the Holy Spirit (which is a logical consequence of the notion of papal infallibility) or that the institutional priesthood is christological while the non-institutional priesthood is pneumatological. Nor can it be said that Christ unifies us within a unity of nature while the Spirit distinguishes us as persons within this institutional or pantheist unity (Lossky). All that Christ achieves, he achieves through the Spirit.

In this respect the Commission on Faith and Order of the World Council of Churches formulated certain things very precisely and correctly at its meeting in Montreal in 1963: "This ministry of Jesus Christ in his Church is made effective by the action of the Holy Spirit promised by the Lord to his people." [43] But this is also reflected in the ministry of the Church. "To serve Christ in his Church means to wait always upon the Spirit of power, holiness and love. It is in this waiting upon the Spirit that the ministers of the Church preach the word, administer the sacraments, watch in prayer, lead God's people, and engage in deeds of brotherly help. The Holy Spirit dwells in the Church. He comes to each member in his baptism for the quickening of faith. He also bestows differing gifts (charismata) on groups and individuals. All his activities are to enable men to serve and worship God. All members of the Church are thus gifted for the common good. . . . The call to the special ministry depends upon the presence and the action of the Holy Spirit in the Church." [44]

If the variety of gifts derives from the same Spirit who is at work in all and is revealed in the service of the common good, then we can conclude that the institution is not devoid of spirituality while spirituality on the other hand is not inevitably lacking in structure and institutional order. An institution with a weakened spiritual life would give proof of a weakening of the actual presence of Christ as well, while a disordered spirituality which does not maintain ecclesial unity would indicate in turn a weakening of the true presence of the Holy Spirit. The true Church is christological *and* pneumatological, institutional and spontaneous at the same time, or rather it is christological because it is pneumatological and vice-versa.

The institution cannot be compared merely to a vessel in which the spiritual life is stirred around; it is also the expression of the real and co-ordinated activity of the gifts (charisms and ministries) which come from the same Spirit, just as the variety of spiritual gifts and ministries is the means of the fullest possible expression of the spiritual wealth of the Church. The Spirit active in the Church through Christ not only imparts the variety of charisms but also creates unity among those who have been given these gifts in Christ. A so-called pneumatological individualism which does not possess Christ because it does not build up the faithful into the Body of Christ, does not possess the Spirit of Christ either. Nor does a non-pneumatological institutionalism from which the Spirit of Christ is absent possess Christ himself as an adequate effective presence.

The Presbyterian theologian T. F. Torrance closes his study "Spiritus Creator" with the following considerations: "It is of the greatest importance to think of the Spirit in his indissoluble relation to the Son, to think of him as the Spirit of God who has pronounced the Word and incarnated the

Son, as the Spirit who, through the crucified and resurrected
Christ and in him, sustains the creative and redemptive work
of the Holy Trinity from beginning to end and brings it to
its perfection. . . . It is of the nature of his action and the mode
of his being to come to us not in his own name, but in the
name of Christ. . . . we must follow this same path in order
to come to know him, reflect upon him and speak of him."

"Otherwise, because the Holy Spirit conceals himself by
reason of his nature and mode of existence, we fall into the
error of confusing him either with the Church at whose centre
we meet him, or with the human heart, since it is in us that
the Spirit is sent by Christ to attest that we are with him the
children of God. One of the great lessons that Athanasius
gives us in his controversy with the Arians and Semi-Arians
is that unless we come to know the Holy Spirit through the
objectivity of the *homoousion* of the Son in whom and by
whom our spirits are turned away from ourselves and directed
towards the unique source and unique principle, God, we inevitably become absorbed in ourselves, confusing the Holy
Spirit with our own spirits and confusing the unique truth of
God with notions taken from our own imagination. In other
words, outside the indissoluble relation of the Spirit and the
incarnate Son, we are incapable of distinguishing the objective
reality of the Lord, the Creator God of the universe, from our
subjective situations or from our own inventive spirituality." [45]

"These have been the permanent errors of Romanism and
Protestantism: the former confusing the Spirit of God and
the spirit of the Church and, as it were, substituting an
ecclesiaque for the *filioque*; the latter confusing the Spirit of
God with the human spirit and substituting for the *filioque*
a *homineque*. Thus the knowledge of the Spirit is dissolved
in the subjectivity of the consciousness of the Church or of
the individual, and the result of this consciousness, in its individual or collective genius, is affirmed as the operation of
the Holy Spirit. Against all this the doctrine of Athanasius
on the Spirit rises up like an immense rock. . . . And it is only
[in this way] . . . that we are thrown forward to encounter
the infinite glory and majesty of God who is revealed in Jesus
Christ; thus we become capable of distinguishing the Holy

Spirit from our spirits and of knowing him in the fullness of his liberty and transcendent power, as *Creator Spiritus*." [46]

We endorse these views of Torrance but find less satisfactory the explanation he gives of the Western transformation of the Spirit into a pure, natural and human subjectivity, whether collective or individual. He is right when he thinks that this has happened because of the attempt to conceive the Spirit in the image of the Father and Son — that is, as a Person able to be grasped in himself — while the Spirit is only the capacity given us to know God the Creator, whether Father or Son. When we try to take hold of the Spirit secretly in himself, apart from Christ, we are left with only our own pure subjectivity, for the Spirit cannot thus be grasped in himself. This too has happened in the West. Hence the Spirit, as the light in which Christ is known, only exists where there is knowledge of Christ. We must not remove the Spirit from his relation to Christ. Nevertheless, Torrance seems to imply that the *filioque* was intended precisely to guard men against such a mistake and therefore that fidelity to the *filioque* and its authentic application in the life of faith would have preserved Western Christendom from this error.

But it is astonishing that it is precisely Western Christendom — both Catholic and Protestant — with its continual assertion of the doctrine of the *filioque*, which has fallen into this error, while the East which has not accepted the *filioque* has been kept safe from it.

The explanation can only be that the *filioque* itself is the cause of this confusion of the Spirit with human subjectivity, collective or individual, and that it is thanks to this confusion that the situation is such in Catholicism that the Church is considered a creator of dogma or that the Church's consciousness is identified with Tradition as part of Revelation, while we see Protestantism on the other hand attribute to the individual the ability to discover the truth in Scripture. Because of the *filioque* the Spirit has come to be conceived in the same way as the Father and the Son, for he is no longer considered as one who abides or rests in the Son (as in the Eastern teaching on the relations between the Son and the Spirit) but as one who himself goes forth both from the Father and the Son for the sake of an existence similar to theirs.

A further reason why the Spirit has been separated from Christ in human knowledge and identified with the subjectivity of the creature is that through the *filioque* Father and Son are identified in a unity which can only be characterized by their common essence and, consequently, this common essence of Father and Son must be distinguished to a certain extent from the essence of the Spirit. For through the *filioque* the Spirit is deprived of something which is proper to the divinity — namely the quality of being a cause — and hence expelled as it were from the fullness of divinity, and placed on an inferior plane. The Spirit is no longer completely consubstantial with the Father and Son, and hence even his relation to the Son cannot be perfect. He can therefore be conceived as remote from the divinity and thus almost included in human immanence.

According to Orthodox teaching, however, since the Spirit shares a perfect identity of being with the Son and Father and therefore remains in the Son, the Spirit remains on the one hand as much transcendent of our being as either Father or Son and yet, on the other hand, it is through the Spirit that we truly know both the Father and the Son.

We see then how the Orthodox teaching — the teaching of the Fathers — on the relations between the Spirit and the Son preserves in a manner far superior to that of the *filioque* both the divine transcendence and our union with the Son through the Spirit who remains permanently in the Son. This teaching saves the creature both from being isolated from God and also from being confused with the Spirit.

Obviously the dialectical union of the Spirit's transcendence and the intimacy which he shows in his relations with us, a union which assures our own union with Christ but excludes all confusion of ourselves with him, will not be an easy thing to understand. It is difficult to understand how the Spirit penetrates into our consciousness and into our capacity for knowing and yet does not become identical with them. A comparison with human relations gives us a certain analogous understanding of this fact: our love for someone is not just *our* love, it also belongs to the one who loves us. The warmth of his love awakens and intensifies our love for him or for someone else. Now where parents are concerned, their initiative in this respect is clear. Thus we understand the presence of the trans-subjective factor in our affection, however intimately our own it has become. And in the trans-subjective character of this factor there is implied both the trans-subjectivity of the one who loves us and at the same time our intimacy with him.

The life of the Church is full of transcendent divine trans-subjectivity which has ultimately become her own by virtue of the fact that it is life in that Spirit who is consubstantial with and inseparable from the Son.

CHAPTER II

The Holy Spirit
and
The Sobornicity of
The Church

EXTRACTS FROM THE REPORT OF AN ORTHODOX
OBSERVER AT THE SECOND VATICAN COUNCIL *

At the meeting of the Central Committee of the World
Council of Churches which took place at Geneva in February
1966, the Greek Orthodox theologian Nikos A. Nissiotis,
Director of the Ecumenical Institute at Bossey and an observer
for the WCC at the Second Vatican Council, presented a remarkable report on the last session of the Council just as he
had done for the previous sessions.[1] The important observations contained in this report have prompted our reflections
here in an attempt to underline their significance and perhaps to develop their content.

While he recognizes that the Roman Catholic Church
has made progress during the Second Vatican Council towards adopting a more positive attitude to the other Christian
Churches and to the world at large, Nissiotis does make certain criticisms of the Council's treatment of a number of
questions.

With respect to the Council's definition of ecumenism
Nissiotis raises the following objections:

1) Despite its world-wide influence the Second Vatican

---

* Originally published in Romanian in *Ortodoxia* 19 (1967), 32-48.

Council was nevertheless not an Ecumenical Council. That would have necessitated convoking the whole Christian world in a Pan-Christian council which provided for real dialogue between all the Churches. The Second Vatican Council was not a council of this kind. Observers from the other Churches did not enjoy a position equal to that of the representatives of the Catholic Churches.[2]

2) In the *Decree On Ecumenism* the primacy of the Pope over the whole of Christendom in the event of any future reunion of Churches was reaffirmed. This demonstrates once more that ecumenism and its principles cannot be adequately formulated by one Church only, and especially not by the Roman Catholic Church which continues to be preoccupied with the affirmation of its own central position. We have to reject the temptation "to play the role of leader (in ecumenism) or take the initiative in having or setting up any centre endowed with historical or juridical primacy." The *Decree on Ecumenism* now in circulation shows the risk "that such publications, good as they are, involve for those who are not fully initiated in ecumenical work, namely to think that this is really the starting point of the ecumenical movement." [3]

3) In its discussion of the problem of ecumenism the Council addressed itself almost entirely to Protestants and gave the impression that discussion is easier between Catholics and Protestants.[4]

The manner in which the anathemas between Rome and Constantinople were lifted shows, according to Nissiotis, that "we have not yet reached the point where we can say a substantial change of attitude has taken place on both sides which will help under the existing conditions towards the easy removal of the real causes of the big schism between East and West. Unfortunately the real motives still exist." [5] "Therefore to limit the validity of the anathema only to the persons immediately involved in it or only to the local Church of Constantinople is an attempt to overcome the great difficulties but does not remove these difficulties between the two Churches . . . If, therefore, the abolition of this anathema means that Rome realizes that one of her official delegates erred, then there is hope that the glorious ceremony in St.

Peter's on December 7th was not simply a showing of good will, but will have further developments and this is something for which everyone wishes and prays in all humility." [6] The Council however has clearly shown that mutual understanding is still difficult by raising once more the various Catholic positions. This can be seen especially in the following instances:

a) "Not one of the documents of the Council has named the Eastern Church in the singular as one undivided Church . . . the Council continues to misinterpret the autocephalicity of the Orthodox Churches . . . the Council does not want to distinguish between the big Church in the East in communion with Rome until 1054 and the Non-Chalcedonian Churches which however split both from Rome and the Church in the East as early as the 5th century . . .they look at all the Eastern Churches separately through the small Uniate Oriental communities which have recognized the primacy of the Pope. . . . It is however very important for the ecumenicity of Rome to accept at least one Church outside her own communion as Church in the full sense of the word in order to break with any kind of self-sufficiency and centralism." For the time being the *Decree on the Eastern Catholic Churches* "gives clear indications that the Churches whose example is to be followed are the Uniate ones." [7]

b) "The great authority over and above the Council was the absent Pope, represented by his empty throne, placed where the Gospel was placed in the Ancient Councils. No Orthodox can understand how it is possible in an ecumenical Council for the decisions of the Council to be prevented, modified or explained in a different way by the *motu proprio* that the absent Pope can send to it by way of intervention, whenever he regards such a move as necessary for the good order of the Council or wants to indicate the right line of doctrine and thought." [8]

Nissiotis makes his most important observations however on the *Dogmatic Constitution on Divine Revelation*. We repeat them here because they touch on a shortcoming of Catholic theology which might well be said to explain the whole difference of conception between the Roman Catholic Church and the Orthodox Church, and this is the vital question in present-day ecumenical discussion.

After he mentions the progress realized by the Roman Catholic Church both in the problem of the relationship between Scripture and Tradition, and in other matters as well, Nissiotis goes on to point out the principal weakness of the Constitution, one which he had noted previously at the third session. This weakness is the Council's neglect of the Holy Spirit.

The Council's progress in treating the problem of revelation consists, according to Nissiotis, in the desire which the Constitution shows "to overcome the traditional separation between Bible and Tradition, as two distinct sources of Revelation, and [to try] to remedy this by introducing a unity between them." [9] But Nissiotis also notes with disapproval the affirmation of a third authority, outside the authority of Scripture and Tradition. In this he sees the anxiety of the Catholic Church that "neither the unity (proclaimed in an excellent way in the text) of the two sources for transmitting the Revelation in the Church, nor the high praise given to the Scriptures as a fundamental basis for understanding it, are sufficient ways of affording to the Church certainty and order in doctrine and practice." [10]

This fear, or this desire to have a "guarantee" for the biblical truth in the magisterium of the Church, points up the absence of a strong pneumatology in the *Dogmatic Constitution on Divine Revelation* just as it explains the exaggerated emphasis on papal infallibility in the *Dogmatic Constitution on the Church*.

"Christologically the Revelation appears to be understood in a monistic way rather than in a full trinitarian sense. It is right to attribute the full revelation of God to Christ, but it is not right to attribute to the Paraclete simply the function through which 'man might in the Holy Spirit have access to the Father . . .' as the text explicitly states in paragraph 2. It is right to say that 'Christ as the Word of God completes the work of salvation' (Para. 4), though I have some hesitation as I do see in the Bible and from the historical point of view that the Holy Spirit performs this work and makes the once for all event a historical reality by setting up the historical Christian community, on the day of Pentecost. It is therefore taking a one-sided position to recall several times only the act of Christ sending the Spirit (Para. 4) to work in us the salvation or illuminate our minds to a deeper understanding of Revelation (Para. 5 and 8) or to secure the already existing harmony of Tradition, Bible and Magisterium and support this idea by the operation of the Holy Spirit... (Para. 8)." [This phrase shows] "the way in which Roman thinking is bound to use the Holy Spirit, that is in a rather unbalanced way as an agent of personal salvation or as confirming the already existing order and harmony [11] between the main principles of Revelation in the Church which with its magisterium directly deriving from Christ's call to the Apostles precedes in time and qualitatively the function of the Spirit. It is, perhaps, here that one has to try to explain the anxiety...to find a clear criterion of authority alongside the Scripture and the Tradition" in the successors of the Apostles to whom authority was given to teach in place of the Apostles.[12]

Nissiotis goes on to ask why it is that Orthodoxy makes no separation between Bible and Tradition, and especially why it feels no need to insist on the hierarchical magisterium as a guarantor of Tradition.

"The Holy Spirit, as the Paraclete of Truth, does not harmonize nor keep the preexisting order of the Church only, and he is not simply an agent of salvation acting in the individuals, but he it is who sets up the historical Church, thus making out of the Cross and Resurrection of Jesus the pivot of history, he it is who leads the Church into the full truth..." [13] "Without Pentecost Jesus' calling to the Twelve Apostles remains an event without completion and fulfillment and his salvation is without possibility of communication in history. It is by the founding of this universal and at the same time concrete, local and historical Church that the Divine Economy becomes reality in time. The Spirit of Truth is he who opens the historical road to the permanent presence of Christ in history, by means of the church community. He gives, maintains and continually perfects us together in the truth in

one family. The Bible is the crystallized form of his action,
and Tradition is the life of those who are living in historical
continuity of the charismata of the Paraclete. The one manifests the truthfulness of the other, they belong together,
witnessing to the one event, namely to the Presence of Christ
in and by the Spirit in the One Church of the Trinitarian God.
All individuals and the magisterium must consciously submit
themselves to this common source of truth which abides with
us." [14] "The certainty for the right biblical exegesis is not to
be found either in the individual exegete or in the Magisterium,
as clear criteria of authentic understanding of Revelation, but
in the interpenetration and mutual explanation of the Bible
and life of the Church as an echo of the plenitude, the wholeness of the community in Christ set up, gathered and led by
the Paraclete into the Truth. It is, therefore, the consciousness
of this whole community as the People of God which pro-
claims to us all, laymen and clergymen alike, as an inseparable whole, the Truth of Christ by the Spirit, and, if necessary, judges everyone from the highest hierarch and the wise
theologian to the simplest layman, if he does not live and
express this truth of the Paraclete and if he separates Bible
and Tradition or opposes them or seeks for an external criterion of security. All these attitudes threaten the unity of the
Church and humanize its authority, neglecting the authentic
understanding of the operation of the Holy Spirit as the
Paraclete of Truth." [15]

"The time of the historical Ecclesia between the first and
second Parousia of Christ is his, as are all institutions of the
visible Church. All criteria are submitted to his uniting operation of all into the One Body of Christ. Bible and Tradition
are the witnessing dynamics of Christ's presence amongst
us in the Spirit, which excludes all qualitative difference between teaching office, its authority and the objective truth,
and gives priority to the authority of the whole community
of the people of God." [This authority of the community]
"does however operate clearly as the most immediate and
binding authority from within the life of the Church. The
Church has only one great principle of authority: her fidelity

to the presence of the Holy Spirit and her conviction that he will lead her in to all truth." [16]

* * *

These observations of Nissiotis have suggested a number of reflections on the role of the Holy Spirit in founding and preserving the Church as community, as the Body of Christ, and in investing the Church with the attribute of sobornicity.[17]

In an earlier study [18] we showed that the defeat of the idea of episcopal collegiality at the Second Vatican Council was due to the fact that the bishops did not derive their collegial ministry of teaching from their role as exponents of the Church and of the community of all its members, but rather from their episcopal consecration, which they thought of as a transmission of power to the episcopal college from a Christ who is absent from the Church. The Pope has been able, following the logic of this conception, to sustain the view that he receives from Christ, through Peter, an even greater power over the Church than that held by the bishops.

Had the bishops derived their collegial ministry of teaching from the entire ecclesial community, from Christ present and active in and through his Mystical Body, a new conception of the origin of ministries in the Church would have asserted itself, and in this case such ministries could no longer have been considered powers over the Church, but powers of the Church, powers exercised by bishops, by the college of bishops, even by the Pope, in obedience to the Church.

Nissiotis goes on to suggest that the profound and ultimate cause of this authority of the entire ecclesial community is, *par excellence*, the activity of the Holy Spirit in the community of the Church. Thus he takes the clarification of the problem one step further, but he stops short of the solution. He affirms the connexion of the Holy Spirit with the community. He affirms that the Holy Spirit is the creator and sustainer of the ecclesial community. But in a brief report he cannot give the complete foundations of these views nor develop them as he should.

In what follows we will try to contribute in a small way to providing the biblical and patristic foundations of these questions and to explaining the spiritual meaning of the special bond which connects the activity of the Holy Spirit to the ecclesial community.

The Holy Spirit And The Church In The Teaching Of The Fathers

The Fathers show a surprising unity of thought in the way they speak of the relation of the Holy Spirit to the Church.

In a commentary on the events of Pentecost, St. Gregory Nazianzen says that either the listeners all understood in their own languages what the Apostles were saying in one single language, or else that the Apostles were speaking in the different languages of those present. (Gregory inclines to this latter view.) In any case, however, just as the appearance of a variety of tongues at the building of the tower of Babel meant that those present were no longer able to understand each other, so at the foundation of the Church the same variety of tongues became the means through which harmony was achieved among all present, for all understood the same thing. "Because from one and the same spirit the same understanding was poured out upon all and all are brought back into a single harmony (εἰς μίαν ἁρμονίαν πάλιν συνά-γεται)." [19]

St. Gregory of Nyssa in his interpretation of these same events of Pentecost, namely, the descent of the Holy Spirit in the form of tongues of fire, and the Apostles' preaching in the various languages of those present, says that through the Holy Spirit "those who were separated into the many various languages all at once shared the same language with the Apostles (ὁμογλώσσων τοῖς μαθηταῖς γεγενημέ-νων). For it was necessary that those who had broken the unity of the language (τὴν ὁμοφωνίαν) when the tower was being built should return to this unity at the moment of the spiritual construction of the Church." [20]

We are dealing then with the birth of a common way of thinking in those who come to believe which makes them understand one another despite all the differences of expression which may exist among them. For those who entered into the Church on the first Pentecost this phenomenon occurred simultaneously with the birth of the Church. We might say that the Church was founded precisely through the infusion into all believers of a common understanding, an understanding which was shared by faithful and Apostles alike. In this way the Church is the opposite of the Tower of Babel: the former united those who agreed to work in its building and to build themselves into it, while the latter separated them, made it impossible for them to understand one another, and so deprived them of this common understanding. We need only mention here that the author of *The Shepherd of Hermas* also pictured the Church as a tower into which are built all who share the same mind.[21]

This common mind which belongs to those who have entered into the Church does not, however, mean uniformity in all things. The fact that all those who received the same understanding preserved their distinct languages is a symbol of this unity in variety.

The same unity in diversity is directly expressed by the difference of gifts which flow out from the same Spirit. For it is the same Spirit nevertheless who binds together all those endowed with the different gifts. One who receives a particular gift has need of another's gift in order to turn his own gift to good account and to complete what he himself lacks. Similarly, the same man contributes with his own gift to the full use of another's gift, thereby helping his brother towards his own particular fulfillment. By virtue of the different gifts they have received all are dependent on the same Spirit and on one another as well.

After his discussion of the "harmony" which was created at Pentecost and which reigned among the Apostles and the crowds, and indeed which still reigns among those who have come after them, St. Gregory Nazianzen goes on to say: "And there also exists a distinction between the gifts, for it requires another gift to discern which is the best gift." Gregory

here completely follows St. Paul who said that some speak
while others judge and interpret, adding, after he drew a
comparison between the different gifts and the various members of the body: "If all were a single organ where would
the body be? As it is, there are many parts, yet one body."
(1 Cor 12:19-20).[22]

The one who makes a single Body of all the faithful, each
endowed with his own different gift, is the Holy Spirit. He
binds men to one another and creates in each an awareness
of belonging to all the rest. He impresses on the faithful the
conviction that the gift of each exists for the sake of the others;
the Spirit is the spiritual bond between men, the integrating
force which unites the whole, the power of cohesion in the
community. Just as the organs of the body have within themselves a force which keeps them all together, so the Holy
Spirit, present within the faithful, is the force holding them
together in one whole and making them aware of the fact that
integration is only possible through the others. This constitutive force of the whole body, the δύναμις τοῦ ὅλου,
or synthetic power, exists in each of the parts and everywhere
in the unity which together they constitute: πάρεστι ἐν τῷ
ὅλῳ. It is this which gives the Church the nature of a whole,
and from all its parts forms one single unity, thereby giving
it the character of "sobornicity" which translates the Greek
word for this notion of wholeness: catholicity (from καθ᾽
ὅλον).

Because of this variety the gifts complement one another,
and satisfy every spiritual need of the faithful and of the
entire Church. This is what makes the Church a well-ordered
whole. All those who have received gifts, and therefore ministries, within the Church are subordinated to and serve the
whole body. In every member we see the Spirit who is present
in the entire Church and who desires that through the continual activity of each individual believer the needs of the whole
Church may be satisfied. The fact that the Spirit who is present in the whole Church is also active in one or other minister does not make this believer any the less dependent on the
Spirit present in the whole Church.

St. Basil the Great expresses these ideas in the following

words: "Is it not clear and incontestable that the order of the Church is maintained through the Spirit? For he has given to the Church, he says, firstly Apostles, secondly prophets, thirdly teachers, then powers and charisms of healing. . . . (1 Cor 12:28) This ordering and endowment of gifts has been decided by the Spirit." [23] The Spirit creates the grace-filled structures of the Church, but precisely as structures of the *Church*, as members of the Body, subordinated to the Body, and in and through which the life of the Body is expressed. The Body of Christ is by no means a chaos devoid of structures, but on the other hand, these structures are not independent of the Body nor does any structure exist which is superior to the Body.

The faithful are able to remain united because of the power of the Holy Spirit, the same power by which he is present in the various different gifts, inasmuch as he is present entirely in each man. St. Basil insists on this idea: "He (the Holy Spirit) is wholly (ὅλον) in everyone and he is wholly everywhere." [24]

But the Spirit is wholly present in every member by a different gift, or by way of mutually interdependent gifts which neither make all members the same nor allow them to work in isolation from one another, for no single member remains unconditioned by the others. St. Basil expresses this idea by adopting the Pauline image of the members of one body held together by the integrating force of the whole: "But the Spirit is also conceived as a whole (ὅλον) existing in the parts through the distribution of gifts. For, although the gifts and the grace which God has given us may differ, we are most certainly members of one another. Therefore, 'the eye cannot say to the hand, I have no need of you, nor again the head to the feet, I have no need of you.' (1 Cor 12:21). But all together make up the complete Body of Christ in the unity of the Spirit, and provide mutually for one another from their gifts the benefit that each one requires (ἀλλήλοις δὲ ἀναγκαίαν τὴν ἐκ τῶν χαρισμάτων ἀντιδίδωσιν ὠφέλειαν)." [25] Here St. Basil resolves faithfully the problem of how to achieve unity among the members of the Church without making all uniform. Just as the bodily functions are attached specifically to the different members of the body, so in the Church charisms and ministries are not passed around from one member to another. Nevertheless, the "benefit" derived from them is shared by all the members, just as in the body the hand remains a hand with its own function and the foot remains a foot, but each of these in carrying out its function draws benefit both from the functioning of the other members and from the life-force of the whole body, and also passes on in its turn to the other members and to the whole body the benefit of its own special function.

St. Basil continues: "God has located each of the members in the body as he wished. But the members share a common concern for the same thing. They care for one another and share a spiritual communion because they possess within themselves a common sympathy. Hence 'if one member suffers, all suffer together; if one member is honoured, all rejoice together.' (1 Cor 12:26) And the same holds for us, we are as parts of a whole (ἐν ὅλῳ) in the Spirit. 'For by one Spirit we were all baptized into one body.' (1 Cor 12:13)" [26]

In their spiritual communion (τὴν πνευματικὴν κοινω-νίαν=communion in the Spirit) and their shared sympathy, the members of the Mystical Body, that is, the members of the Church, experience the unity they share as an integral whole. This unity, produced and maintained by and in the Spirit, extends among them on the plane of spiritual experience.

The Holy Spirit is the "Spirit of communion", that is, of the unity of a whole in which the members are not melted together to form a single part. In this sense sobornicity can also be expressed as communion. Sobornicity is not unity pure and simple; it is a certain kind of unity. There is the unity of a whole in which the constitutive parts are not distinct, or the unity of a group which is kept together by an exterior command, or formed into a union of uniform entities each existing side by side. Sobornicity is none of these. It is distinguished from an undifferentiated unity by being of a special kind, the unity of communion. The Roman Catholic Church has lost this sense of catholicity as communion, for the doctrine of papal primacy and the ecclesiastical magisterium make impossible the communion of all the members of the Church in all things. The Roman Catholic Church remains content with the unity which characterizes a body under command, and it has replaced the unity of communion (catholicity or sobornicity properly so-called) with universality in the sense of geographical extension.

The unity of communion is the sole unity which conforms to the dignity of the persons involved in the union. It is the sole unity which does not subordinate one person to another, or in which the institution is not conceived as something external to or superior to and repressive of the persons involved in it. In the unity of communion persons are united in equality and the institution is the expression of their communion. In the unity of communion structures are communities of persons with identical ministries.

Like Gregory of Nazianzen and Gregory of Nyssa, St. John Chrysostom also affirms that as the difference of languages at the building of the tower of Babel ruined the evil harmony which had existed there, so at Pentecost the diverse languages served to bring the whole inhabited world into unity and to gather into a single thought what had been separated. Pouring out his love into souls, the Spirit has laid the foundations and raised upon them the structure of the Church.[27]

But Chrysostom develops and deepens these familiar ideas of the Cappadocian Fathers, and particularly the notion that the members of the whole are more than merely distinct from one another, but in fact possess a common element which binds them together. The body is characterized precisely by the unity of certain quite distinct members. If the members were not different there would be no body. If the members were only different, they would not form a unity and hence once more there would be no body. Prompted by the words of St. Paul, "If all were a single organ, where would the body be?" (1 Cor 12:19), Chrysostom says: "This is what he asserts: if there were no great differences among you, you would not be a body, and not being a body you would not be one. Moreover, not being one you would not share the same nature. Therefore if you all had the same honour you would not be a body, and not being a body you would not be one, and if you were not one, how could you be of the same nature? But now, precisely because you do not all have a single gift, you are a body, and as a body you are one, and individually you do not differ in the fact of being a body in even the slightest degree. Therefore it is this very difference which itself makes for equality in honour." [28]

Here Chrysostom grasps the paradoxical character of an organic whole which reveals itself simultaneously in its interior differentiation and in its unity. The paradox is that within this organic whole the equality of all the members is due precisely to the fact of their differentiation. By way of concrete illustration Chrysostom tells those who have lesser gifts not to be envious of those with greater gifts: "If you are still upset, consider that most often the other person cannot do what you can do. And so, even if you are smaller, in this respect you surpass the other person. And even if he is greater, precisely in this respect he is smaller. Thus there is equality." [29]

But after he has remarked upon the paradox Chrysostom provides an explanation. Equality of honour among the members is due to the fact that they accomplish a common task, that the lesser members take part in the accomplishment of great things through the agency of the greater members, and that the indivisible worth of the common achievement spreads out like a halo crowning all the members which took part in the work. For in the body even the work of the smallest members is to be esteemed for if these are not present even the greatest members suffer. "What is more lowly in the body than hair? Yet were you to remove the hair from eyebrows and lashes you would have destroyed the entire beauty of the face, and the eye itself would no longer seem so pretty. And even though the harm is slight, the whole appearance has been destroyed. There is even more involved than mere appearances, for much of the use of the eyes would also be impaired." [30]

This implies that the unity of the organism is in all the members and is sustained by them all, and Chrysostom's conclusion leaves no loose ends to his explanation: "*For each*

of our members has both a particular and a common activity,
and likewise there are in us two kinds of beauty: one which
is peculiar to each member, and another which is common
to all." [31]

This is the mystery of organic unity, and it is also the
mystery of the Church as a whole — *this common element
which binds the members together, which shines forth from
them all, and which is served by all.* Chrysostom speaks of
the particular function and of the common function of each
member as of two separate things. But this distinction can
only be made in the mind. In reality, it is precisely inasmuch
as each member performs its own particular activity that it
contributes to the welfare of the whole organism, and this
is the common activity. This can only be explained by the
fact that each member does its own work with the help of the
whole organism, or, rather, that the whole organism works
through the individual member. In the Church it is the same
Spirit who carries out this common activity through each believer. Hence the members are equal in honour because,
whether the work done through one particular member is
great or small, it is the same entire organism which does it,
and each member is necessary in the same way to the constitution and preservation of the whole. "Do not say then that
such and such a one is unimportant, but consider that you too
are a member of the same body which sustains all, and just
like the eye, so this part too causes the body to be a body. For
where the body is being built up, size is irrelevant. What
constitutes the body is not the fact that one part is bigger
than another, but that the parts are many and various. If you,
because you are greater, contribute to building up the body,
so does the other one because he is smaller. When there is
need of building up the body, his littleness is equal to your
greatness because he does exactly what you do." [32]

In virtue of the presence and efficiency of the whole organism in each of its members "the members seem to be separated, but they are strictly interwoven and if one is destroyed
the others are destroyed too. Notice: the eyes shine, the face
smiles, the lips are red, the nose straight and the eyebrows
smooth. But if one of these were to perish, it would ruin the

beauty of all the rest, and all would be filled with sadness. Where before these things seemed beautiful, now they would seem ugly." [33]

The functions of the members are inseparable in the same way, a fact which demonstrates that the particular function of each member is simultaneously a function of the whole, a common function of the one organism and, in a sense, of all the other members too inasmuch as it sustains their own functions. "If you wish to perceive this in the matter of functions, take away a finger, and you will see that the others are more clumsy at their work and can no longer do their task in the same way as before. If therefore the destruction of one member causes a common ugliness while the preservation of all means a shared beauty, let us not puff ourselves up beside our neighbour or offend him in any way, because it is through the insignificant member that the great one is beautiful and comely, as it is through the tiny eyelash that the eye itself acquires its beauty. Therefore whoever contends against his brother struggles against himself. Nor does the damage stop at his brother. In no small measure it will hurt the man himself. . . . Let us transpose this image of the body to the Church and be solicitous for all her various members." [34] Elsewhere Chrysostom speaks of this same reciprocal dependence or communion among the activities of the different members: "Once again, if the eyes suffer from something, all feel the pain and everything stops. The feet no longer move, the hands do no work; not even the stomach enjoys its food although the sickness is in the eyes. . . . Why do all these functions cease? Because they are one with the eyes, and the whole body suffers unspeakably. If it did not suffer, it could not share in this anxiety for the eyes. . . . The opposite is also true: if the head is crowned, the whole man is glorified; the mouth speaks, the eyes smile and rejoice even though the good reputation belongs to the tongue, not to the beauty of the eyes." [35]

Having thus explained the words of St. Paul, "If one member suffers, all suffer together; if one member is honoured, all rejoice together" (1 Cor 12:26), Chrysostom insists on that shared element which all members experience: "Hence he has seen to it that even anxiety is shared by all, and he has made the unity consist in so great a diversity that whatever happens may be shared by all. For if care for our neighbour means shared salvation, then both glory and sadness will also be shared. Thus the Apostle looks for three things: that we do not break apart from one another but become more closely united, that we take care one for the other, and that we consider that what happens to each of us happens to all of us in common." [36]

From these few lines of St. John Chrysostom we should retain the general idea of the presence and the activity of the whole organism in each member. This whole (ὅλον) in the present context is the Church. Through the Church each member completes his own task, but in such a way that it becomes simultaneously a common task, an activity of the Church for the Church. What gives the Church this character of "wholeness" is the Holy Spirit, for, in the last analysis, he is the one who gives the various gifts and causes them therefore to be put to use in the service of the whole and to appear as common gifts for the sake of the whole. "Now there are varieties of gifts, but the same Spirit." (1 Cor 12:4) The Spirit is the same; he is wholly in the whole Church and wholly in each member.

Because the Spirit is present in each believer and as such is the force which holds them all together, we can say that all the faithful are present in him. In this respect the Spirit resembles a kind of spiritual "milieu" in which all are brought together, or a bridge which joins all together. St. Basil says: "For the Spirit is called the place of those who are being sanctified," [37] and certainly he is a lifegiving fluid or "place", an atmosphere in and from which all who make up the Church live and move spiritually.

We meet this idea in a surprising way in the modern thinker Martin Buber who speaks of man's communication with the other within a "sphere" which the two share but which extends beyond the particular domain of the one or the other. According to Buber the astonishing meeting between two is not something sentimental, but "ontic", and this ontic element is not to be found *in* the two existents but *between* them. In the

dialogue between two there is a third which transcends both
the individual and the social, both the subjective and the objective. "On the small border where the 'I' and 'thou' meet is
the Kingdom of Between." This reality permits the transcending of individualism and of the kind of social life which is
destructive of persons, just as it permits the founding of an
authentic community. Only in this living relation is the life
of man renewed.[38]

This living relation is realized in the Holy Spirit because
he himself is alive. He is life, the Giver of life to the two
(or the more than two) who meet in him, on the sole condition that they truly meet in him. One alone cannot enter into
this milieu, for it lies between two or more and is never enclosed within the limits of the solitary one.

At the same time the Holy Spirit is a *Person* between the
two. He is the Person who sustains the relationship, not merely
an impersonal milieu. Perhaps it is precisely because he is the
Person who sustains relations that he is the Person who gives
life. For a person comes alive always and only "within a relationship". The Holy Spirit can under no circumstances be
possessed in individual isolation. Hence the Spirit gives himself in the Church of the New Testament just as he did in the
Old Testament, that is, specifically for the service of the community. He is given for the sake of the priestly ministry. Even
his gifts in the Sacrament of Chrismation are given for the
general priesthood, for the strengthening of service. The
Saviour gave the Spirit to the Apostles in common (Jn 20:22);
on the day of Pentecost the Holy Spirit came down upon the
Apostles in common; in their turn the Apostles, at least two
of them together, conferred the Spirit on those who were
baptized (Acts 8:14-17); and even to the present day the
chrism with which those who receive the gifts of the Holy
Spirit are anointed is consecrated by a group of bishops rep-
resenting the whole Church.

We all have within ourselves the impulse to transcend
self and to be in the other, although without confusing ourselves with the other or the other with ourselves. It is only
sin which tends to confuse others within our own selves by
annihilating them. Because all of us want to be "between"

ourselves and the other, we *are* all, in a manner as yet in-complete, between ourselves and the other.

The Holy Spirit possesses this quality in the highest and most complete degree. He gathers in himself the one and the other. He is between the one and the other, but as more than just a longing between them: he is a living reality. Therefore, "he who fills all things" is also he who fulfills our longing for communion. In him we truly find a position "between" ourselves and the other. He is the mid-point between us, the milieu in which we really transcend both the one and the other. This quality of the Holy Spirit is evident first of all in the internal life of the Holy Trinity. He proceeds or flows continually from the Father to the Son, and shines forth upon the Father from the Son on whom he rests. He does not also proceed from the Son because he remains eternally between the Father and the Son. He does not proceed beyond the Son because he has no place to go. And the Spirit cannot proceed from the Son towards the Father because in their mutual relations the Father must maintain unchanged his position as Father and the Son his position as Son.

Precisely because the Spirit does not proceed "also from the Son", nor beyond the Son, but remains as the bond between Father and Son, he gathers us together in the Son whose face is turned always toward the Father. The communion with us and among us which he effects is not something apart from the Son and the Trinity.

Through the Spirit we who have been united in the Son have a filial relation to the Father, not in exactly the same manner, obviously, as natural sons begotten by the Father, but in the manner of sons adopted through the Spirit, which is to say, we have been gathered into one under the same overshadowing presence of the Spirit in whom is also the Son and through whom the Son is bound to the Father. We are related among ourselves as brothers, and Jesus Christ is Brother to us all in our midst.

The Saviour has said: "For where two or three are gathered in my name, there am I in the midst of them." (Mt 18:20) He is "in the midst" of the two or three (or more) in the Holy Spirit. The Spirit is a kind of "midst", a "milieu" for the faithful. It is in this sense that the priest says at the Divine Liturgy, "Christ is in our midst." When Christ is in the midst of his faithful with his Spirit, he is not in a milieu which is isolated from the existence of mankind; rather, for Christ to be "in the midst" means that he is in a milieu which, like a bridge stretching between them, brings men together into one.

Orthodoxy therefore does not explain the Church from an exclusively christological point of view: the Church is the Body of Christ only because the same Spirit of the Son has united all her members in Christ as his brothers and as brothers among themselves, and by so doing has brought them all together within one filial relation to the Father.

A Contemporary Orthodox Theologian On The Activity Of The Holy Spirit In The Church

The Orthodox theologian Vladimir Lossky has also insisted on the link between Church and Holy Spirit.[39] According to Lossky, as the Church we are placed in living connexion with the Holy Trinity. The life of the Holy Trinity with its unity of nature and distinction of persons extends throughout the communion of the faithful, establishing, sustaining and animating it with the trinitarian love. "Here we touch the very source of catholicity, the mysterious identity of the whole and of the parts, the distinction between human nature and persons, complete identity which is at the same time complete diversity — the initial mystery of the Christian revelation, the dogma of the Holy Trinity . . . If the Church possesses catholicity, it is because the Son and the Holy Spirit, sent by the Father, have revealed the Trinity to her; not in an abstract way, in the form of an intellectual apprehension, but as the very rule of her life. Catholicity is a bond, binding the Church to God, who reveals Himself to her as Trinity while bestowing upon her the mode of being proper to the divine unity in diversity, an ordering of life 'in the image of the Trinity'. For this reason every dogmatic error touching the Trinity must find its expression in the conception of the Church, must translate itself into a profound change in the ecclesiastical organism." [40]

"We know the Holy Trinity through the Church, and the Church through the revelation of the Trinity. In the light of the dogma of the Trinity catholicity becomes clear as the mysterious identity of the one and the many — unity which is diversified and diversity which remains one. As in God there is no one Nature apart from the Three Persons, so in the Church there is no abstract universality but a complete harmony of catholic diversity. As in God each one of the Three Persons, Father, Son, and Holy Spirit, is not a part of the Trinity, but fully God in virtue of His ineffable identity with the One Nature, so the Church is not a federation of her parts: she is catholic in each of her parts, since each part in her is identified with the whole, expresses the whole, has the value which the whole has, does not exist outside the whole." [41]

Lossky is correct when he sees the sobornicity of the Church as modelled on the pattern of the Holy Trinity and sustained by the irradiation of the Holy Trinity within her. Yet he does not assign to the Holy Spirit the role which the Fathers gave him in the foundation and preservation of the Church as unity in diversity, as the bond joining the parts together in unity. In his explanation of the Church Lossky makes use of one of his own theories according to which Christ brings about the Church only as unity, and the Holy Spirit only as diversity. "When, as often happens in the treatment of catholicity, the emphasis is placed on unity, when catholicity is above all other consideration based upon the dogma of the Body of Christ, then Christocentrism invades the theory of the Church. The catholicity of the Church becomes a function of her unity, becomes a universal doctrine that absorbs in imposing itself, instead of being a tradition evident to every person, affirmed by all, at all times and in all places, in an infinite richness of living witness. On the other hand, if the emphasis is placed on diversity at the expense of unity there is a tendency to base catholicity exclusively on Pentecost, forgetting that the Holy Spirit is communicated in the unity of the Body of Christ." [42]

In reality the Holy Spirit is neither a cause of disintegration in the Church nor of mere diversification, and this for two reasons: firstly, because he is communicated within the unity of the Body of Christ, and secondly because he is himself a principle of unity; he does not come into a pre-existent unity in the Body of Christ, but is himself the power of unification, the gift of unity in communion, and hence the factor which constitutes the Mystical Body of the Lord, which is to say, the Church. Christ, in turn, is not cause of some merely indistinct unity within the Church, for he is more than just a human nature. He is a divine Person and consequently also a human person. As such he does not simply represent either the unity of nature proper to the Holy Trinity, nor some impersonal human nature, but in addition to this he represents a Person as a distinctive principle and as such he enters into personal relations with those who form his Mystical Body, affirming their personal reality.

Lossky asserts on the one hand that unity in the Church is a unity of nature and diversity a diversity of persons, while on the other hand he considers Christ to be the principle of this unity of nature in the Church and the Holy Spirit the principle of personal diversity. In this way he encourages the conclusion that within the Trinity the Son is not Person but Nature while the Holy Spirit does not himself possess the one divine nature but exclusively represents the personal principle. This conception approximates the *filioque* theory according to which both Father and Son, by causing the Holy Spirit to proceed as from a single unity, are viewed — in some indeterminate way — as one Being. On the other hand it leaves the impression that Christ did not also become, as man, a person.

Both in its unity and in its diversity the Church comes into being as much through the Holy Spirit as through Christ. And the Son and the Spirit do not work separately but in a perfect unity, bound together as they are both by their essential unity and also by their personal relations.

Nevertheless the Holy Spirit has a particular role in establishing and sustaining the Church both as unity in communion and as unity in diversity. He represents *par excellence* the living relationship between Father and Son, and as such provides the foundation for the living relationship which obtains between members of the Church, as well as between these members and the Father. For it is in the Holy Spirit that both the distinction of Persons in God and the unity between the Persons come to their complete expression. In him the Trinity appears in its "finished" form, to use an expression of St. Gregory Nazianzen. He is the keystone between the different Persons, and he is also the living force of unity among the faithful and between the faithful and the Holy Trinity. Coming to rest from all eternity upon the incarnate Son, the Holy Spirit after the incarnation also comes to rest upon the personal humanity of Christ and then upon all who are united with Christ through faith. But through this coming-to-rest upon Christ he unites the faithful not only with Christ and among themselves in Christ, but also with the Father as sons of the Father together with Christ. The Holy Spirit proceeds no further than the Son, and neither he nor the Son can belong to the faithful apart from the other. The Spirit is the principle of connexion between man and God, not the principle of separation. The Church therefore cannot be conceived apart from the Trinity as a Church which belongs exclusively to Christ or exclusively to the Spirit, ideas which are peculiarly Western (the former Catholic, the latter Protestant). But neither can the Church be conceived as something in which the Son and the Spirit work simultaneously but in isolation from one other, as though the Son stood for the single nature of the Trinity and therefore effected the unity of human nature in the Church, while the Holy Spirit stood for the diversity of Persons in the Trinity and accordingly brought about the diversity of human persons within the Church. At bottom this would reduce the personal reality of the Trinity to a single Person (the Holy Spirit) and the communion of the faithful as persons to an exclusive communion with the Holy Spirit. Were this the case, the presence of the Trinity in the life of the Church would not be represented in its fullness.

Lossky's intuition in constructing his theory of the Son as representative of the essential unity of the Trinity and as restorer of the unity of human nature was correct. He began with the teaching that the Son is the Logos and, consequently, the one who reveals the Godhead as a structure which can be grasped by the intelligence. For it is true that in the Trinity the Father is the unfathomable depth, inaccessible and inconceivable; the Son is the Godhead revealed as a conceivable structure, stable and eternal, while the Spirit is the Godhead revealed as a relation between the unfathomable Father and the Son as structural revelation of the Divinity. Nothing seems more natural for the theological mind therefore than to conclude that the Son as structure is the representative of unity inasmuch as both unity and stability depend necessarily on structure. Lossky has clearly drawn the conclusion (and made it his own) that the Son is the eternal unitary structure within the Trinity and therefore the one who brings about stable unitary structure within the Church.

What Lossky has not kept in mind however is that the divine Son is not an indistinct whole; his unity is at the same time a plenitude of meanings and as such the structure which he creates in his image is also a unity filled with meanings. In the unity of the structure of the cosmos and in the unity of the cosmos re-established as the Church, the diverse complexity of these particular meanings is to be distinguished. Thus the incarnate Logos does not bring the Church into being merely as an indistinct structure, but as a structure which in no way annuls the diversity of the various meanings, elements and persons which it contains.

Every created entity is part of that whole which is the universal "reason" corresponding to and in union with the uncreated Logos. Understood in this way nothing is self-sufficient or complete in itself. Nothing has within itself all that it needs; in fact, everything serves as a complement to all other things. Everything, by itself, is incomplete, "unilateral", and must meet its own needs with the help of all the others, and so it helps in its own turn to meet the needs of all the others. Each has a more particular gift which the others need, and certain undeveloped potentialities in itself which demand the presence of others if they are to be developed. Each is universal in potency only, and can become universal in act, although without ever ceasing to be itself, only when surrounded by and in communion with all men and all things.

Not even in the Church — *pace* Lossky — can sobornicity (catholicity) be understood as an existing plenitude in each member, unless that member is considered as joined to the whole.

The Holy Spirit is the one in whom this communion is, in fact, made real. The Holy Spirit is the one who, through his divine fluidity, re-establishes the weakened unity existing among the various elements of the structure of creation. And the nature of this unity is such that it does not confuse these elements precisely because it is re-established by the Spirit in the incarnate Logos, the divine structure in which all elements and all meanings are contained without any loss of identity. As a Spirit of unified life the Holy Spirit radiates out from the Head of the Church into all the members, just as the blood flows through all the cells and unifies them all. It was not without reason that even from apostolic times the imposition of hands as means and symbol for the gifts of the Holy Spirit given after baptism was replaced in the East by the anointing with chrism which corresponds to the Old Testament usage according to which oil symbolized the power of the Holy Spirit. The chrism symbolizes in the most adequate way possible the fluidity of the Holy Spirit extending into all the parts of the ecclesial organism. He spreads out like an oil, but more especially like a perfume. Whoever receives the Holy Spirit in the Church receives him in the form of a fluid or a fragrance, a breath of life spreading out from him into all the other members of the Church, binding him to them and thereby sustaining the whole organism and its sobornicity. This fluid provides no foundation for rigid structure, but as Spirit in the most precise sense of that word, that is, a wave diffusing outwards, it overcomes every separation and brings things formerly distinct into union among themselves. Whoever has seen the Monastery of Arges admires the harmonious unity of the place. Yet this unity and harmony are formed of ornaments no two of which are the same. Here is a symbol of Orthodox sobornicity, a visible image of the all-encompassing Logos, for it is well known that, according to St. Gregory of Nyssa, Moses on Mt. Sinai saw the Logos as the Church.

When once the Church is conceived as a living organism

preserved in unity by the Holy Spirit who is himself understood as interpersonal relation in the Church, as the personal
fluid flowing from Christ the Head and uniting all the members to one another and to their Head, then it becomes impossible to conceive the exercise of any function or gift within
the Church apart from its relation to the whole ecclesial community. Those who celebrate the Mysteries in the Church
celebrate them in relation to the community with which they
are linked through the Holy Spirit. Those who plumb the
depths of Truth do so in relation to the ecclesial community
with which they are linked through the Holy Spirit. The
Holy Spirit, conceived as the relationship between all believers
and all ministries, makes individualism or hierarchical ex-
clusivism impossible in principle. It also makes the thesis of
infallibility *ex sese non ex consensu Ecclesiae* impossible.
No single believer exists in the Church because of himself, nor
does any believer exercise any gift in isolation. Similarly, in
the visible Church, as the Body of the Lord, there exists no
head other than the supreme Head of the Body who is Christ.
Another head of the Church, other than Christ, would make
the Church autonomous from Christ, self-sufficient. To admit
a head of the Church analogous to Christ and substituting for
him would mean that such a head would be removed from
the life of mutual interdependence and would be thought to
provide for the Body of Christ from within himself and to
receive nothing from it in return. Such a position is claimed
for the Pope when he attributes infallibility to himself *ex sese
non ex consensu Ecclesiae.* But this is an impossibility. It means
that a man is being raised to the level of divinity; it means
that he is identified with Christ or, more exactly, that there
are two Christs.

Returning to Lossky's theory, we must make it plain here
that we are not interested in a unilateral conception of the
Holy Spirit as a principle of diversification. This would make
of the Holy Spirit either a counterbalance to a christological
principle of exaggerated unity (Catholicism) or an anarchical
emphasis (Protestantism) against which the christological
principle would have to contend.

The Holy Spirit is himself the principle of variety in unity, the principle of sobornic variety, that is, of unity in communion. He creates and sustains the whole organism in which individual parts are not suppressed but instead remain alive and active and find in fact the very condition of their life and growth.

Nissiotis has reproached Catholicism with making the Holy Spirit into an instrument of order within the Church. There is no need however to deny that the Holy Spirit is in principle a factor of order within the Church. What we must reject is this order as it is conceived by Catholicism: an order achieved by subordinating the whole body of the Church to one group of her members (the magisterium), or even to one single member who is held to be the very head. Such a conception implies that the activity of the Spirit suppresses natural gifts rather than encouraging their development through the agency of the Spirit's own supernatural gifts. But Church order, the order which the Spirit maintains, is not the order of uniformity. It is the order of symphony, an order in liberty and love, an order of sobornicity and brotherhood. It is an order which does not stifle manifestations of originality arising from the Spirit himself. It is an order in which these movements exist in harmonious correlation and reciprocal obedience because such is the obedience given to the Holy Spirit who preserves the oneness of the Body in the variety of its members and ministries.

CHAPTER III

The Holy Trinity: Structure of Supreme Love*

The Tripersonal Consubstantial Form Of God And Its Manifold Significance

1. God in himself is a mystery. Of his inner existence nothing can be said. But through creation, through providence and his work of salvation, God comes down to the level of man. He who made us as thinking and speaking beings has made himself accessible to our thought and our speech. Touching our spirit he wakens in us thoughts and words which convey the experience of his encounter with us. But at the same time we realize that our thoughts and our words about him do not contain him completely as he is in himself. For us men they are flowers grown up from the depths of his ineffable mystery. Our words and thoughts of God are both cataphatic and apophatic, that is, they say something and yet at the same time they suggest the ineffable. If we remain enclosed within our formulae they become our idols; if we reject any and every formula we drown in the undefined chaos of that ocean. Our words and thoughts are a finite opening towards the infinite, transparencies for the infinite, and so they are able to foster within us a spiritual life.

We are aware of the infinity of the divine ocean but we

* Originally published in Romanian in *Studii Teologice* 22 (1970), 333-355.

do not dissolve in it ourselves. We communicate with it in human fashion, going down into its depths with the diving suit of human nature and human formulae, or sailing on its vast expanse in a boat constructed according to laws based on our experience of the ocean itself and therefore adequate to it but adapted also to our own human limitations.

The Greek metropolitan Emilianos Timiades writes: "We can say that just as the incarnation of the Word in the life and works of the historical Christ is a condescension of the divinity towards human obscurity, a condescension through which 'mysteries hidden from the foundation of the world' are revealed, so the same Word, the Truth himself, comes down in order to 'be incarnate' in our formulae and in the dogmas that serve to guide the Christian through the labyrinth of confusion and ignorance in which he finds himself. In other words, doctrinal formulations have a twofold aspect. On the one hand, they 'reveal' the Truth in terms accessible to human intelligence, and in this sense they have an affirmative or cataphatic aspect and are useful to man both as supports in his spiritual growth into maturity, and as safeguards against the mistaken conceptions which human intelligence is always tempted to adopt. But on the other hand, they are not the Truth itself, only expressions of the Truth in human terms, and in this sense they have a negative or apophatic aspect." [1]

2. God has revealed himself clearly as Trinity in the work of salvation and hence this revelation is clear only in Christ in whom God has come down among men in order to save them. A uni-personal God remains an exclusively transcendent God who does not himself accomplish the salvation of men but issues instructions to them as to the way in which they can save themselves. An exclusively immanent God, wholly identified with the world, is no longer a personal God, or, if he is, then men are no longer real persons but only apparent ones manifesting a single being, namely, their very own essence. A personal and saving God is a God simultaneously transcendent and revealed in immanence. In the Old Testament where God still remains only transcendent, even though he acts upon history from a distance, he is not revealed as Trinity.

The revelation of the Trinity took place in Christ, for one divine Person became man in order to save men, while another divine Person remained above men so that He who had become incarnate might raise men up to that divine Person who was not incarnate but transcendent. The Son becomes man but the Father remains the goal of the incarnate Son's striving and that of all the men whom the Son has united to himself. The incarnate Son could not have been without this goal or else he would not have been able to imprint this striving towards it upon all the faithful.

The Son becomes man in order to be the model and the centre from which a force shines out making men like Christ in their striving towards God the Father. This force, which becomes an intimate principle within all who believe yet always remains at the same time above them, is the third divine Person, the Holy Spirit. In the Spirit God becomes wholly immanent and yet imprints upon all men this yearning for the transcendent God. The Holy Spirit must be a Person in order to make us grow as persons ourselves, yet he must be the equal of the transcendent God in order to lead us into his presence and, by divinizing us, give us a place as true partners with God.

When the God in Trinity reveals himself to us, he reveals himself as a saviour-God, and a God whom we experience in the saving activity that he exercises upon us and within us. He is revealed to us as an economic Trinity.

But in this revelation of itself the Trinity also draws our attention to certain premises about the intrinsic relations between the divine Persons. The theological teaching on the inner reality of the Holy Trinity is based on these indications and on the bond which joins the eternal relations between the divine Persons together with their saving activity.

3. A God who is one and three at the same time is a mystery beyond our logical grasp; it is the supreme apophatic reality. Yet this mode of God's being is the highest stage of the true spiritual life and the goal for which the Christian as a spiritual being yearns continuously. Each and every Christian taken individually and all of us together want to reach a rich spiritual life; we want to achieve a perfect balance between

the unity we share and the separate identities we maintain within this unity. We are aware that the most perfect and most meaningful unity is unity in love, that is, unity between persons who retain their own individual identities. Any other unity is devoid of meaning and spiritual life. Hence the expressions "one in being" and "three in Persons" must not lead us to contemplate the divine being in itself as distinct from the Persons and from their mutual love, but rather as the love existing in persons and between persons.

The Russian theologian Boris Bobrinskoy writes: "The divine unity is not merely one of the attributes of God; more exactly it is the profound life of God and the fruit of the love that exists between the divine Persons. This unity is in no way a depersonalizing confusion, nor a structure of monads, nor the sum of the parts of a whole. Only in God does unity assure a complete union which preserves the distinct and absolute qualities of the Persons." [2]

4. God is pure subject. But the character of being a pure subject is experienced only by one who in no way experiences himself as object of the other, or who does not experience the other as he experiences himself, that is, as his own object. Otherwise this would create a certain opposition between subjects, and every "I" would also experience himself as the object of the other. The divine "I" as pure subject must be experienced as such by another divine "I" and must also experience the other divine "I" as pure subject. Pure divine subjectivity is experienced in the perfect communion of certain "I's" united in a unique subjectivity. Thus, we speak of one God (a unique subject) and of three "I's" (three subjects).

On the basis of divine revelation Christian teaching affirms that the Father begets the Son eternally. This begetting is not the action of one subject upon another since this would in some sense make the latter into an object of the former. Accordingly, while it is said of the Son that he is begotten of the Father, it is also said of him that he takes his birth from the Father. But the fact that this begetting or birth is eternal indicates that the Son enjoys the same character of pure subject. The birth/begetting of the Son from the Father expresses by this term "birth" or "begetting" only the unchanged position of the two Persons and the unity between them. The Son exists eternally in the movement of being born from the Father.

Nor does the term "proceed" indicate any passivity on the part of the Holy Spirit such as to make him an object of the Father in some respect. The Saviour has said that the Spirit "proceeds from the Father" (Jn 15:26). The Spirit is eternally in the act of proceeding from the Father, but neither does this mean that the Father is placed in a state of passivity. The Spirit proceeds but the Father also causes him to proceed.[3] The act of the Son's begetting and the act of the Spirit's procession are acts of a pure common subjectivity, the first proper to the Father and the Son, the second to the Father and the Holy Spirit. But within these common acts each Person has his own place. The Father and the Son are united and yet distinct in the act of begetting as an act of pure subjectivity. They experience this act together yet without their being any confusion of the one with the other. The Father and the Holy Spirit are similarly one and distinct in the act of procession of the Holy Spirit.

5. The divine subjectivity cannot be the subjectivity of a single "I". An "I" without another "I" and without an object, that is, a subject sunk within itself, is robbed of all reality. The content of the divine "I" must consist not in opposed subjects and objects, but in other subjects interior to itself in an internal intersubjectivity. Because they do not each individually possess natures, the divine "I's" can be perfectly interior to themselves. Inasmuch as a divine Person does not possess the other Persons as if they were "contents", properly so-called, the relation of the divine "I's" must be conceived as a communion so perfect that each subject must experience himself as a triune subject, as a triformal subject, yet without changing his own proper position. The Father experiences himself as Father, but he simultaneously experiences, as Father, all the subjectivity of the Son. The subjectivity of the Son is interior to him, but as to a Father. It is infinitely more interior to him than is the filial subjectivity of an earthly son to an earthly father.

This is the potentiality of experience at its highest level, rather like the experience of a mother who can substitute herself for her son and live his own joys and sorrows. But just as the Father experiences the subjectivity of the Son as his own subjectivity, although precisely in his character as Father, in the same way the Son experiences the paternal subjectivity of the Father but precisely in his character as Son. All is common in the Trinity, but in this communion there is no confusion of the distinct modes in which each Person experiences what is common.

The responsibility that one believer feels for another, the prayer that he offers on behalf of another, represent imperfect degrees of this permanent and reciprocal substitution of the divine Persons, imperfect degrees of a permanent identification that is able nevertheless to respect and maintain separate identities.

6. A lone "I" cannot experience the fullness on which complete joy and happiness depend, a fullness which only takes the forms of pure subjectivity. The joy of the lone "I", of that which is by itself, is not complete joy and therefore not the fullness of existence. And the joy of existence communicated by one "I" to another "I" must be just as full in the one who gives as in the one who receives. Hence there is also fullness of existence. But this implies the complete self-giving of one "I" to another "I", not merely the giving of something from oneself or from what one possesses. There must be a total giving and receiving by one "I" to another in order to bring about a kind of reciprocal possession of "I's" which nevertheless remain distinct within this very possession.

But this means that from all eternity God is a common act of love according to the measure of his absolute character and pure subjectivity. In perfect love persons do not merely engage in a reciprocal exchange of self; they also affirm themselves through this reciprocal giving and establish themselves in existence. But the divine love is all efficacious. The Father therefore establishes the Son in existence from all eternity by his integral self-giving while the Son continually affirms the Father as Father by the fact that he both accepts his own coming into existence through the Father and gives himself to the Father as Son. Now God cannot be lacking in a perfect and eternal love. The acts through which this reciprocal establishment of the divine Persons in existence is accomplished are eternal acts and have a totally personal character, although they are acts in which the divine Persons are active together.

Were the love of God directed only towards contingent beings which at some given time have had a beginning to their existence, it would also be a love which once had a beginning and so would be contingent. This would mean that in God love begins to be, thus causing an important change in God, or it would mean that love is not essential to God. This would in turn make the appearance and existence of love inexplicable and accord it a role devoid of importance in all existence everywhere. On the other hand in order to love a contingent world God has to bring it into existence, that is, he must have love for it before it can come to be. Only from an eternal and infinite act of love can we explain the creation of other existing things as well as all God's other acts of love for them. Love must exist in God prior to all those acts of his which are directed outside himself; it must be bound up with his eternal existence. Love is the "being of God"; it is his "substantial act".[4]

It is plain however that love, like goodness too, must not be understood in a way that excludes the whole ocean of qualities and possibilities belonging to the divine being, such as love in the special sense of the word. The act of eternal love which is in God means the reciprocal gift and perfect communion between "I" and "I", together with all that this implies. This communion means both truth and perfect existence and the divine absoluteness. In every divine act or attribute all the others are implied. In the divine love is all.

7. In God the love between "I's" is perfect and therefore the unity between them is surpassing. Even so the distinct "I's" are not abolished within this unity, otherwise the living relationship between them would be impossible.

If love depends essentially on God, then the reciprocal relationship in which love manifests itself also belongs to the divine being. In God there must be relation, but as from equal to equal, not, as is the case among men, from superior to inferior. On the other hand, this relation must not be thought to refer to something outside God. This would imply that God has need of something distinct from himself. But divine relation must take place in God himself. God must relate to himself, but this self with whom he relates must at the same time be another in order for the relation and consequently for the love to be real. The trinitarian structure corresponds to the paradoxical combination of these requirements.

In order to maintain the definition of love as the essential divine act and the simultaneous definition of this act as a relation while the divine essence remains one, we must see the divine essence simultaneously as a relation — unity, or, conversely, as unity — relation. Unity must not be destroyed on behalf of relation, nor relation abolished in favour of unity. Relation or reciprocal reference is act, and this act belongs to God's essence. Reference is common in God although each Person has his own position in this common act of reference. One Orthodox theologian has written in this connexion: "The subject of the truth is a relation of the Three, but a relation which appears as substance, in other words, a substantial relation." [5]

8. Let us return to the notion of giving. All love between person and person reveals itself in giving. To hold on to a thing for yourself, or to possess something for your own sake means that you do not truly give another the joy of it. Your joy comes from the capacity of another to renounce something for your sake, and also from your own capacity to give it to another. Things have meaning as demonstrations of love between persons.

As the love is greater so the quantity and quality of the things given increase until the gift becomes the gift of everything that a person has. Every act of giving transforms the one who gives and also the one to whom gifts are given, not because of the goods received but because of the proof of love shown in the giving. Moreover, in love there is the tendency to give one's own person, to sacrifice oneself in order to promote the existence of the other into the most exalted condition possible. But among men it is never possible for someone to give himself wholly in the sense that his own existence is added to the existence of the other. A man can lose his own existence in the impulse to sacrifice, but he cannot add that existence to the existence of the other. This can only happen in God. A divine Person gives himself to the other in his supreme love, yet it is not possible for him to lose his existence in this way. On the other hand, he does not merely add himself to the other, for this would mean that the divine Person is not himself wholly efficacious. The self-giving of a divine Person, by this very act, establishes in existence the Person to whom he wished to give himself, and thus fashions him completely in his image. The Person established in existence receives everything from the other's act of giving; he is the very existence of the other, experienced by another as gift. But giving is reciprocal between persons who love each other, and so it is between the divine Persons. Thus the joy of a divine Person who eternally possesses the initiative of giving is twofold: firstly, it is the joy of giving oneself and so of establishing the other in existence in order that he may receive the gift and thus the two can rejoice together in the fullness of existence; secondly, it is the joy of receiving back the being that was given, as a sign of the other's love. A human father who gives all to his child has great joy in doing this, but his joy is only full when his child turns back to him from the things which he has received. Each man rejoices in something only to the extent to which he receives it from the other as a sign of the other's love. The essential nourishment for every man's existence is the love of someone else; existence without love is not in itself a source of joy.

In the case of the divine reciprocal giving, however, Father and Son preserve their own positions. The Son rejoices in the gift of existence received from the Father, and the Father rejoices in the gift of his own gift received by the Son.

9. Christians are aware that all men are brothers. But brothers are born from a common father and mother which means that men are brothers because they come from a common source of being, because they draw their existence from the same common source. In every man — my brother — I must see manifested in a different way, a way that is a complement to my own way, the same source of being which is

also revealed in me. Therefore I must rejoice in all those gifts of his which I do not have, and in all his successes, while he must also extend the benefit of his own gifts and successes to me, because in a certain manner I am in him and he is in me, or, to express it in another way, the same source that is manifested in him is also my own. This is our human consubstantiality.[6] But in this consubstantiality we are different, as the divine Persons are not, and we serve as complements to each other, a fact that derives from a certain separation that exists between us and which we can make larger or smaller since human nature repeats itself distinctly in every "I". The separation nevertheless is not total. It is not ontological, as if it were a separation between one nature and another.

Both our consubstantiality and its imperfect realization are visible in the fact that although I can say "I", I am conscious that I am "I" only when I say "Thou", or when I am conscious of a "Thou".[7] But although I seek the "Thou" and I can change the "Thou", I do not bring it forth from myself. Consequently we can speak of the reality of our mutual spiritual birth, or of a coming to consciousness of our complementary belonging to one another which is the arrival at full consciousness.

"Thou" belongest to my existence and without "Thee" I would not have come forth from the state of consciousness, or I would have fallen into despair. But "Thou" belongest to my existence as a "Thou" not produced from within me. When I say "We", I place more emphasis on "Our" unity as on something that cannot be reduced to an "I". When I say "Thou", or "I — Thou", I throw the difference between us into greater relief, but at the same time I am stressing the complementary nature of our "I's".

I can only say "Him" after I have become conscious of "Thee". "He" is the pronoun used to designate the one who ought to become a "Thou" for me, or who has ceased for a while to be a "Thou" for me. "He" is the manifestation of the fact that not every person can be simultaneously "Thou" for me with the others who are "Thou". But "He" is also the manifestation of the fact that, indeed, I do not talk much about "Him" when I am alone, but only when I am together with "Thee".

Therefore "He" too belongs to me, or to the unity "I — Thou", as a complement of that unity. I am not complete even in relation with "Thee", but am still in need of relation with "Him". We all find our fulfillment by virtue of an infinite number of those who are called "Thou" or "He".

In God the consubstantiality of these three Persons is perfect. God is the perfect model of the tri-personal, consubstantial form of human existence, of the perfect mutual interiority of three persons.

10. Perfect consubstantiality can exist only between subjects who do not drag behind them any of the burden of being "thing" or "object", that is, between subjects who share a perfect love. Whereas irrational things are composed of parts, the subject is a whole, simple, and not open to disintegration. One subject cannot contain another subject except wholly, though the degree to which this is achieved may be larger or smaller. But a subject cannot contain objects wholly, though there does exist a bond between the subject and the things of the cosmos, or between the subject and everything in the cosmos, a bond which makes them one composite whole. Human persons cannot be contained wholly because they also have bodies. It is to a greater or lesser degree that, as subjects, human persons are contained, because their bodies — although these also enter into a relation — cannot become totally interior to themselves, and therefore neither can human persons become totally interior to themselves. The Christian looks even upon his body, which belongs in the greatest degree only to himself, as a part of himself, and as something which is, to a certain extent, outside himself. Complete love among men would have as a result that each man cared for all the others, and even for their bodily needs. Moreover the transfiguration of bodies through the resurrection introduces the faithful into a truly consubstantial existence. As one who is perfectly consubstantial with us, transfigured in body and wholly pure, Christ gives us his body in Holy Communion.

11. But there is another obstacle in the path of our full

human consubstantiality. Every individual experiences himself
in relation with all other persons as "I", and experiences the
others either as "Thou" or "He". But each person is experienced in turn by these other persons as "Thou" or "He". To
every individual person there is this simultaneous threefold
aspect or position precisely because on the one hand he views
himself from within in relation to the others who are situated
in the other two positions ("Thou" — "He"), and on the
other hand he is viewed from these two positions in which the
others are situated. But because the individual cannot see himself from these other two positions which belong to the others,
he cannot imagine exactly how he himself is experienced as
"Thou" and "He", nor can he experience himself as both
"Thou" and "He". However in his experience as the "I", he
knows the repercussions of the fact that he is viewed as
"Thou" and "He" by the others. These are able to treat him
to a greater or lesser degree as a subject, and accordingly
(and in proportion to this treatment) to a greater or lesser
degree also as object. Moreover, he is able to treat them in
the same way. The more he is treated as object the more he
feels a stranger to these others; and the more he treats others
as objects, the more he feels them becoming estranged from
himself, closing themselves to him and becoming enclosed
within themselves. My transformation of others into objects
and their transformation of me into an object is a weakening
of consubstantiality, a decline into an inferior kind of consubstantiality, the decline of real love through communion
into a facsimile only more or less faithful to the original.

One who feels himself treated as object not only feels that
he is an instrument, but he is also humiliated and repelled.
This humiliation is different from that humility or modesty
which is voluntary and which itself derives from a refusal
to treat others as objects. Humility is experienced in communion, whereas humiliation is the sign of a lack of communion.

On the other hand one who is viewed as subject feels himself simultaneously attracted into the inner world of the others
and cherished in his own subjectivity; consequently he in turn
makes room for the others within his own interior world. In
the same way, if he views the others as subjects, he makes

room for them in himself and they open their inner world to him. The subjectivity of each person grows to the extent to which he is open to others as subjects and they to him. Only in this reciprocal interiority, which is an experience of the subjectivity of others, is our own subjectivity fortified and do we thus make progress in consubstantiality.

God is from eternity and to all eternity this kind of perfect consubstantiality from which the consubstantiality of created subjects draws strength and towards which it progresses.

12. There was a time when the coincidence of opposites was considered incompatible with reason. Whenever a synthesis of such a kind was encountered — and the whole of reality is like this — reason would break it up into contradictory and irreconcilable notions.

But more recent scientific knowledge of the unitary-pluralist constitution of the atom and of all material reality has so accustomed reason to unify the principles of distinction and unity in its attempts at understanding the world, that it is no longer a problem to accept an antinomic model for all being. It is an accepted fact for science today that plurality does not break apart unity, nor does unity do away with plurality. In fact, plurality necessarily exists within unity, or, to express it in another way, unity is manifested in plurality. It is a fact that plurality maintains unity and unity maintains plurality, and that the decline or disappearance of either one means the weakness or disappearance of the other, the disappearance of the life of some kind of entity. This conception of the mode of being of reality is recognized today as superior to former ideas about what was rational, while, under the pressure of reality, the idea of what is rational has now become more complex and antinomic. Assertions formerly considered irrational because of their apparently contradictory character are now recognized as indications of a natural stage towards which reason must strive, a supra-rational stage that constitutes the natural destiny of reason, and which, although it does not take over the normal daily functioning of the reason, does call for sustained efforts on its part.

This effort towards the supra-rational as the natural destiny

of reason in its desire to become ever more subtle and sublime
is also required in order to understand the Christian teaching
on the Holy Trinity.

Obviously the effort of reason to elevate itself by climbing
the rungs of its own natural possibilities does not produce a
result that corresponds in all respects to revealed faith. It is
necessary in addition that rational effort also be an effort to
transcend reason's own present possibilities through humility
and respect for the data of revelation, in order that, by accepting the teaching on the Trinity through the grace which
is faith, reason may also share in the grace of that understanding which is greater than reason, understood here as our own
act and our own effort.

For on the spiritual plane in general, unity and distinction
are of a different order from that found on the plane of natural things. Material things do not have an indestructible
interior unity, and for this reason they are consistent in their
unity only in virtue of their component elements, or else they
merge together indistinctly. Persons however are in the first
instance interior "I's", non-composite (simple) and indissoluble. They are able to unite in their entirety as interior unities
without losing their character as unities. At the height of a
certain spiritual development we can conceive of their consubstantiality, of an identity of content experienced in common which yet preserves the distinct identities of individuals.
This is eminently what takes place in the case of the Holy
Trinity.

"Raising itself above the limits of its own nature the 'I'
emerges from its temporal-spatial limitations into eternity.
There the whole process of the reciprocal relation of those
who share a mutual love is one and the same act in which the
infinite chain of single moments of love finds its synthesis.
This unique act, eternal and infinite, is the essential unity of
those who love one another in God, in whom the 'I' appears
as identical with the other 'I' and yet as distinct from it. Each
'I' is a non-'I', that is, a 'Thou' because of its renunciation of
self in favour of the other, and it is an 'I' because of the self-
renunciation of the other in favour of it. In place of isolated
'I's', split apart and persisting in their isolation, a duality

emerges, a being which is both one and two, and which has its principle in God." "This duality has as its essence love." [8]

13. But the fact that material things, even if they are not completely interior to each other as "I's", do stand nevertheless within a certain continuity is visible in the fact that by memory and thought the "I" not only contains them but is even able to control and arrange them in large groupings. The "I" is able to contain virtually and to control in an ever more comprehensive and actual way the whole universe of material things, precisely because of the connexions which exist between them, not merely because of some greater or lesser likeness. [9]

The "I" is a concentrated whole which in its own way contains all things and in which the universe — viewed from a certain perspective and in a certain manner — is also contained, if not actually, at least virtually. Hence, an "I" containing another "I" contains it as a universe more or less actualized and as a complement to the universe of its own.

The aspiration and, in part, the realized capacity of the human "I" to be an unfragmented whole and simultaneously to contain all things, and especially to contain other "I's" as integral wholes within a similarly integrated whole, is a reality perfectly achieved in God, for otherwise the mode of being of the human "I" which we have discussed above would be inexplicable.

God is by nature the all, and — even prior to their coming into existence — he contains in his thought all the origins of things within a perfect unity. After they come to be he contains them in their reality. The divine love and happiness of God consist in the fact that in God an "I" which is the all contains other "I's" which are also the all, and that each of these "I's" contains the other. These "I's" do not encounter one another from the outside as is the case with human "I's". From eternity they are completely interior to one another just as human "I's" aspire to become. The divine all is not multiplied externally as is true with men, since if this were the case the divinity would no longer be absolute. It remains perfectly one and nevertheless there are three modes of being, each mode containing perfectly in itself the other modes as well. Each is, so to speak, the infinite divine "universe" in interior unity with the other divine "I's". No divine "I" can separate his divine universe from the other "I's". The divine "universe" belongs to each divine "I" in reciprocal interior communion with each of the others.

The Father, as the divine "universe" lived in one mode, contains the other two modes of being which belong to this same universe, not in the sense of being perfectly equal to them but of being identified with them. It is as if another "I" within my own "I" had title to all that I am, although I myself do not thereby cease to have title to all that I am. For us the difficulty of understanding this rests in the fact that in God an "I" does not have title to what belongs to another "I" as if to something distinct from his own "I", but as the content of this same "I". Hence in God it is not possible that one "I" should assert himself over against another "I"; instead he continually considers the other as a substitute for himself. Each divine "I" puts a "Thou" in place of himself. Each sees himself only in relation to the other. The Father sees himself only as the subject of the Son's love, forgetting himself in every other aspect. He sees himself only in relation with the Son. But the "I" of the Father is not lost because of this, for it is affirmed by the Son who in his turn knows himself only as he who loves the Father, forgetting himself. He affirms himself only implicitly in so far as he affirms the Father. This is the circular movement (περιχώρησις = *circumincessio*) of each divine "I" around the other as centre. They are three, yet each regards only the others and experiences only the others. The Father beholds only the Son, the Son only the Father, reducing themselves reciprocally by love to the other "I", to a single "I". But each pair of Persons in the Trinity, reduced in this manner to one, beholds only the third Person, and thus all three Persons are reduced to one. Each Person does not disclose his own "I", nor does each pair of Persons disclose its own "I", but whether individually or in pairs, the Persons place the other "I" in the forefront, hiding themselves (as it were) beneath him. Thus in each hypostasis the other two hypostases are also visible. St. Basil writes: "You see, consequently, that sometimes the Father reveals the Son, sometimes the Son reveals the Father . . . hence the whole divinity addresses itself to you at one time in the Father, at other times in the Son and in the Spirit." [10] "The character of the hypostasis of the Holy Spirit is to love by eclipsing himself, as the Father by forgetting himself loves the Son in whom he has placed all his joy, and as the Son is beloved because he puts off his own 'I' in order that the Father may be made manifest and the Spirit shine forth." [11]

The Trinity is the culmination of the humility and sacrifice of love. It represents the continual mortification of each "I", for it is the self-assertion of these "I's" that would make the absolute unity of love impossible, and thus give birth to individualism. And it is the sin of individualism that hinders us from understanding fully that the Holy Trinity is a complete identification of "I's" without their disappearance or destruction.

15. The affirmation of the filial "I" by the paternal "I" and vice versa is manifested concretely in the fact that all the works of the Father are effected by the Son, and vice versa. This is how we are to understand the idea that all the divine activities are common to the three Persons. In the eternal act whereby the "I" of the other reciprocally replaces the "I" of each other Person, it is the Father who continually has the initiative. He makes the Son the real possessor or the actual bearer of the act of intellection which rises up essentially from the Father. St. Athanasius says: "then, because the Father, as St. Paul says, is the only one who is wise, the Son is his wisdom." [12] The initiative of the Father in considering himself represented by another "I" is implied in the act which is known apophatically as the "begetting" of the Son from the Father. The Son is so completely the one who takes the Father's place and reveals him, though always by virtue of the Father's will, that St. Gregory of Nyssa calls the Son another "self" of the Father. "But he who sees the Son, sees the Father, the Father has begotten another Self of his own (ἄλλον ἑαυτόν), not by going outside himself, but by revealing himself wholly in this other." [13] The Saviour says: "Whoever has seen me, has seen the Father." (Jn 14:9)

This representation of the Father by the "I" of the Son,

and vice versa, is able to achieve such a degree of perfection
because the "I" of the Son, this other mode of being of the
divine universe, is begotten by the Father.

16. The meaning of the divine begetting goes beyond any
human power of understanding. But although the begetting
of the Son conforms to the will of the Father, it is necessarily
bound up with his divine existence, for it is only by communicating this existence to the other "I" that God the Father can
possess the full joy of the plenitude of divine existence. God
cannot be happy except as Father and Son. St. Basil the Great
says that it is good for the Father to have a Son and that, as
God, he cannot therefore be without such a good. Nevertheless
the Son is not begotten of the Father without the Father's will
but in conformity with it. For the Father cannot not will what
is such an essential good for himself. In conformity with the
eternal correspondence of this good with the divine existence
and with the eternal will of the Father's "I", a will which corresponds to his own Godhead, the Son is begotten from all
ages. Again St. Basil: "The good is eternally in God who is
above all; but it is good that there be a Father of such a Son.
Hence this good is never wanting to him, nor does he wish
to be Father without the Son. Now he is not without power
when he wills, and inasmuch as he both wills and has the power
it is natural that he possesses the Son eternally, because eternally he wills the good." [14] The Son comes forth from the
"being of the Father" not, as is the case with creatures, from
his will. But at the same time he is begotten of the Father in
accordance with his will. The divine being is absolutely free
existence. Even the love between the divine Persons can only
be conceived "in the context of freedom", [15] but clearly, this
freedom is in harmony with that good which is the divine
existence or "being".

The fullness of the divine existence is necessarily linked
with its communication to certain other "I's" in interpersonal
communion and with the joy which comes from this communication, a joy that no single "I" can experience in isolation.
Only thus is this fullness known and experienced completely
because only through this sharing is it a fully actual reality.
Thus the Son is also for the Father the one through whom the

Father knows himself, for the Son is the image and eternal radiance of the Father. The Son is the Wisdom of the Father; he is the Word which reveals the fullness of the Father just as the Father is the source of this Wisdom and of this revealing Word.

17. This is why it has become normal to consider the begetting of the Son from the Father as the thought which the Father thinks about himself, and to consider the Son as a "likeness" of the Father which the Father has thought, as the Eastern Fathers say, or as the Word gone forth from the Father's Mind (νοῦς). It is clear that in the "truly existing existence" of God every act is substantial and shares in existence. In God thinking is not one thing and existence another. By thinking himself, the Father duplicates himself hypostatically yet without becoming two in being. By thinking himself, he knows himself both as thinker and as the one who is thought and known by himself. He beholds the Son, the hypostatic "Truth", that is, himself as another "I", and simultaneously knows himself as the source of this his perfect Image.

18. The Swiss writer Ramuz has said, *"exprimer c'est agrandir"*. But expression is thought communicated. Hence thought "manifests" the reality which has been conceived in the mind. On the other hand, whoever enlarges things through thought also enlarges himself. God however does not just enlarge existing realities by thinking them, he also creates them. Moreover the very enlargement of a reality which occurs when someone thinks it is itself a kind of creation because of that which the thinker gives to the thing which he has thought, although it is not also true that the thinker thereby deprives the thing of its own originality or diminishes himself. When he thinks, the Father creates things — if he so wills — and gives them part of his power, or better, makes them exist by his power without making them identical with himself.

But when the Father thinks, it is principally the Son that he begets from his being. This is thought communicated in the very highest degree, thought in which, out of supreme love, a Person gives himself completely. We feel how much another person causes us to grow by the thought which he communicates to us, and we are aware how much he changes us and attracts us towards the good, bringing us to a rebirth through the benevolent imagination he exercises on our behalf. I am "reborn" and confirm the other in an ever expanding and deepening existence through the imaginative and loving thought about him that I communicate to him. At the same time I cause myself to grow. My consciousness and hence my existence on this higher level of conscious being is conditioned by what the other is thinking. We can say that God is both supreme being and therefore conscious being because he thinks himself, which is to say, he is an "I" who thinks another "I", an "I" whose consciousness is eternally full of another "I". Although it is not true that at some one moment God became both Father and Son because of this shared loving thought, God nevertheless is eternally Father and Son because of it.

The Procession Of The Holy Spirit From The Father And His Relation With The Son

1. The Father begets the Son by an act of intellection, but he also loves him. The divinity is an eternal act, one and triune at the same time, a unique act in a continual condition of triuneness, the Father thinking himself or begetting his image, and loving himself or loving his image.

This means a double relationship of God the Father to himself, and because the Father is God, this relationship is therefore real or hypostatic. Moreover knowledge or consciousness itself can only occur where there is relation. Where there is knowledge and hence where there is consciousness in general, there is implied a content which on the one hand is different from the "I", and yet is at the same time bound up ontologically with the "I". Even more, where there is relation, each sees the other directly, and only indirectly sees himself. The Father knows himself in the Son and the Spirit, and here we see the supreme humility of supreme love.

2. The communion of two "I's" is necessary in order to

experience the fullness of existence, but it is not sufficient. This fullness is experienced totally only in the communion of three "I's". Communion between two does not open up an unlimited horizon; considered in itself it represents a certain act of limitation. The simple presence, or the awareness of the presence, of a third enlarges the dimensions of existence to include in principle all that can exist.

If the "I" without any other dimension can be represented as a point, and the "I — Thou" relation as a line drawn from one point to another, this relation to a third can be represented as a triangular surface, or, when there is more than one in the role of third, as the circumference of this line or as a sphere. And the sphere represents the whole.[16]

3. The Father gives himself wholly to the Son and the Son wholly to the Father. One who loves is not content with halves; he desires the other wholly and gives himself wholly. Hence the Son is the "only Son of the only Father". On the other hand, any idea of an egotism *à deux* is far removed from the love between Father and Son. Such an egotism limits the horizon, keeps everything else outside, holding it fast within an eternal nothingness, or at the most, treating it only on the level of object. Only when there is a Third does the love of the Two become generous and capable of extending and diffusing itself. It is only because there is a Third that the Two can become one not through the reciprocity of their love alone, but also through their self-forgetfulness in favour of the Third. Only the existence of a Third in God explains the creation of a world of many "I's", and the fact that these "I's" have been elevated to the level of partners with God in love. Only through the Spirit does the divine love radiate to the outside.[17]

The Two, Father and Son, love each other wholly because each sees the other in his capacity as a love which is unlimited by any narrow boundaries. If one "I" closed in on itself remains in a dream-like subjectivity, the absorption of two "I's" into a mutual love which is indifferent towards the presence of any other also preserves, to a certain extent, this same character of dream-like subjectivity and uncertainness of existence. Now this incomplete unity and lack of certainty fosters a greediness for the other in each of the Two which transforms him into an object of passion, and this is beneath the level of true love.[18] Complete unity and the full assurance of existence are possessed by the two "I's" when they meet in a Third by virtue of their mutual love for the Third. In this way they transcend that particular subjectivity which is fraught with the danger of illusion.

4. If, in order to remove from God any suggestion of the character of object, we have made use above of the term "pure subjectivity" to describe God's mode of being, we have understood by "subjectivity" not an illusory mode of existence but one which is absolutely free, existing in itself and determining itself. In God however this means the most consistent mode of reality, an objective subjectivity, or a subjective objectivity.

This objective — subjective consistency is provided in the Trinity by the Third. The Third represents the "object", the whole "object" of that existence which is only fully grasped in the communion of two "I's". But in God all is according to the mode of perfect existence of a subject. Hence even the "object" is all subject, even if it occupies the position of object.

The Third occupies the position of object only because he unites the Two in himself, because he is recognized together by the Two and is the cause of their common joy in knowing and possessing him. He plays the role of "object" because the Two transcend their common subjectivity in the Third, and it is this which manifests the fullness of existence and hence of truth. We can say that if the Two do not meet in the Third, their subjectivity is not truly a common subjectivity. It becomes a common subjectivity, true and objective, by this meeting of the Two in their common "object" which is the Third.

5. The Third also fufills his role as "object" or horizon because he keeps the Two from becoming confused within an indistinct unity because of the exclusiveness of their love for each other. In his love for the Second, the First does not forget the Third and so is prevented from becoming confused with the Second. And the Third also fulfills this same function

vis-à-vis the Second. Among men this means that an "I" preserves a certain detachment from the fascinating abyss represented by the other "I" because each is thinking of the third. Therefore where love exists, the third maintains the consciousness and the distinct personal character of each of the two. But from the third, who has become the second for one or other of the two, the two return to the communion between themselves, for meanwhile each of the two has taken on the function of the third *vis-à-vis* the other. This return is experienced as a rekindling of love enriched by a new reflection. Thus, as a general rule, the third serves as a factor rekindling love and causing human subjects to grow in love.

In the case of God there can be no question of a rekindling or growth in love, but only of maintaining a personal distinction between those who love and of keeping them at the very apex of their love, a love which remains nevertheless united with reflection. God is personal and exists within a love which is eternal, for he is threefold in Persons. Now the meeting in the Third coincides with the confirmation in existence of the subjectivity of the Two. For existence confirmed as truth is existence experienced not only by one subject, or by many isolated subjects, but by two subjects in common and in relation to a Third. Truth can then be defined as existence experienced in common, that is to say, among Three. This truth or this mode of experiencing existence represents the confirmation in existence of each individual "I".

6. A Fourth is not needed to experience the fullness of existence and to confirm the Two in existence. The Third represents all that can exist over and above the Two, the entire reality in which the Two can be confirmed. The Fourth is himself also a Third, and so the conjugation knows only the three persons: "I — Thou — He". From the perspective of the "I" or of the "I — Thou" relation, there can be no movement in principle beyond the Third, because there is no place to go. Florensky says: "I will be asked, 'Why are there exactly three hypostases?'. I am speaking of the number three as of the one immanent to the truth and inseparable from it. No less than three can exist for only three hypostases together make up from all eternity that which is. Only in the

unity of the three does each hypostasis receive an absolute confirmation . . . Apart from three there exists no confirmation (in truth). But could there be more than three? Yes, there could exist more than three by the reception of certain new subjects into the bosom of the trinitarian life. But these new hypostases would no longer be members through whom the subject is preserved as the subject of the truth and so they would not appear as internally necessary for its absoluteness. They would be conditioned hypostases which, as far as the subject of the truth were concerned, might be or not be. Hence they cannot be called hypostases in the proper sense of the term, and might better be named deified persons." [19]

7. We have seen that the Third is a bridge between Father and Son, a bridge which not only connects them but also keeps them distinct. In the case of men the third calls one of the two towards himself and always has the effect of rekindling in each of the two desire for the third and for one another. In the case of God, the Spirit keeps this love in a state of constant intensity. This position and role of the Third corresponds to the understanding we have of him as Spirit or as Life creating a bond between the Two Living Ones, and hence also as Love. St. Maximus the Confessor calls the Holy Spirit the "consubstantial Life of the Father" just as he calls the Son the "consubstantial Wisdom of the Father." [20] Of the three Persons he says: "For in himself God is unknown Mind, unuttered Word and incomprehensible Life." [21] Certainly this Life springs up wholly from that which, while itself without beginning, is nevertheless the beginning of all, namely, the Father. It springs up unceasingly because it springs up from the depth of that abyss [22] which is never diminished. This abyss of being is at the same time the abyss of the "Mind" from which Reason, or the Word, is eternally begotten.

When the Father sees his hypostatic image in the Son, he loves this image. His love which is the most proper expression of the life of the spirit is another mode of his act of self-revelation. But it is a mode which reveals the Father as completely as his image reveals him. And each of these hypostatic modes carries in itself, together with the entire divine being, the other modes as well. Thus each hypostasis bears the whole

Godhead but in its own mode. And all three are necessary in order to hypostatize the fullness of the Godhead. The mode of the "Image" or of the "Truth", and the mode of "Love" are particularly necessary in order to reveal the Father in whom the fathomless depth of the Godhead is an unoriginate mode which is itself at the origin of the other revelatory modes.

Hence it can also be said of the Spirit that he is the "Truth" inasmuch as he makes possible complete knowledge of the Truth, and inasmuch as he is intimately bound up with the Truth and himself binds others to the Truth in his character as Life and inspirer of the Truth. At the same time the Truth is Life or is intimately connected with Life and Love as one who is Truth and worthy of love. It is in this sense that the Byzantine theologian Joseph Bryennios speaks of the reciprocal relation between the Son and the Holy Spirit, considering the Spirit as the Spirit of the Son, the Spirit of Truth and of the Word, and considering the Son as the Word of the Spirit.[23] More especially, the Son is the "Image of the Father" or the mode in which the Father knows himself, while the Spirit is the Life or Love of the Father, that is, the mode in which the Father experiences and loves himself, and this means that he loves himself also "in his image".

The Father cannot but love his "Image". Love is a "sighing", a Spirit which is connected with the Truth and which is sought out by the Truth, a Spirit to which the Truth is bound. Love, as the Spirit of Truth, forges the link between one who knows the Truth and the Truth itself, which means, in this case, between the Father and his Image which he thinks from all eternity.

But we must give equal emphasis to the role of the Holy Spirit as bridge between the Father and his Son, and to his origin from the Father as the Father's love of the Truth which is his hypostatic image.

The Father cannot know his Image without coming to love it. Love is the necessary relation when we are in the presence of the Truth, provided that the Truth exists. Love is even the mode of the full knowledge of the Truth, and the identifi-

cation of love and knowledge in Orthodox teaching comes
from this manner of understanding the Holy Spirit.[24]

Existence is not exhausted in love; rather it is essentially
a source of love; it reveals itself as love just as it is a source
of truth and reveals itself as truth. Truth and love for the
truth are the two inseparable aspects under which this same
unique and fathomless existence is revealed.

8. The distinction between truth and love or between the
Image and the Love of the Father consists in the fact that
the existing, revealing hypostatic Truth or Image is begotten
by the unoriginate existence because this latter wills to know
himself and because at the same time love radiates from the
unoriginate existence for the sake of the Image of that existence which is the Truth, and therefore of course, also for
the sake of the existence from which Love radiates. Love is
directed always towards another person; it does not exist for
its own sake. This is the "generosity" of love which the Fathers have observed as a special characteristic of the Spirit.[25]
In this sense the Spirit is thought of as a light going out from
the Father which shines forth also from the Son in whom he
abides. The Spirit, then, as the Third, is also the atmosphere
of infinite life and love in which the divine "I — Thou" relation is bathed, similar to the sphere of the third or integral
objective reality in which the human"I — Thou" relationship
occurs. It is in this sense that we are to understand the statement that the Spirit is "through the Son", that is, the Spirit
shines forth "because of the fact that the Son exists, and for
the sake of the Son." It is "through the Son" or due to the
fact that the Spirit shines forth from the Father for the sake
of the Son, that he also shines forth for the sake of the Father,
inasmuch as the Father by loving the Son also knows himself
as one who loves.

The term "procession" of the Spirit from the Father —
completed sometimes with the phrase "through the Son" —
conveys this role of the Spirit as bridge between Father and
Son, with the further distinction that the Spirit has his existence from the Father but that he also has a relation to
the Son.

On the other hand the Son cannot be understood without

the Spirit, and this implies that the Son is to be considered bound to the Spirit. It is only in this context that we can understand the statement of the Fathers that no Person of the Trinity exists for the sake of any goal or for the sake of any other thing at all. By this the Fathers wished to stress the equality of the Persons of the Trinity, but they did not of course exclude love between them.

9. When we characterize the Spirit as the "Love" between the Father and the Son, we must not only avoid identifying him purely and simply with love; we must also not neglect that the Spirit is a Person. Just as when the Fathers call the Son "Wisdom" they do not understand wisdom as belonging only to the Son, or as being the only thing proper to the Son, nor as being a non-hypostatic wisdom, so we must proceed similarly in the case of the Spirit. The Spirit plays the special role of "bearer of love" from the Father to the Son and from the Son to the Father.[26] The Spirit is the hypostatic form of the eternal actualizing and conveying of the Father's love for the Son and of the Son's response to this same love. In the hypostatic character of the Spirit another of the Father's acts of self-transcendence is revealed, this time as the love he has for that image of himself that he knows; it is in his eternal knowledge of this Image that the Father realizes his first transcendence as Person. In the Spirit, the Father — transcending himself through love — transcends himself before someone, before his Image, before his own hypostatic Truth. There is no question of a transcendence towards something higher, but of a transcendence in virtue of which the "I" does not remain only in himself, but relates to another. When the Father transcends himself through this reference to another, the Son, he does not however possess this other apart from himself but in himself. It is in his very self that he transcends himself, and although the relationship is a real one, it is within himself that he realizes it.

10. Through the "procession" the Spirit "starts from a certain place and sets out on the path towards a goal" (ἐκπόρευσις). The "procession" does not mean setting out on a way which leads nowhere. The Holy Spirit sets out from the Father towards the Son, for he "comes to rest in the Son",

he "abides" in the Son (Jn 1:32-33). The abiding of the Holy
Spirit in the Son does not have its cause in some weariness of
the Holy Spirit but in the fact that the Son is his goal. More
exactly, the Father causes the Spirit to proceed and gives him
the Son as his goal. The Father himself through the Love projected from himself comes to rest upon the Son.

The Spirit is distinguished from the Son by his abiding
in the Son, for the Son does not come to rest in any Person.
But this abiding also expresses the special relationship between the Son and the Spirit, a relation in which each of the
two Persons has a special position and which at the same time
excludes the movement of the Spirit any farther afield. This
"rest" or "abiding" of the Spirit in the Son does not express
a temporal relation of the Spirit to the Son but an eternal one,
and in fact it is this eternal relation which is reflected by the
temporal one. St. Gregory Palamas says: "Therefore we must
ask ourselves: when the Spirit goes forth from the Father in
a movement we neither see nor understand, can we say that,
according to the evidence of Scripture, he has someone in
whom he comes to rest in a manner which befits God?" After
he recalls the passage in John 1:33, Palamas continues: "And
that no one may think that these things were spoken and accomplished by the Father with reference to the incarnation of
the Son, let us listen to the divine Damascene who writes in
the eighth of the Dogmatic Chapters, 'We believe also in the
Holy Spirit who proceeds from the Father and rests in the
Son.' " [27]

11. But the "procession" like the "projection" (προβολή)
also implies an act. The Spirit is in a state of eternal motion
from the Father towards the Son. This means that when the
Spirit arrives at his goal he also remains with the one who
causes him to proceed and who sends him forth. He is the
breath of Life which the Father breathes out upon the Son.
Now breath is found both in the one who breathes and in
the one upon whom he breathes. If the Spirit comes to rest in
the Son, he goes no farther than the Son. He does not also
proceed from the Son to some point beyond the Son in order
to constitute a mode of existence on the boundaries of the
Godhead. He is eternally "between" Father and Son. "The

Holy Spirit stands in the middle between him who is the Unbegotten and him who is Begotten, and he is united with the Father through the Son," says St. John Damascene.[28] Any progress of the Spirit beyond the Son, through the Son, would make it impossible to explain why the divine processions stop with the Spirit. Just as the Son who is caused could in turn be a cause, so the Spirit, caused wholly or partially by one who is himself caused, could in turn himself be the cause of another divine Person, and so on to infinity. But the Spirit is no "grandson" within the Holy Trinity, and thus a possible means for the production of an infinite series of greatgrandsons. Nor was the Spirit caused to proceed in order to stand alongside the Son though without any relationship to him. In this case too there would be no reason for the divine processions to stop at two instead of multiplying to infinity and undergoing a continuous dilution in the process because of the increasing remoteness from the one who himself has no cause. Both Son and Spirit are exclusively from the unique uncaused source, the Father, and both partake directly and eternally from his unoriginateness.

The Spirit represents the return of the Godhead into itself, the reunion of the divinity, so to speak, its reunification on the level of a mode of existence in personal communion, without thereby destroying this mode of existence. Through the Spirit the divinity is revealed as structure, as the interpersonal matrix of infinite divinity, thus avoiding both the lack of "generosity" of a being hermetically sealed in the darkness of impersonal existence, as well as the disorder of an infinite plurality. Both of these ultimately represent an existence lacking in structure and in that meaning which is bound up with structure. St. Gregory of Nazianzen says: "A complete Trinity is formed from three perfect elements, for the monad is in motion because of its richness, but it transcends the dyad for it is beyond [the distinction of] matter and form from which bodies arise, and defines itself as trinity (for this is the first [stage] of synthesis beyond duality) in order that the divinity be neither too restricted, nor overflow to infinity." [29] Both the first and second of these alternatives would fill all with a Godhead which was not free, but pantheistically conceived and incapable of either love or creation.

12. The Holy Spirit is what unites the Father and the Son, not as essence but precisely as Person, leaving Father and Son at the same time as free Persons. Hence the Spirit is also the one who unites men among themselves, but as a Person himself he leaves other persons free.

13. The movement of the Spirit between the Father and the Son as a living bond between both that permits us to consider the Spirit especially as the Love between Father and Son, also allows us to see a relation between the Spirit and the Son. But how do we reconcile a continual movement of the Holy Spirit between Father and Son as the reciprocal love between them with the fact that the Spirit proceeds only from the Father? St. Gregory Palamas gives the following explanations: "No sensible person can conceive of the Word without the Spirit. (Gregory wants to suggest here the indissoluble personal bond between the Son and the Spirit.) The Word of God from the Father therefore also possesses the Holy Spirit who comes forth together with him from the Father. . . . Now this Spirit of the supreme Word is like an ineffable love of the Begetter for the Word which was ineffably begotten. The Word, the beloved Son of the Father, avails himself (χρῆται) of the Spirit in his relationship with the Father, but he possesses the Spirit as the one who has come forth together with him from the Father and who abides in him (the Son) through the unity of nature . . ."[30] The Son has the Spirit from the Father as the Spirit of Truth, of Wisdom, the Spirit of the Word . . . and through the Spirit the Son rejoices together with the Father who has his joy in the Son (ὃς τῷ Πατρὶ ἐπ'αὐτῷ χαίροντι συγχαίρει) . . . For this joy of the Father and of the Son from before all ages is the Holy Spirit who is common to both in what concerns their inner association (ὡς κοινὸν μὲν αὐτοῖς κατὰ τὴν χρῆσιν); this also explains why the Spirit is sent forth by both upon those who are worthy, but why he is *of* the Father alone in what concerns his existence, and therefore proceeds from the Father alone with respect to existence."[31]

14. If we put this idea together with the idea of the Fa-

thers that the Spirit proceeds from the Father but shines forth through the Son and in the Son, we can say that the shining forth of the Spirit from the Son is only the joyful response of the Son's love when confronted with the loving initiative of the Father which causes the Spirit to proceed. The love of the Father coming to rest in the Son shines forth upon the Father from the Son not merely because the Father knows and loves the Son by virtue of this love, but also because the Son reveals himself to the Father as the one who responds to his love. Through this love the Son is known by the Father not as a passive object, but as the one in whom the Love of the Father is reflected back as Love for the Father. This Love does not have its source in the Son but in the Father, but when it is projected upon the Son as upon an active subject, it reflects back upon the Father, engaging the subjectivity of the Son in this act of reflection, this return of Love towards the Father, just as the Spirit of the Father by communicating himself to us also turns back towards the Father, having engaged our own loving filial consciousness. The Father projects himself in his love wholly towards the Son. This love of his is imprinted on the Son and shines back upon the Father, or turns back towards the Father imprinted on the subject of the Son, revealing itself in the movement of this subject towards the Father. For the love of the Father is also movement and is imprinted as movement on the Son as subject who is himself also active in his quality as Son. Thus the Spirit of the Father is ceaselessly made the Spirit of the Son as well. The fact that the Son loves the Father through the Spirit of the Father does not mean that he does not love him personally through the Spirit. The Spirit has become the Spirit of the Son too, which means that he has also filled the Son with the love that comes from the Father, although the Spirit belongs to the Son only because by origin he (the Spirit) belongs to the Father, and only because he receives the Son from the Father. This is also what occurs in our case, although on an infinitely reduced plane: the fact that we love the Father through the Spirit who comes to us from the Father does not mean that it is not we ourselves who love through the Spirit. The Spirit of the Father penetrates

within us as paternal love and kindles our own subjectivity
so that it may become a loving filial subjectivity in which at
the same time the Spirit himself is evident. Inasmuch as he
has been actively imprinted upon us, the Spirit has become
our Spirit (of sonship), inseparable from and coloured by
our own subjectivity as sons. Here we see illuminated the
truth that every time a person is truly aware of someone else,
this feeling does not belong to that one person only but is
also experienced by the consciousness of the other because it
has been provoked by it.

15. There are only two other explanations — apart from
the one we have given — for the love which the Son has for
the Father and for the expression "the Spirit of the Son";
both of these explanations however are unacceptable. The
first is that the love of the Son for the Father is other than
the love of the Father for the Son, and hence "the Spirit of the
Son" is also other than the "Spirit of the Father". But this
explanation, which corresponds to one form of the *filioque,*
cannot be accepted. The second is that which follows the
official Catholic interpretation of the *filioque,* according to
which the Spirit proceeds from the Father and the Son "as
from a single principle". Corresponding to this interpretation,
the divine love is no longer the love which passes between two
Persons but an overflow from the common essence of Father
and Son directed not as from one Person to another, but towards something else. This is an explanation which confuses
the Persons and makes the divine essence a source of personal
being. Moreover in both these explanations the Spirit loses
his character as Spirit of the Son received by the Son from
the Father, and even more does the Son lose his character as
Son in the manifestation of the Spirit within him, since the
Son becomes the source and hence the Father of the Spirit, in
which case it would have to be said of the Spirit in relation
to the Son that he is the Spirit of another Father. It follows
that the Son would no longer find himself in a filial relation
to the Father through the Spirit.

On the contrary however the explanation which corresponds to Orthodox teaching preserves the position of the
Father and of the Son in the eternal love between these two

Persons, and therefore also preserves their personal distinction. At the basis of this teaching we find a reciprocity between Son and Spirit which is not due to the fact that one has taken his origin from the other, but is due instead to the simple fact that both come forth from the Father, and that there is a certain connecting relationship between them. The begetting of the Son from the Father produces as a consequence the love of the Father for the Son (this is the procession of the Spirit), and the Spirit turns back from the Son as Spirit of the Son, that is, as filial love. Consequently, the fact that the Word of the Father, which is also the Word (spoken) to the Father, or better, the response to the Father, is a Word or response full of the Spirit; it is the Word of the Spirit.

16. This non-causal reciprocity resembles a kind of passage of the Spirit through the Son and vice versa, as is also the case with reciprocal spiritual encounters among human persons (*perichoresis*) where each person as a consequence bears the other in himself. This notion has been expressed by the Byzantine theologian Joseph Bryennios who demonstrated that in addition to their causal relation to the Father and in addition to the names which correspond to this relationship, the Son and the Spirit also possess a non-causal relation between themselves, and names which correspond to this other relation. He writes: "The Son, because he is the one who is Son, alone possesses the name of Son *vis-à-vis* the Father, for he is the Son of one Father only, not of two; but the name of Word which belongs to the Son alone within the Holy Trinity has reference not only to the Father as the one who is Mind, but also to the Spirit in another way. . . . For the Word belongs to the Father as one who exists from within him, but the Word belongs to the Spirit not as one existing from within the Spirit but as one who has his existence from without, and in fact from the same source whence the Spirit has his own existence, and as one who is consubstantial with the Spirit. The same is true of the one who proceeds. He truly is He Who Proceeds and is so called only in reference to the one who caused him to proceed, that is to say, to the one who is and who is called Father with reference to that other Person who shares with him the character of being caused, namely, the Son. But the

Spirit is not and is not given the name of Spirit with reference
to the Father alone, but he is Spirit and is called Spirit correctly and truly with reference also to the Son. However, the
Spirit belongs to the Father and is named Spirit as one who
exists from within him, while in reference to the Son he is
Spirit not as one who has his existence from within the Son,
but as one who through the Son, that is, together with him,
comes forth from the Father and shares one being and one
glory with the Son." [32]

17. The intimate union of the Holy Spirit with the Son,
and his reciprocity with the Son (which does not mean, however, his procession from the Son) are also reflected in the
activity of the divine Persons upon human persons. Because
the Spirit "abides" in the Son and moves no farther afield
within the divine order, it is only when we are gathered together in the incarnate Son that we too have a share in the
abiding of the Spirit within us. We cannot possess the Spirit
apart from Christ nor Christ apart from the Spirit. We do not
know Christ without the Spirit nor the Spirit without Christ.
We possess the Spirit because we are united in Christ, recapitulated in Christ, and as those who are united with the only-
begotten Son of the Father, we too have become by adoption
sons of the Father. We have the Spirit of sonship because
the Spirit of the Son becomes our Spirit too. In this way we
are, in the Son, placed in direct relation with the Father just
like the Son. The Son became man, was crucified, died, rose
and ascended not just to save us purely and simply, but to
make us sons of the Father and co-heirs with himself. By
making us sons of the Father inasmuch as we are united in the
Son, the Spirit is our power of communion and the bridge of
communion among ourselves, and yet he does not destroy the
liberty we have as sons who are equal in honour before the
heavenly Father.

18. In general, Orthodox teaching on the Holy Spirit is
distinguished by the following characteristics: a) the ir-
reducibility of the Spirit to the Son and the affirmation of his
equal importance with the Logos; b) the inseparability of
Son or Logos from the Spirit, in fact, their indissoluble connexion; c) the preservation of the filial relation of the Son

towards the Father together with the affirmation of the Spirit as Spirit of the Son: this makes of the presence of the Son a source from which filial response, life and divine movement radiate upon men; d) the understanding of the Spirit as a unifying factor, a bridge, a communicative movement between "I's" which nevertheless does not do away with their liberty.

All these characteristics find their reflection in Orthodox ecclesiology, while to a great extent these same things are missing from Catholic ecclesiology and from Western Christianity in general because of the *filioque*. In the West ecclesiology has become an impersonal, juridical system, while theology, and in the same way the whole of Western culture with it, has become strictly rational.

The decline of the importance of the Spirit compared to that of the Son, a decline which can be traced to the *filioque,* and the near-reduction of the Spirit to the Son together constitute one reason why in the Roman Catholic Church there has been such infrequent mention of the presence and activity of the Spirit. Christ the Word transmitting his power to Peter and his successors, and in part to the successors of the other Apostles, and withdrawing at the Ascension to some remote and transcendent place, keeps the Spirit also with him. The character of a juridical society has been imprinted upon the Church, a society conducted rationally and in absolutist fashion by the Pope while neglecting both the active permanent presence of the Spirit within her and within all the faithful, and also the presence of Christ bound indissolubly to the presence of the Spirit. The Pope, the bishops, the priests occupy the place of the absent Christ who is not present through the Spirit in the hearts of the faithful (the vicarial theory); the faithful are not the images, the visible signs of the invisible sacramental and pneumatic presence of Christ as they are in Orthodoxy.[33] The character of the filial relationship of the faithful towards the Father, and of their intimate communion among themselves in Christ who is present within them through the Holy Spirit, has also fallen into a similar decline.

Protestantism has also experienced this same weakness,

for, having rejected the direction of a vicarial hierarchy it has lost even that unity which was maintained by largely human means. From the *filioque* Protestantism has at times deduced a separation of the Spirit from Christ and, consequently, having preserved the idea of the transcendence of Christ, it has substituted the presence of the Spirit for the presence of Christ. But the presence of the Spirit without Christ has become a presence devoid of the "Truth", of Christ to whom the Spirit is bound. It has become a presence that cannot create ecclesiological communion, a presence which is variously individualist and sentimental, or psychological and immanent.

CHAPTER IV

Revelation Through Acts, Words and Images*

A group of Protestant theologians influenced by the thought of Rudolph Bultmann assert that the ideas we have about Christ and the acts we attribute to him, like the ideas about God found in the Scriptures as a whole, are mythological objectifications of certain existential references man makes to God whom he conceives as that which transcends man. Hence the Bible must be demythologized.[1] The theologians in question have also been driven to this conclusion by the idea that modern man no longer accepts the traditional notions of Christianity and that therefore a radical change in Christian language is necessary. Thus Paul Tillich proposed that the idea and the name of a transcendent God be abandoned and in its place the idea and name of "ultimate reality" or "ground of being" be adopted, inasmuch as for the man of today God is nothing other than creative nature, the creative ground of all objects. The Anglican Bishop John Robinson also believes that the idea of a transcendent and personal being, and even the name of God, must be given up. He proposes they be replaced either with the names suggested by Tillich, or by another, "the Unconditional". Christ is only a man who, in a more marked manner than anyone else, experienced union with this "ground of being" or "Unconditional" in his love for men.[2]

The question thus arises of the possibility and limits of any change in the language of Christianity.

---

* Originally published in Romanian in *Ortodoxia* 20 (1968), 347-377.

Christianity is based on the revelation which is contained, according to one view, in Sacred Scripture and Tradition and preserved by the Church, or, according to another view, in Sacred Scripture alone. Any change of language which implies the rejection of this revelation can no longer claim to preserve Christianity, and theologians who suggest that the Christian revelation be abandoned can no longer claim for themselves the name of Christian theologians.

When confronted with the fundamental significance of Sacred Scripture and Tradition the aforementioned Protestant theologians have two replies: the first is that Scripture was an historically determined creation which conveys the ideas of the times in which it was written, using the expressions and literary forms of its own age; the second is that revelation is patient of many interpretations and that the changes of idea and language which they themselves have proposed are also supported by one of these possible interpretations.

A further question arises: does there not exist an inner core of revelation which must be considered to have remained intact, unquestioned by all possible interpretations as long as these can still be called Christian? And is not this essential core of revelation also expressed by certain definite means?

In a report on the evolution of Catholicism after the Second Vatican Council presented in August 1967 to the Central Committee of the World Council of Churches, Dr. Lukas Vischer, the Secretary-General of the department of studies for the Commission on Faith and Order, observed that theology in general has reached the conclusion that any expression of the Christian witness, even that found in the books of Sacred Scripture, is determined by the historical conditions of its respective age. It was Dr. Vischer's belief, moreover, that precisely for this reason hermeneutics must have a large role today if we are to establish what it is that constitutes this inner core of revelation and what are only the outer historical garments — the images, language, concerns — in which it has been expressed.[3]

In order to make our position clear at the outset let us say first that we think the Apostles in their preaching, the authors of the New Testament — and the prophets and writers of the Old Testament as well — doubtless made use of the language, ideas and literary forms of their own age in order to express the divine revelation. But these words, ideas and literary forms have been transfigured in the very way in which they were combined in order to express a content which transcends their normal content.

In any case the divinity of Christ and his saving acts cannot be treated as an outer shell or a form peculiar to the time in which the New Testament was written.[4]

We will deal with the problem of language below. Here we will only observe that, in our opinion, there exists an apostolic typology which has proven that it occupies a privileged position over against all later typologies, and has in fact partly determined the shape of these later typologies because the Apostles were under the immediate influence of Christ, that is, of the God incarnate. Their human capacity for understanding the divine was raised to a supreme degree and so, consequently, was their capacity to express the divine element which they had understood. Hence the means by which they expressed the divine revelation have to be preserved. Obviously there must be a method of adapting this Christian language to the language of today while still taking into account the core of revelation that has found expression through these privileged means. If we can anticipate the results of our exploration we can say now that if "demythologization", and with it the abandonment of those means which are bound up essentially with the expression of divine revelation, are not acceptable because they mean the destruction of revelation, a "spiritual understanding" of these means can, on the other hand, most certainly be accepted because it corresponds to their very meaning. To speak more precisely we can say that revelation received essential and authentic expression through words and images that always convey a true spiritual core which they allow to be glimpsed and which must be preserved even if other words and images are used apart from the ones first used to express the revelation. "Demythologization" on the other hand begins from the idea that popular imagination created a series of myths with no kind of content. These myths therefore must be wholly done away with and we must look for a core other than the one which they express.

The essential unchanging core of Christian revelation is identified with the series of acts through which the revelation was effected. These acts moreover were expressed without alteration by a number of particular words and images. Even were we to use other words and images they would have to express the same essential core of acts which the original words and images set forth without any deception, and we should always have to rely upon these.

We will try to show here that this unchangeable core of Christian revelation in fact responds even better to the needs of modern man when he wishes to become a Christian than do the modern ideas with which certain "theologians" want to replace the very content of revelation.

Revelation Through Acts And Words

Christian revelation consists of a series of acts accomplished by God or promised by him in relation to the world and to human history. More recent theology has emphasized this dimension of "act" in divine revelation in contrast to the older theology which saw revelation as a "disclosure of teachings" from God, meant to satisfy man's interest in knowing the truth and living according to it. In the Dogmatic Constitution on Divine Revelation of the Second Vatican Council the idea was adopted that revelation consists especially in the acts of God. In this the Council follows a Protestant school of thought which is much concerned with "the history of salvation" (*heilsgeschichtliche Schule*) and which sees revelation as a series of the acts of God in history and understands salvation as something achieved by stages in history.[5]

These acts distinguish God clearly from the world and also from the gods of mythology who are, ultimately, personifications of the forces of nature and of the human passions. Even if these gods were projected beyond this world by the folk imagination, their mode of acting upon the world had a certain routine regularity and was closely bound up with the same phenomena of nature and the same human passions. Their activity was cyclical.

This too suggests that Christianity is not mythological and as such does not need to be demythologized.

The great need which does exist is for a spiritual understanding of Christianity. God in Christian teaching is not an objective entity, or a force of nature acting upon the world as object but remaining more or less like those in the world, and so, as it were, merely a stronger force among the others. This would be the mythological objectification of which Bultmann speaks and it would demand demythologization. In reality God is a subject of free and spiritual energy, and his acts are spiritual. They produce effects upon man only in conjunction with man's own will, and in general we can say that God's influence acts in much the same way that spirit, ideas and beliefs exert an influence upon the body, upon human relations or even upon the material world as a whole. In other words, when God at some one point within the universal causality of a contingent world makes choice of one or other of its many causal polyvalencies, he does not deprive the world of its own causality, nor does he hinder human liberty by the acts whereby he infuses new spiritual energies into man or guides him in other directions. As inexhaustible source of energy, God shares his energy with the world and with man without upsetting the orderly rule of the world or reducing man's freedom. This is so because God is a personal source and, as creator of both world and man, he has by this very fact established them as their own realities, confirming nature with its laws and man with his freedom (within, that is, the framework of this world). All revelation through divine acts takes the form of a dialogue between God and man. God has regard for what man needs but he also has regard for man's acceptance or rejection of revelation.

In fact the first act of God towards the world, which can also be considered as the basis of all his further acts and of God's continuing revelation, is the creation. This is an act most difficult to grasp, but here let us dwell in particular on the fact that by virtue of this act the world is established as a reality by the very will of God. On the one hand it has its own laws; on the other it is a contingent reality and its causality can be directed either by God or by man in order to achieve its end of communion between God and man. To the free energy of God responds the free energy of man; or, more exactly, human energy takes its beginning and has its growth from the divine energy.[6]

Bultmann proposes the demythologizing of Christianity because he thinks that it has already been mythologized and that in this process it has transformed God into a transcendent "objectified" creation which does not offer man the possibility of realizing himself authentically and "existentially". In Christianity, according to Bultmann, we are dealing only with man's return to self. Revelation does not speak to man about nothing; it opens his eyes to see himself and enables man to see himself as a claimed being. It places him in a situation where he can make the decision of faith, the decision to break with an ordinary and automatic life and to achieve in different situations an understanding of himself at his most authentic.

It is Bultmann's view that man can realize himself authentically only on the plane of an existential experience, one that is free from all constraint of that objective reality which includes the divine and which pulls man down to a common life. The objection however has been put to Bultmann — and rightly — that man cannot realize himself authentically if he is not open to the world. This implies however that the world is also open to him. "Only in his going out towards the world does man experience himself truly."[7] For the world is not so rigid as is sometimes claimed; on the contrary it too is open to the transforming power of man. Liberty is no abstract quality, continually unverified and uncreative; it grows stronger and proves itself in dialogue with the world and in the affirmation of those creative acts which introduce beneficial changes into the world, society and human relations.

Moreover, man cannot grow in freedom if he is not in dialogue with a personal God. An impersonal ground of the world would carry man along through the meanderings of a destiny devoid of all design. The existential experience of man apart from dialogue with a personal God can only be the tragic experience of a fate which leads man inevitably to death.

The Christian believes that the impulse for such a vigorous affirmation of freedom comes to man precisely from God, as personal partner in dialogue with man. Nothing makes a more powerful claim upon man, nothing more sustains his strength to live a life of response than a God who is not subject to the automatism of this world. A God who was subject to this world's automatism could not give man the strength to liberate himself from it, to be free to accomplish new acts, acts creative of greater good.

Only a God unconditioned by nature, because not a part of it, only a God who represents for man the support of his freedom, the source of strength in unconditioned freedom, can help man to achieve his authentic self-realization. Bishop Robinson suggests to the man of today "the Unconditional" as a name for God, thinking of it at the same time as the "ultimate ground" of the world, ultimately not distinct from it. But this is no longer to be unconditional, and such a God could not help man accomplish unconditioned acts which would not be subject to a strict determinism.

Today's Christian — who is also today's man — does not seek an authentic existence if this means an existence cut off from the world. However, in order for him to do the world a service which may help it transcend the automatic repetition of the old patterns, he has need of an unconditioned effort which can come to him only from a God who is not conditioned by the world but is nevertheless full of love for it.

It is precisely Bultmann and his followers who, while believing that they are "disobjectifying" God, are in fact making an object of God, or, better, are leaving man more or less completely prey to the omnipotent object which is the universe.

The whole revelation of God through free acts shows him to be a God who is not conditioned by the world, yet has regard for the freedom of man and calls man to the unconditioned exercise of his freedom.

Even the first act of revelation is, as we have said, a bringing into existence of a world which has its own laws, and of a humanity which is free. We cannot grasp the innermost meaning of the act of the creation of the world. It is clear that our own inferior understanding has introduced many an element of objectifying mythology into this act. We must therefore eliminate these elements insofar as we can, but unlike the "demythologizing" theologians we cannot do away with the very idea of revelation and throw out the baby with the bath water. What is required is not "demythologization" but a spiritual understanding of the divine acts and the relations of God with the world. Creation does not have to be understood as an act by which God creates a reality separate from himself, like some object exterior to himself who is the primal object. God creates the world in himself, through a manifestation of his energy and his Spirit. Clearly God must in no way be confused with some part or power of the world, but God is not separate from the world nor is the world separate from God; he is the unconditioned cause of the world.

God is an endless source of spiritual energy open to the world and the world is capable of being open in its own innermost depths to this energy. The intimate openness to each other of these two interior realities makes them, in one sense, into a kind of unity. The world is open to God and God is open to the world, but each preserves its own freedom. As a result the world is able to close itself to God — though not on all levels. There are channels through which God communicates his energy to the world. For example, God, as a matter of course, communicates to the world the energy required to keep it in existence, but it is only if the world, through the mediation of man, actively desires it, that God communicates to it his transfiguring energy.

God took the Hebrews out of slavery in Egypt "with strength of hand" (Ex 13:14) and brought them into Canaan, but always and only with the will of the people. As often as the Hebrews refused to obey God, they were bereft of God. Consequently it is not God who makes history directly, it is the people. But in all their great deeds the people are helped by God because they willed to follow his advice and receive his aid. Every act of God's revelation is followed by a free act of the Hebrew people and makes allowance for their free decision. The more an individual act of divine revelation is characterized by energy and seriousness, the greater the consequent effort on the part of the Hebrews. Moses was a powerful historically creative personality because God gives and seeks great deeds. The efforts of the Hebrews at the time of the Exodus from Egypt, the wandering in the desert, and the conquest of the promised homeland — all efforts which followed upon numerous acts whereby God revealed his power and his commandments — were remarkable precisely because the commands were insistent and the help provided was so great.

The intention behind the act of delivering the Hebrew people from Egypt and of settling them in Canaan was to make them a people devoted to God who had shown his own devotion by his deeds, and confirmed these by the Law he gave through Moses. In this way an "alliance" was established, a special bond, a "covenant" between God and the Hebrew people which was struck in complete freedom.

This covenant passed through all manner of changes because of the fickleness of the Hebrews. As often as the people did not fulfill their obligations in this covenant they were left without the help of God. As often as the people returned to the fulfillment of the obligations which they had assumed, God came back to them and helped them with new acts of his power. It is man therefore who makes history both when he fulfills the will of God and when he does not.

Through this alliance with the Hebrews God does not seek an extension of worldly power over the whole earth, that is, domination over history in the strict sense. Had this been his purpose he could have achieved it. But in that case it would not have been the human factor — which in this particular instance was disproportionately small in relation to the desired purpose: a tiny people meant to dominate great nations — but rather the divine factor which would have achieved the historical purpose in question. Through the Hebrew people God was seeking the fulfillment of a universal spiritual mission, and was helping and guiding the people only with this mission in view. His intention was to raise this people to a higher conception of God and to a correspondingly higher moral life, and so to spread a similar conception and a similar life throughout the whole world, thereby uniting mankind in the higher principles of thought and action.

As a result each moment in God's revelation and each affirmative response from the Hebrew people is a stage in an action which represents a rising series of these stages. When the people as a whole definitively refuses to go up another step in this ascent, God directs his guiding activity towards a small portion of this people. And now he no longer accomplishes acts with a positive consequence for the collective history of the whole people, but instead he guides those who desire to make the ascent with words and descriptions of the higher goal towards which he is leading them. In place of the distinction between the Hebrew nation and the other nations, the prophets increasingly distinguish between those who are good — whether from Israel or from the Gentiles — and those who are not: "For I will leave in the midst of you a people humble and lowly. They shall seek refuge in the name of the Lord" (Zeph 3:12); "Seek the Lord, all you humble of the land, who do his commands; seek righteousness, seek humility; perhaps you may be hidden on the day of the wrath of the Lord." (Zeph 2:3)

Because God wishes to lead the world towards the goal of ever deeper knowledge and life, every act and every word through which he makes known what he expects from the Hebrew people or from the remnant of those who are willing to do his will, at once opens up the wider perspective of these goals, that is, it has a prophetic sense which discloses the progressive meaning of history. Even the ceremonial acts of the Law keep this progressive perspective open and have a more or less hidden prophetic meaning. For all the sacrifices kept alive in the consciousness of the people the idea that higher acts of sacrifice were necessary for a more intimate union with God and a loftier moral life. This unceasing upward guidance of the Hebrew people, or of that "remnant" of it which remained devoted to God, implies a continuous action of God, namely, an action adapted to every stage of history, to the problematic of each historical period. From this it follows that we must necessarily understand the activity of

God in the world as always adapted to the moment in which it occurs. This adaptation does not envisage only a subjective change of the understanding under the influence of certain new conditions and problems of historical life; it looks also for a response to an action of God which is in a continual state of adaptation, and this response must come on the new plane where mankind finds itself under the upward direction of God.

God acts continually upon those men who wish to open themselves to this activity and in general his activity follows the direction of progress. Not all this activity however is normally called revelation. We have revelation in the true sense when the Word of God discloses actions which are directed towards history. Revelation presupposes this action and action is a component act of revelation, for God is not just a teacher of men allowing them to work exclusively with their own powers. But the action of God is only one component of revelation. A second component is the word whereby man's attention is drawn to the action. The word comes after or goes before the more important and decisive moments of those actions of God which move history forward; sometimes the word both goes before and also comes after these moments. The Word urges men to give themselves to the energy communicated and promised by God in order to fulfill certain more important historical acts, and to make use of this energy with all their powers in order to fulfill these acts or to respond with gratitude and trust to the help given by God, and so raise themselves up to a life in which the will of God is ever more perfectly accomplished. But it is often the case that the word of God is also revealed when the people have ceased to accept the will of God. This happens in order to explain why they have been left without God and to urge them to the fulfillment of his will that they may receive new acts of help. This abandonment is itself also an act of God but it is not a total abandonment. In any case, even then the word is at least accompanied by the promise of some future help from God. A word of God is never given that is devoid of any support drawn from some past, present or future action of God.

In the period of the prophets revelation was not so much
a matter of the present acts of God as of words which promised future acts. Here the words are predominantly prophecy
rather than disclosures of certain present divine acts moving
history towards new moments of decision. At the most they
disclose an activity of God which promotes some unobserved
historical advance. In this sense the words of the prophets are
also an "apocalypse", that is, a disclosure of the hidden meaning of history and of the divine energy which aids unobserved
in the unfolding of history. They do not point any longer to
great acts of God in the present because the Hebrew people on
the whole refused to be open any longer to those divine acts
intended to carry history forward by leaps and bounds. The
people became fixed on the prescriptions of the Law as a system of forms able to preserve them as a nation intent on
earthly power and avid for history, understood in the sense of
their own exaltation to increasing worldly dominance, a history
to be fashioned by their own powers alone. The people no
longer saw the prophetic meaning of the Law and no longer
made use of the Law for the sake of their spiritual and moral
progress or to grow into that condition of fraternal openness
to all nations which alone would enable them to communicate
to others God's promises and his higher expectations for all
men. They were no longer interested in contributing to the
realization of this kind of history.

But God guided the obedient "remnant" of Israel to the
promised condition in which he would intervene with new
acts that would be decisive in raising up the world to a totally
new spiritual level. For by the effects they produced in men's
souls and by the incentives contained in the promises which
they were making more and more clearly, the prophetic words
too were acts. These words, by their promising description of
the conditions which God would bring about in the future,
created a certain anticipation, a certain foretaste of these
future conditions. But in order that souls might be capable
of this foretaste and of the anticipated experience of this
promised future state, it was necessary to make the promise
of these conditions at the moment when souls were raised to
the required capacity by some divine act. From this point of

view the moments of revelation are adapted to the moments
through which the human spirit passes in its ascent, inasmuch
as, besides its divine origin, prophecy also corresponds to
a certain level of a man's ability to see. Prophecy is fulfilled
more completely when the spiritual condition of at least certain persons has become capable of experiencing those new
states which the fulfillment of prophecy effects.

The acts prophesied and prepared for by the entire revelation of the Old Testament are these: the incarnation of the
Son of God, his crucifixion, resurrection and ascension as
man, the sending of the Holy Spirit together with the founding
of the Church, and the continual activity of the Holy Spirit in
and through the Church. All these acts, apart from the last
named, are acts of divine revelation and are accompanied by
words that draw attention to them and elucidate their meaning.
The activity of the Holy Spirit in the Church is no longer
revelation strictly speaking, because it is no longer accompanied by new divine words interpreting and demonstrating the
Spirit's adaptation to new human circumstances and problems.
The reason for this is that the incarnation of the Son of God
as man, his other saving acts and the descent of the Holy
Spirit contain in themselves on a broad scale all that will be
realized until the end of time in the way of spiritual progress
and union of the human with God.

Neither Moses nor his generation had the knowledge or
state of soul attained by the pious Jews at the end of the Old
Testament era as a preparation to receive Christ. The necessary condition had to be approached in stages by means of
new acts of God's revelation. In Christ himself, however,
through his resurrection and ascension there is to be found
all that those who will believe in him until the end of time
must obtain. In Christ is revealed all that we will become, not
just until the end of time but to all eternity, for he is that
eternal goal towards which our yearning must be directed.
In Christ the revelation is closed. It is closed not only by those
acts which have brought about in him the final and eternal
state for which we yearn, but also by words. For Christ always
explained in words not only the meaning of this final and
eternal state which he has achieved by his acts, but also the

necessity we are under to strive towards making this state
our own, the way in which we can make it our own, and how
he will help us through the Holy Spirit to do so. The teaching
of Jesus is prophecy for all time until the end of the world,
just as his incarnation, sacrifice, resurrection and ascension
have created in the Christ-Man, and the descent of the Holy
Spirit in the first Christians, that state which is to become
proper to all those who believe. Hence this teaching has a
prophetic meaning and a dynamism which overshadows the
whole span of history and even what lies beyond the end of
time.

This prophecy has also been made by the Apostles under
the inspiration of the risen and exalted Christ. St. Paul says:
"When Christ who is our life appears, then you also will
appear with him in glory." (Col 3:4) Until then the faithful
strive according to the words of St. Paul: "that I may know
him and the power of his resurrection, and may share his
sufferings, becoming like him in his death, that if possible
I may attain the resurrection from the dead." (Phil 3:10-11)
But this striving is sustained in the faithful by the Spirit of
Christ: "And I am sure that he who began a good work in
you will bring it to completion at the day of Jesus Christ."
(Phil 1:6) They have made this prophecy not only (in part)
for the sake of the individual believer, but also for the sake
of the whole of history. This is especially true of the Apostle
John in the Apocalypse, the only exclusively prophetic book
of the New Testament, the only book which shows the hidden
meaning of history to its very end, as well as what will happen
after the end of historical time.

To the eyes of faith and to the Christian vision there are
three stages in the self-disclosure of God, in the *rapprochement* between God and creation, and in the spiritualization
of creation. There is the period from the fall of the first
parents to the time of John the Baptist, then the period from
the incarnation, crucifixion, resurrection and ascension of
Christ and the descent of the Holy Spirit until the end of time,
and finally the life which follows after the end of time for
all eternity.

The first period was a period in which God acted rather

from a distance, more through commands and the creation of certain legal and theocratic premises to help men abide in their belief in one God by means of external motives, earthly and political, and to prepare themselves and the world in general for the condition of a greater intimacy with God and a period of greater spiritualization. This was more a period of messianic expectation, a period of shadowy knowledge and anticipation, of riddles and symbols of the God who was sending his aid from afar.

The second period is the period when complete union of God with man and complete spiritualization are achieved but only in one person, Jesus Christ. For all others this is the period in which the first fruits of this complete union with God are received and the complete union itself, realized in its fully developed form in Christ, tends to become general. The period until Christ was the period of messianic expectation, the period in which preparations were made to receive the Messiah; the period after Christ until the end of the world is the period of eschatological expectation, the period in which preparations are made to extend to all the complete spiritualization realized in Christ.

The revelation in Christ is a new stage in comparison with the revelation of the Old Testament. It is brought about by a new group of acts of a quite different order for which, however, mankind was prepared, and the power of these acts will be active in more and more men. The revelation of the end of time will be, in a certain sense, a new face of that revelation which is already known to us from the time of the incarnation, resurrection and ascension of Christ and the descent of the Holy Spirit. In another sense, however, it will be the same as the revelation in Christ; it will in fact be, in the persons of the faithful, the experience of what has already been realized in Christ, and what the faithful themselves have received as first fruits here in their life on earth. Thus we read in the New Testament that in Christ we have come to the end of time (1 Cor 10:11; 1 Pet 1:20). On the other hand this explosive extension of the state of Christ which will occur in all men at the end of time will be a new act of revelation, the supreme act — not just the simple completion

of some teaching. It will lead to a deeper and increased knowledge only because by a new act it will bring about a new
state.

In order to prepare themselves for this condition men are
called to free efforts of a higher spiritual kind in order that,
as far as they can, they may make the condition of Christ their
own, not simply in order that they may offer worship to the
one God. This period no longer requires the support of a
theocratic state to sustain by force the spiritual efforts of
mankind.

The incarnate Son of God, risen and exalted, is the bridge
between the earthly life of the faithful and their eternal life.
In him is given all that we can possess as long as we are on
earth and all that we will possess in the eternity to come.
In him we make progress in this life, and through him we will
progress in the life to come. In him all prophecy, both for the
time of our earthly life and for eternity, is realized.

This is why the complete revelation has already been realized in a certain sense through the acts of the incarnation,
crucifixion, resurrection and ascension of Christ and the descent of the Holy Spirit upon the world. It is this revelation
in Christ, which is at the same time the condition of the
Christ-Man, that has been realized through these same acts
of revelation, that we make present and active for ourselves.

In this we see that revelation is not only a simple communication of teaching but a continuous new state man
achieves by drawing near to God. The revelation in Christ
is a new condition of the humanity assumed by the Son of
God, while the revelation of the life to come is a condition,
similar to that of the Christ-Man, which is found in all who
believe.

Thus we see that Christian revelation is given in a Person,
the divine-human Person of Christ, and that it is the consequence of the acts of the Son of God in becoming man, being
crucified, raised and exalted as man, and in sending his Holy
Spirit upon the world. *There can be no Christianity without
revelation understood in this way. An adaptation of Christianity to the world which would reject these acts of Christ,
acts which are essential to the Christian revelation, would be*

equivalent to abandoning Christianity. Any theological language which, from a desire to bring Christianity up to date, would no longer express the content of these acts of revelation, would no longer be a Christian theological language.

In other religions the deeds of their founders are not constitutive of the religions themselves because they have not created in these men a risen state which, once assimilated by their adherents, becomes for them a source of salvation. They are not the deeds of God become man and as such a bridge or means to salvation. These religions consist only of the teachings of their founders and the methods which they have recommended to their adherents as the means to procure their salvation. Consequently these methods can be perfected as the consciousness of man deepens and grows richer. Given the fact that in these religions divinity and humanity are identical in essence, the formulation of these methods is due definitively to a more profound experience and grasp of the specific character of the human essence, and this process of growth can continue until it brings about certain revisions of the established rules.

But beyond this state of the risen Christ no higher condition is conceivable nor can we conceive of any other salvation except for the faithful themselves to attain to Christ's risen state; anything else is no longer salvation at all in the Christian sense. The saving condition has been realized in the Christ-Man through divine acts and we conceive our own salvation as an overflow from his risen state.

Each of the acts of Christ represents a spiritualization of the humanity which he assumed, and this implies a growth of this humanity in freedom and authenticity. This is demonstrated for us in the incarnation of the Son of God by the constancy of the will of the assumed human nature and by the free subjection of Christ to the conditions of human life. The act of incarnation is an act beyond our powers of understanding, but in any case we must understand it as spiritually as possible and in a manner as little given over to "objectification" as possible. "The spiritual foundation of reality", that is, the free and unconditioned divine power, makes human nature its firm and consistent medium for acting upon creation.

It achieves such a close unity with this medium that together they form a single person acting upon creation in human fashion but to a supreme degree of intensity and spiritual elevation. From one point of view this is a *kenosis* (humiliation) of the divinity; from another it is a divinization of humanity. Yet neither does the *kenosis* change the nature of the divinity, nor does the divinization change the nature of the humanity. What is human is raised up in freedom to a supreme degree of spiritualization, to the capacity of being a subject of the divine activity, while the divinity comes down in freedom to a mode of manifestation which uses human acts and forms. The supreme humility of what is human is one with its highest exaltation, and this humility is the point at which man encounters the Godhead who descends. The humility of what is human means that man's will is placed at the disposition of the divine will. But the divine will does not coerce the human will to rise to this act of willing, rather it aids the human will in its efforts to win through to this supreme exaltation, and it renounces kenotically the exercise of any coercion. All here is spiritual relation. There is none of the mythological domination of a superior force manifesting itself by means of an "objective" pressure brought to bear on an earthly reality which is then physically overwhelmed. The incarnation raises the human element assumed by Christ to a supreme level, but this is a level of freedom and authenticity, that is, of human spirituality. We must understand the incarnation of the Son of God in the light of this spiritual framework and we must maintain the doctrine of the incarnation as a reality with permanent and general significance, rather than "demythologizing" it and treating it as something capricious and unreal, the imaginative product of an inferior mentality.

There is no need to discuss the crucifixion of Christ at any length because it is accepted even by Bultmann and all his more or less immediate disciples. We ought to say however that the crucifixion of Christ has a unique, universal importance, one which is definitive for the salvation or spiritualization of all men, only if it is treated in close connexion with the incarnation and as a consequence of the latter. Only if it was accepted in full liberty and perfect love for men is the meaning of the crucifixion that of the supreme spiritualization of human nature. But the premise of this kind of acceptance of the crucifixion was laid down in the incarnation. This was the decisive act of a human will elevated to the highest level and freely willing, in the conditions of a feuding and estranged humanity, the higher goals of God's own will as the means of achieving the unification of human wills through their conformity to the will of God.

The effect of this free and supreme spiritualization of the human will in God has its repercussions in a spiritualization of the whole condition of human nature which the soul, elevated to such vigour by the help of the divine power, raises up from the process of decomposition.

If the God-Man through his incarnation, life and crucifixion was acting completely within the framework of the conditions of historical man — though a man raised up to a culminating spiritualization of human will — the act and condition of resurrection no longer belong to history strictly speaking, that is, the history that all men experience and endure with their varying strengths of will. The risen Christ no longer acts in history directly as he did until the crucifixion, and as all men do while they live. If the earthly life and crucifixion of Christ are not myths because they were real historical acts, if his incarnation is not a myth because through it there appeared in history a real man who is the fundamental means whereby the "supernatural ground of being" acts, then neither are the resurrection and the risen state of Christ myths, because it is no strange being that they bring into history as we know it. The Apostles recognized the risen Christ when he wanted to show himself to them and leave his invisible supra-historical plane. The risen Christ exists at a level of spiritualization to which the whole world will be raised, and only those who had opened themselves in some manner to this level through faith were able to "see" Christ on this level. The risen Christ proved himself to be just as real as the historical Christ but on another level, one which we cannot experience and know. We do know that the risen Christ is the historical Christ raised to the higher level of present history, beyond our present experience and action. He has advanced to the future plane of the present life. In a certain way, those who believe exist continually between the life of history and the supra-historical life, between their passing life and the life of the resurrection. The risen Christ is not separated from all connexion with our historical life, nor is our historical life separated from all connexion with the life of the risen Christ; the two are complementary. Nevertheless historical life remains in its own autonomy and freedom. It moves towards the life of resurrection only if it so wishes; it obeys the calls of this life only if it so wishes, and it accepts the perspectives opened up by this new life only if it so wishes.

But if history were only a repetition of certain human acts, essentially identical, if history did not lead somewhere beyond itself, it would not be greatly different from the repetition and lack of purpose that characterize nature, and hence would have no meaning and, strictly speaking, would not be history at all. History is truly history only if it progresses towards some goal beyond itself. This goal has been opened up for it by the resurrection of Christ. The risen Christ leads history towards the resurrection of all men. "The revelation of the possibility and power of God in the resurrection of the crucified one, and the direction and intention of God recognizable in this act, form the horizon of what is to be, and so can be called history", and it is this which truly supports the anticipation of something new in history.[8] Obviously we do not approach this new thing through miraculous acts produced by God either in nature or in history, but by an upward growth in spiritualization which is most certainly visible in an exterior way in the perfection of social relations and the mastery of nature by the spirit of an evolved mankind. To advance towards the resurrection of Christ means to move forward towards the Kingdom of God which, as a perfect community, must be prepared for by a development of the spirit of communion.

If it is true in general that a process is now underway whereby the "spiritual ground of being" is penetrating gradually into creation, this process has now been made easier by the fact that at one point in creation it has achieved its climactic result, and that in this same point creation has advanced to the very heart of this "spiritual ground of being". We are each of us in a particular manner attracted by the risen Christ towards his risen state, because, although he exists on a plane superior to our own, he is on the other hand one of us and is bound up with us both spiritually and ontologically.

This is the way in which God, the "spiritual ground of being", functions at the point where we are ontologically connected, our own invisible centre. And all of this is also true of the ascension of Christ.

The bond which links Christ with us, his outpouring upon us, our gradual assimilation to him, our spiritualization which is like his own — all these are effected by Christ through the Holy Spirit in the Church. This is the prolongation of the divine act revealed on the day of Pentecost.

Revelation Through Images

But revelation did not come about only by means of acts and words through which it continues to be active in souls; it also used images, a fact much emphasized in recent years by some Anglican theologians.

Strictly speaking, there is no relationship of pure independence between acts and words on the one hand and images on the other, and it is by exploring the nature of the relation between them therefore that we feel the solution lies to the problem of the relationship between word and image in revelation and in Christian preaching, a problem which the Anglican theologian Richardson thinks will loom larger in the future.[9] Word and image are interior to each other, so much so that in the word meaning predominates and in the image form, but meaning does not exclude form nor is form devoid of meaning. And even words are icons of things, as Patriarch Nicephorus the Confessor reminds us.[10]

To anticipate, we consider the appearance of a "theology of images" in the West significant and able — possibly — to soften the nearly exclusive dominance of the word in Protestant theology. It could also lead to an openness towards the sacraments, the *locus* of Christian life as an encounter between word and image.[11] The majority of the acts and words of revelation take the form of images, and images are devoid neither of *logos* nor of the substance of certain acts. Almost every word of revelation is a word-image, a meaning made graphic, while the acts of revelation in turn are real acts, but acts which have assumed a plastic form and expression inasmuch as they affect the visible world and have a meaning.

Among the various problems raised by images as a means of revelation our interest here centres on two in particular: the kinds of images through which God is revealed, and the way in which these images are born in the mind of the instrument of revelation under the divine influence, in short, their subjective-objective character in contrast to myth, which is the product of the imagination and which hides an objective void. It will be seen that images are the inevitable way in which God discloses himself to the human spirit.

The Kinds Of Images Through Which God Is Revealed

The Anglican theologian Austin Farrer, the first in the West to rediscover the importance of images as a means of revelation, says: "There is a current and exceedingly stupid doctrine that symbol evokes emotion, and exact prose states reality. Nothing could be further from the truth: exact prose abstracts from reality, symbol presents it. And for that very reason, symbols have some of the many-sidedness of wild nature.

"The purpose of symbols is that they should be immediately understood, the purpose of expounding them is to restore and build up such an understanding. This is a task of some delicacy. The author had not with his conscious mind thought out every sense, every interconnexion of his imagery. They had worked in his thinking, they had not themselves been thought. If we endeavour to expose them, we shall appear to over-intellectualize the process of his mind, to represent an imaginative birth as a speculative construction. Such a representation not merely represents, it also destroys belief, for no one can believe in the process when it is thus represented. No mind, we realize, could *think* with such complexity, without destroying the life of the product of thought. . . . Let it be said once and for all that the convention of intellectualization is not to be taken literally. We make no pretence of distinguishing between what was discursively thought and what intuitively conceived in a mind which penetrated its images with intelligence and rooted its intellective acts in imagination." [12] What Farrer says here is valuable but it does not sufficiently explain the birth of images.

It is our belief that revealed images are produced inevitably at the point where spirit and visible form meet. Because man himself is an incarnate spirit he is unable to grasp and express the spirit in all its purity; he must use the screen of a visible form. The human spirit itself is by nature accustomed to such a screen and is indissolubly bound up with the whole world of visible forms through which it knows and expresses its own knowledge and reflection. Spiritual reality in particular cannot be grasped and expressed as it is in itself by man who is an incarnate spirit. Material reality through which no spiritual presence shines is not conveyed by man through images, but directly or scientifically. Only when it is called upon to help convey a spiritual reality does a visible form receive the function of image.

The divine reality, as the spiritual reality *par excellence,* cannot by virtue of its own nature be comprehended and expressed in its very essence. This is so precisely because man's every approach towards the divine reality and his every human contact with it is a contact made by one who comprehends and expresses his own spirit and all spiritual reality in forms borrowed from the visible material world. Only a completely apophatic theology, that is, a theology of silence, of the negation of every statement about God, is free of images.

But let us examine first the kinds of images used in revelation. On the plane of revelation various categories of images exist. Some are ontological, that is, they are definite unities constituted by the real and definitive abiding of the

divine Spirit in a visible form. This is somewhat analogous
to the human face or body which is an image of the spirit
that is definitively united with it. These images are the results of certain acts from the moments of revelation. In this
sense, the most real, vital and ontological image of the Godhead was the humanity of Christ, an image brought into being
by the act of the incarnation. The icon, so honoured in Orthodoxy, is the artistic conveyance of this image of God assumed by the Son of God. Christ as man is the human image
of himself as God since he is at the same time God himself.[13]
The incarnation is not a myth, not a subjective human creation; it has accomplished a real and definitive union of divine
spirituality and visible human reality. We do not have in
Christ the divine reality fully revealed, and therefore we are
not able to comprehend and express it in the fullness of its
infinite complexity and richness. But neither does the living
image which is his humanity hide the divine reality completely; in fact it reveals it to the extent to which it is possible
for men to grasp it.

In his risen state Christ as man is similarly a human image
of the divine life unconquered by death, an image in which
the divinity is even more transparent. Even now, as God, the
risen Christ does not abandon his character as image for then
he would be abandoning his humanity itself. And it was this
human image of the divine life, unconquered by death, that
he showed to the Apostles.

In the same way the ascension of Christ into heaven is an
image of the exaltation of risen humanity in Christ to the
level of the divine glory. Again, man cannot grasp or express
what this divine glory is in itself. The Apostles saw it in the
image of the body of the Lord which ascended and which
shone whiter than snow on Mt. Tabor. All these are divine-
human realities, stages of the growing spiritualization of the
human drawn towards the divine. They are not myths, that
is, subjective creations devoid of content.

They convey realities beyond our intelligence and therefore
we must beware of understanding them too narrowly, of
reducing them to the level of objects, of that which can only
be seen. These realities have unfathomable spiritual depths

and yet their depths are correctly — even though very suc-
cinctly — expressed by the terms: incarnation, resurrection,
ascension, etc.

In the Old Testament, however, before the time of Christ,
God did not dwell in a created human form to such a complete
and definitive degree. He appeared only in passing, in one or
other of his energies, within a visible form. These were different kinds of images of the divine revelation: for example,
the cloud or the pillar of fire which led the Israelites in the
desert (Ex 13:21-22), or the fire which consumed the sacrifice of Elijah, or the still, small voice revealed to the same
prophet (1 Kgs 18:38-39; 19:11-13). Some of these modes of
the divine were more permanent, but even these were only
remote appearances of the divine energy, not personal incar-
nations making a continual manifestation of God possible
in unequivocal personal acts. Such a presence was the in-
dwelling of God in the ark of the Law, in the volumes contained in the ark, and in the whole tabernacle (itself an
image of God) seen by Moses on Sinai. Similar to this were
certain images which contained a still more reduced divine
presence, and which had the character of images because they
were the products of divine acts, the graphic expression of
certain means of satisfying spiritual needs, or because they
were signs of God's good will, such as the water from the
rock, the manna, etc.

All these images were like fleeting shadows compared
with the consistent image of the humanity of Christ (Heb
10:1) in which the Son of God is wholly to be found in a
manner both personal and definitive. Their character was
prophetic. In themselves they possessed no full divine reality,
but were foreshadowings of a divine reality which was yet to
come. God, who in his revelation indicated these as images,
also disclosed through them a project which was to be accomplished in the future, a project to be perfected historically.
Through these images God created an historical and mission-
ary consciousness in his people Israel, an anticipation, or
more precisely, a messianic tension. The people knew that
they were moving or being led through history towards a
higher spiritual goal and that the foreshadowings which

contained a pledge of the presence of God in miniature would in the future give place to the full reality of this presence. Mythology on the contrary follows no historical plan. It is a cyclic repetition, for its gods are the personifications of the cyclic repetitions of nature and of the passions; they are in some sense not free, and they lack the capacity to pursue diverse goals.

It is because of the lack of this fullness of the presence of God in the images of the Old Testament, and hence also in the men of Old Testament times, that the images themselves were taken from the elements (στοιχεῖα) of nature and even from the animal world. Man's development did not yet allow him to do without the use of certain natural elements as images of God. It is correct to say that in general these images did not fulfill their function by themselves but in virtue of a special divine act — a clear indication of the distinction between God and these images. Thus just as in Genesis, Daniel, and the Apocalypse, the Son of Man appears after the wild beasts have already appeared (Gen 1:26; Dan 7:13; Rev 14:14), so in the climax of revelation God takes on the image of man after he has already made use of the elements as fleeting and incomplete symbols. The history of revelation is bound up with the history of mankind. As man progresses spiritually or grows in the awareness of his superiority over nature, he comes to the realization that man himself is the most adequate image of God and so he becomes this image in fact. As long as he did not understand his own dignity and feared the imposing nature and power of the elements, he was unable to represent God worthily over against nature. Clearly, dominion over the wild beasts did not mean only dominion over them as zoological species; it also included mastery over man who continued to retain much of the beasts' manner of acting. When man became conscious that he was the image of God, and when on this plane God in Christ truly fashioned his own most satisfactory image from human nature, there began the development of the human element in all that is specifically human, all that distinguishes the human from the animal. And so too began the eternal and increasingly perfect dominion of man, or of the human element, over the whole universe and over all that is animal. The goal which this dominion pursues, and the power which attracts and penetrates it, is the risen and exalted Christ. Nothing can be more spiritualized than man who is spirit (although the agent of this process is obviously the incarnate God), and no one can place the seal of spirituality more categorically upon all things than man. And it is God who intends this dominion.

When this image of God and supreme pattern of human existence which is Christ was raised up before the eyes of man, the purpose of the prophetic and inconsistent images, the foreshadowings, came to an end (Heb 10:1). There now exists a model connected ontologically with every man and exercising real power over all men. "The shadow of the Law has passed" in order that the substance of the reality may appear, full of efficacious power over all mankind. "The good things to come" could only be indicated from afar by elements borrowed carefully from nature. But in order that these "good things" might more easily be understood in their ineffable beauty, a beauty which has nothing corresponding to it in the present reality, the Old Testament also made use of "visions". These visions combined a number of facets of present reality in bizarre and contradictory fashion and projected them to gigantic dimensions to show that the good things to come are not exactly similar to these facets since the latter are drawn more often than not from nature and the passions, but that they are a kind of ineffable dimension of these component elements and have a scope which transcends all known dimensions. However with the coming of Christ in whom these visions were fulfilled and even surpassed in all their magnitude, the visions themselves no longer had any purpose. When any description of these "good things" in their final and complete extension over all men is given, the point of departure is always the reality of Christ, and it is through words that the sense of this general extension is conveyed. This is so often the case with St. Paul (Eph 1:3-4). St. John alone uses visions, insisting both on the universal appearance of the glorified presence of Christ and also on the distance already travelled on the way to this goal. But even these visions are concentrated around Christ the Lamb who was slain, the Son of Man who will win the final victory, the Bridegroom who will celebrate his wedding feast with the bride who is the Church universal.[14]

St. Gregory of Nyssa says somewhere that the angels have no need of imagination because the divine reality which they see is far beyond any imaginings. Perhaps this is the reason why the spiritual Fathers (Diadochos of Photike for example) warn against all images, pictures and visions, because in Christ Christians have more than they could find in any imagining. The Fathers even warn against images or visions which have Christ as their object, because we know more from faith and from the experience of the theandric depths of Christ than we do from any help we may receive through images or visions of him.

Farrer speaks of a kind of "rebirth of images" through Christ, and points by way of illustration to the preaching and writings of the Apostles. Farrer does well to limit this rebirth to the Apostles; nevertheless, it is our view that this rebirth must be understood in certain definite ways. The first of these is that Christ becomes the true image of God, and the second is that he is the centre of all verbal images. We will see further dimensions of this rebirth below, but nowhere will we find the idea that after the time of Christ and the Apostles any activity of the imagination — in the sense of visions and imaginings either about Christ directly or about other things independent of him — is to be encouraged.

Christ has brought about a rebirth of images firstly because he has given a real character to the image of God, and secondly because all our words about God have now no other task than to describe Christ who is the true image of God. As in the whole history of revelation so in the revelation of Christ, the Word remains indispensable, but its principal function is to describe the human image with its various acts, through which God has revealed himself in Christ. Without this image and the acts which belong to it words would be unable to describe the richness and power of the divinity which is revealed. And contrariwise, without the help of words, the acts, images and visions of the revelation in Christ would remain, more often than not, unobserved and incomprehensible. In general the words which convey the divine acts and the divine presence manifested in images and visions, bear in themselves the imprint of imaginative expression, and are always less than what the acts and images themselves contain.[15] The word "God is mighty" is an imaginative expression because some act of the powerful working of God was experienced. Certainly religious thought has sometimes detached the imaginative word from the image or vision itself, and it is possible that on occasion God has made a self-disclosure by describing himself in this kind of imaginative language. Nevertheless it is hard to find a single word about God which does not have an imaginative character or some sensible form as its point of departure.

Words also accompany the revelation of the Son of God in Christ who is the consistent, intimate and definitive image of the divine Person. And these words reflect the imaginative character of the revelation of God in Christ. But the words themselves which describe the revelation of God in the image of the humanity which he has personally assumed are able to change; we are not obliged to remain exclusively with the words of Jesus or the Apostles, even though we must always consider them as normative.

In this sense therefore we cannot accept Farrer's statement that in Christ a "rebirth of images" has occurred. It can be accepted in the sense that all our words are based on the real image of God in Christ, on the description of the human as the most adequate image of God, an image that is filled with God. Understood in this way, there can even be an adaptation of the words used about Christ at any given time; various different symbols and verbal images can be used to convey the image or the fundamental and definitive images of God in Christ. What cannot be admitted, however, without abandoning Christianity completely, is any attempt to do away wholly with these fundamental images. Theological progress consists only in the explanation of these images by the use of other words. But this is, strictly speaking, no longer revelation, because there is no further disclosure of any essentially new

images of God, images which make the image of the humanity
of Christ obsolete.

Words must always be rooted in the perfect image of God
which is the humanity of Christ, that is, Christ as man. The
icons of Christ serve this same purpose. Protestants who have
done away with icons of Christ have deprived their words
of a support and a solid guide. It might seem that there is
contradiction between the Fathers' statement that the faithful must be careful not to force the formation of an image of
Christ in their imagination, and the assertion of the value
of icons. In fact, the Christian *is* liable to introduce subjective
elements taken from his own interior imagination into the
image of Christ, and these may well represent a decline from
the true image of Christ. It is for this reason that icons are
always painted according to fixed canons which make no allowance for the addition of even the least subjective element.

This fidelity to Christ whose humanity is the real and definitive image of God, and the formation of the faithful
according to this image, are both maintained and achieved
through the imitation of his acts in the sacraments, and in the
entire effort which Christians make to live a life similar to
Christ's. The imitation of these acts of his represents both
a desire for and an effort at imitation of him, and it achieves
to a certain extent what was intended by his own acts, the
more so as the effort is aided by energy radiating from him
whom the faithful desire to imitate, and who already exists
in that risen state which the faithful yearn to share by pattern-
ing their own acts on his.

Icons and sacraments therefore keep the real, ontological
image of God, which is Christ, or more precisely the humanity
of Christ, always present and active in the consciousness and
the lives of the faithful. They are modes by which the central
and definitive image of revelation exercises a continual effect
upon the life of man.

The word of preaching must stand in closest connexion
with icons and sacraments, as in the period when God first
revealed himself through this central image and through its
different moments, acts and stages.

Because Protestantism has not kept this image alive and

active by the use of icons and the imitation of its various stages in the sacraments, and has thereby retained only the word cut off from the practical activity of the image, it comes as no surprise that some Protestant theologians have even espoused the idea of replacing the fundamental image itself, because they consider the incarnation of the Son of God to be a pure myth.

The Objective Core Of Revealed Images

We are not concerned here with the real, fundamental and definitive image of divine revelation (the Person and acts of Christ) which was established by the objective action of God quite independently of human subjectivity. Nor are we concerned with transitory images produced by the manifestation of God through certain exterior visible forms, such as those of the Old Testament, which were likewise brought into being apart from human subjectivity. With respect to these images human subjectivity has no creative contribution to make; aided by the divine activity at work in it, it can only grasp the divine presence which is already in these external and objective images. It is this recognition of the divine presence (realized objectively) in images that constitutes in these cases the inspiration of the human instruments who are the first to recognize the divine presence in these images, just as it constitutes the faith of those others who assimilate this recognition from them as their own.

The objective core of these kinds of images is guaranteed in a certain sense by the fact that their exteriority is recognized not merely by one instrument of revelation but by many, in fact, by all who accept their primordial witness. We will speak about this role of subjectivity in the recognition of the objective reality of these images immediately after we treat a prior difficulty. This can be formulated in two questions: a) What is subjective and what is objective in those kinds of images that are wholly produced within human subjectivity? and b) How can we achieve certainty about the objective core present within these images?

A. What for example is subjective and what is objective in the vision of the prophet Isaiah (Isa 6:1-13) in which the prophet saw God seated on a throne, high and lifted up, in a house filled with glory and surrounded by seraphim each with six wings, two to cover the face, two to cover the feet, and two for flying? Or what is subjective and what is objective in the vision of the holy tabernacle which Moses received on Mt. Sinai (Ex 25:8-9), or again, what of the numerous visions in the Apocalypse?

The subjective elements in these visions or images are all those concrete forms that cannot exist in the divine spirituality, and which the instrument of inspiration introduces from his own world of preoccupations and reading, and from the preoccupations of the age and social milieu in which he lives. Farrer has shown in his commentary on the Apocalypse the connexions between the visions in this book and certain themes from the book of Genesis, visions from the book of Daniel, Jewish feasts, and also certain rabbinical exegetical treatments of all these elements. At the same time Farrer has shown in what an integrated fashion this material has been organized and concentrated around the person of Christ, how it has received new meanings, and how it has been penetrated by the idea of a development of history and of the end of history in the eternal kingdom of light.

The force and clarity of the dominant idea causes all the means of expression and all the images stored in the memory of the instrument of revelation to be brought together and marshalled in such a way that the idea itself is expressed as adequately as possible.

The feeling of the presence of a reality of supreme authority, surrounded respectfully by other realities, pressed down insistently upon the spirit of Isaiah. The image of a sovereign seated on a high throne in an exalted house, surrounded by powerful kings showing supreme respect, took shape within the prophet as the most proper form for seizing and expressing this presence. It was the awareness of this presence which provoked the recollection of an image which he had seen or recognized from reading or report, but which has received here extraordinary dimensions. The throne is "high and lifted up", the house is exalted, the beings which are standing round the throne are not of this earth, etc.

What has occurred here is in some ways opposite, in other ways analogous to what occurs in the imagination of the artist. In the complex of organs, attitudes, movements, look and form of a man the artist sees an intention, a tendency, a dominant air. Abstraction is made from the mass of motions, attitudes and forms under the powerful impression of the dominant intention or tendency made concrete in them, and in the imagination a few more concentrated, more essential forms appear in which the artist captures the dominant spiritual note of this particular man more expressively and more clearly.

This dominant note is something other than the concrete form in which the artist catches and expresses it. But between it and the forms in which a true artist has rendered it, the conformity can be so great that we are able to say that these very forms pre-exist virtually in the original reality, and that once the necessity arises for the reality to reveal itself naturally or to be captured in the concrete world of sensible forms, then it must inevitably be revealed or expressed in the forms in which it has in fact been expressed.

Thus we can say that on the one hand this spiritual dominant note that presses down upon the capacity for precision which the artist or instrument of revelation possesses, has within itself certain "forms", but that, on the other hand, these forms are not material and as a strict consequence they mould the spirit of the "seer", artist, or instrument of revelation, impressing upon him their own "air" and provoking within him a process whereby those forms most adequate to the expression of the reality in question are gathered together from the memory and brought into place. Obviously this process does not go on without the effort of the "seer" himself, and this effort is especially important in giving style to the dominant form that presses down upon his spirit. In this sense, what the artist or instrument of revelation does when he captures that dominant spiritual note can be called "spiritual sight" or a "super-visual sight".

We already meet a similar description of this procedure of the birth of visions in the Fathers. St. Gregory Palamas

brought together a series of patristic statements on this theme
and added to them his own explanations.

In his analysis of what Moses expressed when the model
of the holy tabernacle was shown to him in the dark cloud on
Mt. Sinai, St. Gregory Palamas says this: "Can we say that
when Moses had torn himself away from all that sees and is
seen, all realities and all concepts, and when he had transcended the sight of the place where he was and penetrated the
darkness, he saw nothing there at all? But he did see the
immaterial tabernacle that he later showed in a material
imitation to those who remained below.... Thus the tabernacle, the priesthood, and their appurtenances were sensible
symbols and veils, covering the things which Moses saw in
the divine darkness. But the things which he saw were not
themselves symbols." [16] Palamas goes on to cite Dionysius the
Pseudo-Areopagite in this respect: "O super-essential Trinity,
direct us towards the highest peak of the mysterious where in
the superluminous darkness are the simple mysteries of the
knowledge of God, stripped of everything, unalterable." [17]
Taking up a position opposed to that of the monk Barlaam
who held that the instruments of revelation deduce the invisible realities from various visible symbols, Palamas continues: "But Moses saw what he saw in forty days and forty
nights, participating as St. Gregory of Nyssa tells us, 'in the life
of eternity under the cover of that darkness'. Hence these visions were without form. (The juxtaposition "visions without
form" — ἀνείδεα ἦν τὰ θεάματα — should be noted here:
author's note.) But how then are they symbolic? They were
seen in the darkness at that time. And in the darkness all is
simple, stripped of everything and unalterable. But among
symbols properly so called, things sensible and composite, is
there anything that it not alterable, composite, and bound
up with beings, that is to say, with created things? But because
Moses saw them they were visible.... At the same time, everything there was simple." [18]

But this "super-visual sight" imprints its own "air" on
the spirit, an air that contains in itself an image or a complex
of virtual images and stimulates their expression in certain
definite symbols. St. Gregory Palamas adduces a series of

Biblical and patristic texts that point in this direction: " 'The prophets saw', says St. Basil the Great, 'because they were marked by the Spirit in the intellect.' Hence the Holy Spirit is the one who takes up his abode in the minds of the prophets, and, by making use of their intellects as material instruments, foretells in the prophetic mind — by his own agency — those things which are to come, in the first place to the prophets themselves, and through them to us." [19]

The divine spiritual reality makes this imprint not in a partial fashion or while remaining totally exterior to the instrument of revelation, but by moulding the whole spirit of the seer, by emptying itself into him. Even the angels are modelled after the divine reality. In support of this view Palamas cites the following words from the Pseudo-Areopagite: " 'Their sovereignty (the reference is to one of the choirs of angels) is full of longing for the source of their sovereignty, and it models both itself and what is with it after the good according to the likeness which it has to that sovereignty.' You see then that there are also spiritual types (τύπους νοητούς)?" [20] Clearly, these are impressions which are imprinted by one spirit on another and which permit the modelling of one spirit after another, and the modelling of the present state of one spirit after that of another. The discernment of these τύποι (spiritual forms or types) must be compared with the *Wesensschau* of which Husserl spoke, although this latter is more properly applied to the poet or the philosopher who discerns the essence of something or of someone in sensible forms, while the instrument of revelation discerns it quite apart from any forms, and afterwards forces himself to express it in forms. Nevertheless it happens that the divine "spiritual type" itself is clothed in images taken from the seer's own treasury of images. But between the spiritual type and the forms in which it is clothed the connexion is adequate to such a degree that it is as if the forms were potentially inscribed in the type and gradually became more precise for the benefit of the seer whose own sensitivity has accustomed him to cast the whole into some concrete form. The images found in the memory of the seer are polarized as if under the attraction of some kindred magnetic force found in the spiri-

tual type. Another difference from poet or philosopher is that
the instrument of revelation is himself moulded by the ethical
power of the type and becomes a different man, preaching a
different life.

The divine types are not visual objects devoid of thought;
they stimulate insights of a spiritual kind that are combined
with thought, or they directly stimulate thought despite the
fact that they are in themselves beyond all that is merely
thought. Palamas says: "For I do not consider the visions of
the prophets to be inferior to human intellection. They are
superior to our mind and I accept that their visions are similar
to those of the angels. For by making themselves capable of
union with the angels through purification and by uniting
themselves with the angels in virtue of their striving for the
divine, these men themselves, like the angels, receive the mould
and impress of other angels higher in rank and so transform
their intellectual image more and more into a divine form.
Moreover by this form they cultivate the holy knowledge
that has descended upon them from above. And what cause
should there be for surprise if the prophetic purity is a form
which has been modelled after the types of the angels, since,
as theology teaches us, this purity is a fellow minister with
the angels, and is attested therefore as able to receive the
types of God himself (καὶ αὐτοὺς τοὺς τοῦ Θεοῦ τύπους
αὕτη δέχεσθαι)? For the purified soul is the one which
presents itself to God without any form (ἀνείδεον), prepared
to receive the impress of the types of God (τοῖς αὐτοῦ
ἕτοιμον ἐνσημαίνεσθαι τύποις) through which God is
accustomed to make himself seen." [21] "Now when Moses
passed day and night in that life without forms, did he not
see the divine forms (ἐν τῇ ἀνειδέῳ ἐκείνῃ ζωῇ, οὐ
θείους τύπους εἶδε)? Nevertheless it says, 'And see that
you make them after the pattern for them, which is being
shown you on the mountain.' (Ex 25:40)." [22]

For in general the heart, that is the inner man within each
of us, is moulded by God, as the prophet David says. [23]

Clearly this "air", this "approach" or "intention" of the
spiritual reality which is seen by an instrument of revelation
(or by an artist), or which is impressed upon him to such

an extent that the instrument is himself modelled after it, does not always stimulate a mobilization of sensible images, or some new combination or restructuring of them, or even the discovery of new meanings within them. Often enough it is only words which are mobilized or put into new combinations so that from these new and often contradictory combinations meanings might emerge which will be adequate to the spiritual reality that has been "seen". But these words too have something "graphic" in them, if in no other way, at least by the fact that they were originally used to convey sensible and graphic realities.

However, when it is not just a case of prophesying what is to come but also of prophesying what must be fulfilled by men, it is always true that the first one to be modelled after the visible pattern and to force himself to conform to the pattern is the instrument of revelation himself. Only thus is the revelation easily received. The word used in the writings of the Fathers for the "form" disclosed to the instrument of revelation is taken from the New Testament where it is used precisely in the sense of a "pattern" on which the faithful must model themselves. St. Paul says: "Brethren, join in imitating me, and mark those who so live as you have an example (τύπον) in us." (Phil 3:17) The same Apostle tells us elsewhere that he does not want to command his listeners how to act but wishes instead to give them himself as "an example to imitate" (τύπον εἰς τὸ μιμεῖσθαι: 2 Thess 3:9).

St. Peter too asks the priests not to lord it over the people but to become "examples to the flock" (1 Pet 5:3). Paul urges Titus to be a "model" in those attitudes which belong to the spiritual order in all "gravity", confirming the idea that there are spiritual models or "forms" (Tit 2:7 and *cf.* 1 Thess 1:7).

We can turn now to the real, definitive images of revelation, the stages of the life of Jesus Christ, or to the exterior images of a transitory character in order to see their connexion with human subjectivity.

In its relations with these images and from both perspectives, that is, theirs as well as its own, the human spirit must attempt a process of modelling in order to discern in them images of the divine reality. In this way they are extended in human subjectivity, and a link is forged between their external reality and the inner being of the seer. That is to say, the images are not purely exterior. Were they to remain so, they would not be discerned as forms of the divine presence. This is analogous to the situation of the artist who has the gift of capturing a meaning within a form thanks to some experience, while other artists, not having had this experience, are unable consequently to capture this meaning.

The difference between the exterior images of revelation, whether definitive or transitory, and those which are purely interior is that the first can also be disclosed to others or be seen by them. If not all are able to see them as images of the divinity, they are at least visible as real exterior forms. Their formation is not produced within the interior subjectivity of a single individual. Yet without an openness of subjectivity, what lies beyond the material plane in these images cannot be seen. Thus the knowledge of God in exterior and historical reality is an interior vision of faith and does not compel the assent of anyone. In fact, as St. Gregory Palamas says, "faith is a supra-intelligible vision." [24] Even when it is not merely faith but also vision, the knowledge of God contains in itself an element of faith, and so implies a certain contribution from subjectivity. It does not however compel recognition by all. Palamas observes frequently that though the light of Tabor shone forth more brightly than the sun, it was not seen by those at the foot of the mountain.

B. But if the subjective factor is absolutely necessary in order to discern an objective core of revelation, how does the instrument of revelation, and above all the believer, find the certitude that he is in fact confronted with an objective core? This is the most difficult question of all, and in spite of the fact that these same instruments decisively assert its certitude, it is only from the indirect witness of these instruments of revelation themselves that we can deduce certain signs by which this objective character is manifested.

One sign which points to the objective character of the core of these visions is the experience of a state of receptivity to this objective core in which the instrument of revelation is usually found. The seer realizes that he has not invented this core, but that it has been given to him to contemplate, to understand, and to express, even though that expression also requires an effort on his part.

Man experiences himself in these moments as one who has been stripped of the substance of his ideas, emotions, and attempts at thought. Hence he comes to realize that what he sees is not caused by the intensity of his own spiritual and intellectual resources or by his own efforts at deepening and combining them. The "spiritual model" or "type" appears to him immediately as something different from all that he himself is. This state is also experienced as a kind of passivity. The seer "sees" but he makes no effort to discover what he "sees", not even to see the "model", the "type". It is a gift, indeed it even compels its own reception, and exerts pressure upon the spirit of the seer.

If certain images or words are brought into play and organized within the seer in order to interpret what he "sees", this again occurs principally without his effort and comes about under the power of that reality which has been "seen". The effort of the seer is only required to touch up points of detail.

The force by which a "type" or "types" compel the recognition of their reality is for the seer a commanding force that constrains him firstly to acknowledge its presence and secondly to communicate what it is that he "sees". "Woe to me if I do not speak!", is a familiar cry of the prophets. The experience of the objective character of the core of the vision is now as accentuated as possible. The instrument of revelation hears these words like a command: "Do what you have seen," or, "do as it has been commanded you: go and speak!" For the sake of the instrument of revelation, the compelling power of the objective reality has been clothed in the aural image of a voice or word.

Indeed this objectivity has such power that the image or sequence of images achieves a species of autonomy in the spirit of the seer, although, on the other hand, it is within him that everything is taking place. There is in this an objectivity of subjectivity, something which goes beyond the

borderline that separates the two. Nevertheless, this phenomenon has nothing in common with hallucination, which is
symptomatic of the sick man and in which everything happens in a sequence devoid of coherence and lucidity. Moreover
the effect of hallucination is a continual aggravation of the
unhealthy condition of the individual, whereas the instrument
of revelation is characterized by lucidity and an acute consciousness of self together with an ethical coherence in the
whole of his behaviour. His vision is not a pastiche; it is
something new and points to a new phase of man's ethical
progress. Because the divinity is spirit and the self-disclosure
of the divinity is addressed to the human spirit, it is not surprising that in this meeting of the purely divine spirit and the
human spirit there occurs a transcending of that exteriority
associated with every man's relation both to material realities
and even to other men who are also clothed with bodies.

Aware of this passivity of the instruments of revelation,
the Fathers speak more often of the action of moulding or
imprinting exerted upon them by these "visions", and less
of the effort of the seers to mould themselves. We have cited
several passages of this kind above.

* * *

The explanations we have given above from the works
of St. Gregory Palamas can also be found in essence — though
applied to poetic knowledge — in the works of the Romanian
philosopher Mihai Sora, especially in his exposition of the
manner in which human subjectivity meets reality which,
though it is objective, becomes interior to the subject in this
encounter. According to Sora, reality is experienced as a plenitude which fills the empty subject, a fullness which forms a
unity with the emptiness that it fills. The reality which fills
and moulds the subject offers itself to the subject at the beginning as a kind of general "pre-word", which later becomes
specific in images and words. In order to describe this moulding
of the subject by the content which fills it but does not cause
it to cease to know itself as distinct from the content that has
filled and moulded it, and which the subject itself simultane-

ously expresses when it expresses itself, Sora uses the image of two circles, one blue (B) and the other red (R), which by a partial intersection produce in the area where they intersect (V) the colour violet.

Subject B, moulded in area V by object R, has united with object R in this intersecting space, and, in the same space, object R has become one with subject B, giving a common result in V. This means, to return to our own question, that there have appeared in the subject certain "impressions", "intentions" or "airs" of the reality which in this case is the divine reality that has accommodated itself to the human subject's meagre powers of discernment and expression, humanized itself and raised up the human element to the level of the divinity. In this "pre-word" the human subject perceives himself as much as he perceives the reality which has moulded him or which has modelled itself after the human subject. But at the same time the human subject preserves his awareness that he himself is distinct from the divine reality, for he simultaneously distinguishes himself and the divine reality as factors which have come together without the loss of their own identities. "In that space (the area of intersection V) there is no question of something which is purely and simply the colour violet. In this violet exist an indissoluble unity and an always radical duality. In it exist two inclinations, the one leading without interruption towards blue and the other towards red; in the violet these are both present 'in person', each with its entire *ratio formalis*." "In the speaker there now spreads the gentle and diffuse light of a pre-word, of a soft whisper, enclosed like a seed in the immediateness of its own sonority, and — like a seed — open towards the branching tree of significations whose uncontainable dynamism is contained — *totum simul* — within it." In this "pre-word" existence begins to be experienced consciously "not only with the five senses, but also with the sixth; not only with the mind but also with the heart, with the welcoming embrace, the impulse which transcends all boundaries. . . . Thus the 'pre-word' (in the full dynamism of its progressive development as well as in the reality it represents to external perception) would furnish the speaker with the one model of the correct usage of the articulated words." [25]

What distinguishes the encounter of subject and divinity from our model above, consists especially in the fact that here the pre-word is experienced by man not only as something inspired by the presence of a reality that is objective in nature, but also as an echo of a claim, of a word above words, of a God experienced as person. The human word corresponds to the divine reality not only as meaning become conscious in man, but in a more complete manner, as discernment of the divine command and response to it. In the encounter with the divine reality the whole man experiences himself as one engaged in a dialogue with God as a partner obedient and responsible to the divine word. The whole man is thus moulded as an obedient and responsive being in the encounter with God, and the experience of these qualities causes the word to spring up in him as a remembrance in human form of the divine word, and as a response to it. This is the experience of man as one who carries the impress of God and yet is at the same time distinct from him.

From this experience of God as commanding word (not articulated in human words but articulated as intention) there follows the necessity for a man to convey this word of God to other men in his own human words. And it is only because man has this capacity and experiences this obligation to convey the word of God in human words, that he experiences the further capacity and obligation of perceiving this reality as object and conveying it in human words for the sake of his fellow men.

Conclusions

Because Christianity is the religion of the revelation of God in human "substantial form", and because all revealed images are born from contact between the divine spirit and the incarnate human spirit, we see that in Christianity man has been raised to the highest level of the discernment of God, that is, to the stage at which God is discerned as a reality distinct from objects, as a reality which is spiritual but which can only be revealed and discerned through the mediation of sensible images. For only man, as spirit, is superior to objects, while as a substantial image, all his spiritual life is bound up with images. Images are the necessary form of the manifestation of the human spirit, and the human spirit exists in the image of God. Man can only discern God through image and symbol. Human images are the highest form of discerning the divine spirit, for, as images in which the human spirit is expressed, they are simultaneously symbols of the divine spirit after which the human spirit has been patterned.

But man must not confuse his images or even his body with his own spiritual reality. That is to say, he must not impose on the spirit, much less on the divine spirit, that dimension of images which he perceives as "object". When he does this we have the birth of an idol, a myth. In this sense any image can become myth whether it is historical event or something borrowed from nature. Even the images of revelation can become myths in such a case.

Thus on the one hand man cannot avoid images when he thinks about God, and on the other hand it depends on man's own spiritual level whether these images will be myths which betray God, or symbols of the God who transcends this world of objects.

Emil Brunner has pointed out the inevitability of the Biblical images: "To the thinking which seeks to obtain final truth purely from man's reflection about himself and his world, and consequently repudiates dependence on a historical fact—revelation or saving history — the very thought of a personal God, a divine Thou who addresses us, is mythical. This thinking is opposed by the faith which knows its dependence on such a historical happening, because in that happening it recognizes the revelation and self-communication of God. This means the acceptance of what we wish to name the 'fundamental myth' of the Christian faith, which is identical with the content of this *kerygma.*

"We agree with philosophy in this point, that we call the decisive *kerygma* of God's self-communication in Jesus Christ 'mythical' inasmuch as we concede that in faith we are aware of the inadequacy of all our speaking about God. The language of the Bible — of the New Testament as well as the Old — is symbolic and mythical in a manner that is inadequate for the abstract thought of philosophy and therefore seems unacceptable. What the philosopher calls inadequate and 'primitive' is marked by two characteristics: by the symbolism of God's Personal Being (anthropomorphism) and by His intervention in history (miracle).

"But when in rejoinder we inquire for the concepts by which this philosophy seeks to replace the Biblical symbolism and mythology in the interests of spiritualization, we discover that they lie in the direction of abstraction. . . . The world of God of which the Bible speaks is transformed into Plato's world of ideas, into the ontology of timeless Being, into the Absolute of the Advaita doctrine, the Absolute which has nothing confronting it but which is at once the eternal ground of everything and its negation.

"It also becomes evident that this abstract system of concepts is not, as was intended, unsymbolical and adequate, but that all that has happened is the replacement of the symbolism of time and personality by the symbolism of space and of things. There is no philosophy, however abstract, which can evade the necessity of speaking of ultimates symbolically even if the abstractions of impersonal being and timelessness are used as such symbols. This is the quintessence of the spiritualization which is aimed at: the symbolism of personalism and of happenings in time is replaced by that of the impersonal, of the 'It' and of timelessness. When we have once realized this fact, our zeal for 'demythologizing' will have cooled remarkably." [26]

What Brunner says here seems to us essentially correct but we would like to draw attention to certain distinctions and nuances which he has passed over.

In the first place, images of God as a person who enters into relation with man are not merely the products of the incommensurability of God and man, but also of the likeness between man, as spirit, and God. Therefore these images possess in themselves an eternally valid truth and can never be made substantially obsolete. Understood in this way, moreover, they are not, strictly speaking, myths. God will be eternally known as Person, although the meaning of his Personhood — as also the meaning of our own — will constantly become deeper for us throughout all eternity.

In the second place, everything that man says about God which takes as its point of departure man's knowledge of his own spiritual qualities possesses a certain truth, but the truth value of such statements is, as it were, "second class" compared to those images of God which have been revealed by God himself. Here not even the attributes of God which philosophy has propounded, such as his absolute existence, eternity, etc., can be totally rejected — as Protestant theology sometimes rejects them — provided they result from divine revelation, and are conceived in a manner which corresponds to that revelation. God does possess these attributes in reality, although the sense in which he possesses them will eternally become more profound for us. Even the concept of images need not be opposed after the manner of the "demythologizing" philosophers and theologians, nor need we oppose the images which accompany concepts as certain Protestant theologians do. What we must do is to join all of these together.

With respect both to revealed images and to the attributes of God based upon these images, there is no need to embrace unilaterally either the cataphatic attitude which can degenerate into a mythical mentality, or the apophatic attitude which can tend to produce a complete lack of belief in the possibility of any connexion between God and man, and even a complete lack of confidence in man. It is, moreover, confidence in the ability of man to grasp what God reveals about himself which is the basis of any confidence in our own word about God — a confidence so cultivated in Protestantism.

We must always unite the cataphatic and apophatic approaches. After all, even the word itself is a human image of God, based on the bond between the human spirit and the divine spirit, an image which, with the help of revealed images, is sometimes sharply focussed and at other times enlarged.

We should also add that Christian revelation as the encounter between God and man, realized through the means that result from this encounter, aims at the growth of man from and in the surrounding atmosphere of the source which is God, who, once free and unconditional, must also be personal. Experience of this bond and communion with that source, and the experience which man has of his growth in it, are expressed inevitably in images, but these images convey a true reality in the most adequate way available to our incarnate condition.

Mythology is completely different from this. There is in mythology no concern for the gradual spiritual growth of the individual or of mankind, either on the part of man or on the part of the supposedly miraculous forces, for they themselves are far removed from what is meant by spirituality in the proper sense of the term.

The Gospel is not in essence a mythology because it does not personalize certain natural forces. In the Gospel the divine person cannot be reduced to some force of nature, and hence neither can the relationship of man with the divine person be reduced to his relation with some natural force. Instead the bilateral personal character of this relationship is always stressed. Moreover the Gospel does not present this relationship as an illusion. Here is the non-mythological core of the Gospel which even Bultmann recognized. Hence he proposed only a demythologization of the mythical dress in which this non-mythological core had been covered while retaining the inner kernel. The Gospel can be demythologized by Bultmann and his school because it is not essentially mythology, but Graeco-Roman or German or Hindu mythology cannot be demythologized because they are in their very essence myths. To demythologize them would be to dissolve them. But the Gospel can neither be dissolved now during mankind's earthly existence, nor through all eternity.

CHAPTER V

Revelation as Gift
and Promise*

In recent years Western exegesis has begun to place strong
emphasis on the prophetic character of revelation. This development has occurred in connexion with the emergence of
a theology of hope, an eschatology which is tending to give
a new stamp today to the whole of theology. Emphasis on
the prophetic side of revelation and on the importance of
hope in Christian theology is welcome because in the past
both these elements have been far too lightly regarded. But
it is our impression that this tendency, which is clearly Protestant in origin inasmuch as it sees the Christian as receiving
virtually nothing in this earthly life, does not take into account the fact that revelation is not just a series of promises
but also a series of gifts or graces given even now during this
life to those who believe.

There is a great difference in this respect between the
revelation of the Old Testament and the revelation of the
New Testament. If it is true that in the revelation of the Old
Testament the benefits of salvation are almost all promises,
and that any fulfillment of them accorded in this life consists
almost always of earthly goods which are types of the promised spiritual goods, it is clear nevertheless that the revelation
of the New Testament represents, even during our life on
earth, the fulfillment of certain important promises of a spiritual order which were made in the Old Testament.

---

* Originally published in Romanian in *Ortodoxia* 21 (1969), 179-196.

Recent exegesis and the theology of hope do not seem in our view to grasp the full importance of the striking difference between the Old and New Testaments in what concerns man's spiritual situation under the two dispensations.

Our attempt in these pages will therefore be to restore the balance a little between revelation as promise and as gift, emphasizing in a special way the existence of such a balance in the revelation of the New Testament. In an earlier study [1] we have already looked at revelation from the point of view of the means whereby it is brought about, and therefore in what follows we will try to show how by these means revelation at once bestows certain immediate gifts and also transmits certain promises for the future.

The Prophetic Character Of Old Testament Revelation And The Predominance Of Types

More recent exegesis rightly underlines the predominantly prophetic character of revelation in the Old Testament. The fulfillments accomplished by *acts* of revelation in the course of the Old Testament are types, on a lower plane, of certain higher spiritual fulfillments. "Thus the whole history of the Old Testament presents more and more completely the character of a fulfillment which points in its turn to the need for a still deeper questioning. The whole history of the Old Testament is guided by the Word of Yahweh. It is a history which is given as gift and has the nature of a fulfillment, yet in that fulfillment there appears a new kind of promise." [2]

Revelation in the Old Testament more or less coincides with the history of the people of Israel because it is by fulfillments of that history which are of an earthly historical order that revelation moves forward — as it were by certain "types" — towards the fulfillment of promises which are of a spiritual order and which are the final goal revelation is seeking, although it does not reach this goal in the period of the Old Testament. No single fulfillment from the time of the Old Testament, nor even all the Old Testament fulfillments put together, represent "the fulfillment *par excellence*" which the revelation of the New Testament brings. In what concerns salvation, the people of the Old Testament live exclusively under the dispensation of the promise. Clearly the promises themselves are a gift, and Israel from this point of view stands in a better situation, one closer to God, than do "the nations". The promises were given to the Jews, the Law was given them, the worship, even a certain sonship and glory, and it was from them that Jesus was to come according to the promise (Rom 9:4-5). They were truly "the children of the promise" (Rom 9:8) as the members of other nations were not. They lived by hope and their hope gave them consolation. But while there exists only hope the fulfillment has not yet come. When Jesus came, firm perseverance in hope was to bring salvation, even to those who died before his coming.

The historical acts of the Old Testament were not just types of the spiritual fulfillments of the New Testament; they also served as preparations for them. God sustained the people of Israel because it was from them that Christ was to come forth according to the flesh. God chose David, the son of Jesse, so that from his descendants Christ might be born. It was from among those Jews who were educated spiritually in the school of the Law and in expectation of the Messiah that the Apostles were to arise, the men who followed after Christ and witnessed to the world on his behalf. In Israel a certain level or perspective of spirituality was created without which Christ could neither have appeared nor been understood. Thus, although the birth of Christ radically transcends the level of the Old Testament fulfillments as types, from another point of view his birth is the capstone of that series of fulfillments. Christ is born as man because before him Abraham was chosen and Isaac and Jacob and Judah and David, and because God willed that the people of Israel should carry his promises to completion. "The law was our custodian until Christ came" (Gal 3:24); "Christ is the end of the law" (Rom 10:4); he was born as man "under the law" (Gal 4:4), prepared by the Law.

The acts of the Old Testament revelation prepare and condition the act of the coming of Christ, and this in turn crowns the former. The acts of the Old Testament revelation

lay history open for Christ who descends and enters into it.
They constitute all the different preparations for the realization of the promise of a Messiah to come. They constitute
that history which prepares for the entry into history of one
who himself transcends all history. They succeed one another
on the path leading towards the gleam of that heavenly light
which shone when God came to dwell among men and history
was fulfilled by what lies beyond it.

In this sense the Old Testament revelation as a whole
is also a gift and not simply a promise, for it throws open
the shining light of the fulfillment in Christ. It does not leave
the people in total darkness, nor does it move in darkness
to the very end. This also is a gift, not simply a promise,
although the gift is more like a light shining at the very end
of a road. The Old Testament revelation moves toward this
light until it reaches the end of the road and comes up along
side it, but this gift is not the same as the very light itself illuminating the road from above. It is more like an oasis; we
see it from afar and we move towards it until we come right
up beside it — but we never finally reach it.

The Old Testament revelation appears predominantly as
a revelation of promise not only because the *acts* of God accomplished within the framework of the Old Testament are
generally fulfillments of earthly wishes, and, as such, types
of the fulfillments of the New Testament, but also because
of its words. Almost all the words of the Old Testament revelation are in the future tense and hence prophetic. Those
in the past tense refer to fulfillments of an earthly kind as
foundations for belief in the fulfillments promised for the
future. The very fact that God speaks to the people through
the prophets shows that he has not yet come among men.

But the prophetic words of the Old Testament, like the
acts of revelation accomplished in the course of it, also represent a divine solicitude for Israel, a certain intimacy of
God with this people. The very fact that God speaks to this
people indicates such a solicitude and intimacy. Abraham was
called "the friend of God" (Jas 2:23). It is true that the
"Word of God" is directed to one or other of the prophets,
but this is in order that it may be spoken by him to the

people. Through the words of the prophets God teaches his will to Israel; he encourages and sustains hope. Thus the people are raised to the level of the knowledge of the truth and achieve some vision of the future. Israel is strengthened to lead a life which is fitting and pleasing to God. God indeed showed his glory to the prophets, but they made it known to the people.

Although the words of the Old Testament generally contain promises only, nevertheless through them God has entered into a dialogue with the people of Israel and he sustains this dialogue. Now this dialogue between God and Israel shows God's appreciation for Israel and through it Israel is maintained at a certain level of knowledge, spirituality and power, and is strengthened in its relationship with God.

The people have the feeling, indeed the assurance that "God is with us." The Word of God addressed to Israel is often a blessing. The Psalms, the prophets, the Old Testament in its entirety, all constitute a dialogue between God and men, the words of God given to men and the responses of men to God. They express the conviction that it is God who sustains and guides the people.

In a dialogue the partners communicate what they themselves understand, but they also manifest their reciprocal love and interest. God brings his judgements down to the level of human understanding just as he condescends to accept human thoughts, because he wishes to have communion with Israel. In the closest connexion with this wish God confesses his own love for men and his desire to hear men confess their grateful love for him and to see them disclose their sorrows and cares to him in filial confidence and to ask for his help. By so doing men are raised up to a higher light and life. God lives, and men live too. Both sides manifest this life of theirs in an exciting dialogue. God is not cold and indifferent nor does he want man to be cold and suspicious of him. God created men as beings who would yearn for spiritual light and warmth. He created them as spiritual sparks and it is he himself who is the spiritual fire.

It is the dialogue which feeds the fire of the spiritual life in men, and it is in dialogue that God is manifested as the fire of love.

The communion which God brings about between himself and men even in the Old Testament carries the name of "covenant", in which — as the name suggests — each party freely engages himself to display continually a loving concern for the other. Obviously, before God establishes a covenant with men for a communion freely accepted and contracted as between equals, there must be an earlier action whereby God comes down to the level of this kind of relationship, that is to say, an election of Israel with whom God wishes to conclude and maintain his covenant.[3] An act of benevolent *kenosis* is demanded which has as its other side the elevation of the people to partnership with God and to a certain level of the knowledge of God and the ability to conduct themselves fittingly before him. In general two things are required for the people of Israel in this covenant and for their continued part in it: the effort to *know* God more and more, and to give him in their worship an *adoration* which corresponds to this growing knowledge. Within the covenant are included both the knowledge of God and the worship which must be offered him. But both this knowledge and this worship are based on divine revelation; they are not simply produced by men.

If the acts of history through which God is revealed in the Old Testament do not, strictly speaking, represent the fulfillment of the descent of God among men, but are simultaneously types of that fulfillment and steps leading towards it, then in the same way the dialogue and ever-renewed covenant of God with Israel do not, through the agency of this knowledge and worship, achieve complete communion between God and men, but only symbolize it and lead toward it. Already through the prophet Malachi God denounced his covenant with the people of Israel which he had made through the mediation of the Levitical priesthood, and replaced it with the covenant which he made with the assembly of the people,[4] that is, directly with the whole of the people. But this act had still another prophetic character: the bond between God and men through the mediation of the Old Testament priesthood would be done away with entirely and in its place and in the place of the symbolic cult maintained according to the covenant, there would be at the very moment of the coming of Christ, that is, at the end of the Old Testament, a direct and complete bond joining the incarnate God to every man and to the community of the faithful, the Church.

Let us not forget, however, that the knowledge of God was preserved among the people of Israel not only by the priests but also by the prophets. In fact it was due to the prophets that there was a continual increase in the knowledge of God in Israel. This knowledge was not however drawn from each man's inner union with God. Even the prophets enjoyed communication with God only at intermittent moments and they transmitted this communication to the people as though from some external source.

The word through which God communicated himself in the Old Testament revelation was not a permanent conversation with himself in the prophet's heart of hearts, still less in the hearts of all men. God did not reveal himself as a word which remains forever. The Word of God had not yet become incarnate as man and had not come to dwell among men "full of grace and truth" (Jn 1:14), and therefore men were not raised up to the level at which they could constantly listen and respond to the divine Word that was constantly being heard, or at least was always to be found among them. Consequently man was not elevated to, nor did he operate within, the condition in which he himself was a permanent word immediately dependent on the divine Word. The dialogue was intermittent; the divine and human partners remained separated by a certain distance. From time to time words of God came to men and were deposited in the Law and in the writings of the prophets. But as soon as Christ had come, the divine subject of these words became incarnate as man and entered into intimate and permanent communion with mankind. "Before his visible coming in the body, the Word of God used to come spiritually to the patriarchs and prophets prefiguring the mystery of his Advent." [5]

This predominantly prophetic character of a fulfillment which was incomplete but which was at the same time a prep-

aration for the true fulfillment, is also shared by the types
or *images*, properly so called, through which the Old Testament revelation was communicated. (We must here abstract
from the fact that the acts by which God helped Israel are
also types of higher fulfillments to come, and also from the
fact that certain types also have the nature of acts by which
the people received immediate help.) The Paschal lamb is
a type of Christ, the Lamb who will in fact take away the sins
of the world. The crossing of the Red Sea is a type of Baptism and of escape from the tyranny of Satan. The cloud
which guided the Israelites through the desert is a type of the
Holy Spirit. The manna is a type of the Eucharist; the water
from the rock is a type of the grace of the Holy Spirit; all
the sacrifices of the Old Testament are types of the sacrifice
of Christ; the holy tabernacle is a type of the Church, and
the ark of the Law found within the tabernacle is a type of
the presence of Christ within the Church on the holy altar.

Yet all these things were not just signs empty of any content. They also represented a certain presence and a real near-
ness of God to Israel. The glory of God was hidden inside
the Law and inside these different types but it was covered
over with the letter, with forms. A veil hung over the face
of Moses for the sake of the people of Israel who were not
able to look upon the dazzling brightness on his face, that
is to say, on the profound divine meanings contained in the
Law (2 Cor 3:12-18). "The grace of the New Testament was
hidden mysteriously in the letter of the Old. Therefore the
Apostle says that 'the law is spiritual' (Rom 7:14). . . . The
Gospel however has shown us through the letter the very truth
itself that has come to us foreshadowed through the Law and
prefigured in the prophets." [6]

The clearest and most apt of the prophetic images through
which Jesus Christ was announced was, however, the human
image. Already in the Book of Genesis we see that man in
his fully actual state, that is, as the embodiment of the heavenly model of man, was to make his appearance after the
creation of the natural world and the animals and was to
exercise dominion over both of them. The whole Old Testament revelation is not only a prophecy of the perfect man

who is Christ and of all who believe in him; it is also a preparation for him. Because of the nature of its own intrinsic development Christ does not appear in the Old Testament. But his appearance, which is from above, is nevertheless the crowning point and keystone of the Old Testament and of all the accumulated contributions which Old Testament mankind, aided and guided by God though not yet united with him, was able to make.

And so just as all the historical acts of God in the Old Testament had the same objective, which was the return of Israel to its own land, and just as the covenant of God and man was renewed many times [7] but always with the same intention of bringing the people back to their obedience to the Law — thus remaining at the level of a revelation of promise rather than fulfillment, though it is true to say that each return of Israel to obedience did serve to broaden the context of God's plan — so, in the same way, the type of man which we find in Genesis appearing as master over the animals after their creation is taken up once again by Ezekiel's prophecy of the shepherd David who destroys the beasts who were tyrannizing the sheep (Ezek 34:20-25; 37:24-26), and by Daniel's prophecy of the Son of Man who appears after the empires of the beasts (Dn 7:1-14). The same type can even be discerned in David who follows after Saul, or in the many other human images in the Old Testament who function as types of Christ.

The Revelation Of The New Testament As Pledge And Promise Of The Perfect Abiding Of God Among Men And Of The Perfect Fulfillment Of Mankind

The Old Testament revelation projects God's promises into the eschatological conclusion of history, to the perfect dwelling of God among man and to the establishment of the Kingdom of Heaven (Isa 9:1-7 etc.). Within its prophetic sweep, therefore, it contains the whole of history including that which follows upon the coming of the Son of God in

the body. In this sense the Old Testament always preserves
its contemporary character. Strictly speaking, this character
is even more contemporary now in the era of the New Testament when the time of the spiritual — and hence more real —
fulfillment of what was prophesied in the Old Testament has
finally arrived. The words of the prophets encourage us especially to put away what is evil in the world and to set out
to accomplish what is good, for after the coming of Christ
and his dwelling among us and in us, we have the power to
accomplish these things.[8]

In the Old Testament era revelation still remained only
prophecy or promise. Real fulfillment begins in and through
Christ. The New Testament revelation therefore represents
the plane of fulfillment but a fulfillment of what was prophesied in the Old Testament and in other sources as well.
Old Testament prophecy in this sense keeps its validity in the
New Testament era also, for the coming of Christ in the
body is only the beginning or foundation of the total fulfillment. "The message of the New Testament does not remove
faith's orientation toward the future, nor does it take away
hope in the future as the necessary and essential structure of
faith." "It would be a mistake to believe that after the Christ-
event the future is found entirely before us as though the
history after Christ had no other meaning than simply to pass
by, rather than to find its own realization. On the contrary
the Christ-event intensifies this orientation towards a future
as yet unrealized . . . and this gives an impulse to Christian
mission. This mission is achieved in the degree to which the
Christian modifies and 'renews' the world in the direction of
the divine future that has been definitively promised and assured in the resurrection of Christ." [9]

If the Old Testament revelation was only promise or hope,
or a prophecy that God would dwell in and among his people
and that their relations with God would be brought to perfection, the New Testament revelation is both fulfillment,
promise and prophecy. There is the promise that this fulfillment already begun will be extended and deepened. Now
life is lived not only in hope but also in joy for what has
been received. But precisely for this reason hope is stronger

because it has received assurance from what has already been given. What has been given us through the New Testament is of the same order as what we hope we will receive fully, while what was given in the Old Testament always remained completely inferior compared with what was promised for the times to follow the coming of the Messiah.

Through the New Testament revelation a pledge is given already in this life, the first fruits of what is to be. And this pledge is of the same nature as the complete fulfillment in the Kingdom of Heaven. In the age of the New Testament we receive the pledge of the Holy Spirit (2 Cor 1:22), "the first fruits of the Spirit" (Rom 8:23), whereas in this respect the Old Testament remained always a promise (Eph 1:13-14).

Let us examine how the New Testament revelation is presented as pledge and as promise by the three kinds of means that it uses: acts, words, and types.

The *acts* of the New Testament revelation no longer possess the nature of historical acts, strictly speaking, as did those events in the life of the Israelite people which were types of the saving acts. Instead, they are acts of salvation in the strict sense, although it is true that they are not without effect on history, and indeed their effect is even greater.

At the present time God does not merely guide history towards that stage in which he himself will make his appearance, but he has come in fact directly into history in order to work from within it at every moment.

He becomes incarnate, is crucified, rises, ascends as man to heaven, sends the Holy Spirit, founds the Church as the place of his sacramental but real presence — all this in order to work continually upon the world. He truly raises up our humanity to the natural condition of his divine hypostasis, frees it from sin on the cross, elevates it to eternal life through the resurrection, and exalts it upon the throne of God. Yet he does not preserve this condition only for himself as man, but he makes us part of it to a certain extent even now, granting us his Holy Spirit who was poured out from his divinity into his humanity. Therefore, "it is now no longer I who live, but Christ who lives in me." (Gal 2:20) "We are his workmanship, created in Christ" (Eph 2:10), and in him there rises

up the whole edifice of those who believe in him. (Eph 2:22)
We reflect his glory with unveiled faces (2 Cor 3:18), and
the Saviour himself encourages us: "Abide in my love . . .
as the branch cannot bear fruit by itself, unless it abides in
the vine, neither can you, unless you abide in me." (Jn
15:9,4)

Christ is without doubt a prophet as well, but he is also
the one in whom the prophecies are fulfilled. For he does
not merely announce to us prophecies of what is to come, he
is himself their perfect fulfillment. "For all the promises
of God find their Yes in him." (2 Cor 1:20) Yet he is also
prophet for "in him shall the Gentiles hope", as Isaiah
prophesied and Matthew and Paul both repeated (Isa 11:10;
Mt 12:21; Rom 15:12). He is "the guarantee of our inheritance" (Eph 1:14), and in his own person he is the
prophet of our perfect gifts, "the hope of glory" (Col 1:27).
He is our ultimate future. And therefore after him can come
no prophet announcing anything superior to what Christ has
announced to us. He is the permanent prophet in his own
person which is not only God most intimately near to us, but
also perfect man risen from the dead. In him we see fulfilled
what will also be fulfilled in us. In his own person he is the
assurance of our ultimate fulfillment, not just talk about that
fulfillment. But precisely on account of this the words by
which he promises us these things also serve to interpret him
to us.[10] Christ is not only the prophet "of the good things to
come" who has entered into the heavenly Holy of Holies, the
"pioneer" who goes before us to open for us "the way" there
(Heb 9:11; 12:2; 10:20). He is also the one who communicates to us new life now (1 Jn 1:3). If St. Paul maintains the
balance between the presentation of Christ as prophet of the
good things to come and as giver of certain present goods,
St. John places special emphasis on our present life in Christ.
Thus we have in Christ not only the "past" of God and his
"future" but also his "present." [11]

The Orthodox Church, preserving the balance between
these two sides of the New Testament revelation, neither
empties the sacraments of all content nor considers them
merely as signs of certain simple promises. Instead it teaches

that through the sacraments we receive a pledge of the life
of Christ; we receive his grace, his Holy Spirit.

We also see the same tension between the affirmation of
certain goods given already in this life and the hope of future
fulfillments in the *words* of the New Testament revelation.
Christ himself does not promise us through his words only a
fulfillment to be achieved in him in the future; he also communicates to us teachings for our spiritual life on earth and
describes some of the good things that he gives us here and
now. Through his words he not only teaches us the conditions
we ourselves must fulfill in order to reach his own state,
that state in which he now exists, but he also gives us the power
to reach it. He is therefore more than just the *prophet* in the
strict sense of the word; he is also the *teacher* who teaches
with power. Men feel that he teaches them "as one who has
authority" (Mt 7:29), and the Saviour himself says: "The
words that I have spoken to you are spirit and life." (Jn 6:63)
And his disciples turned to him and said: "Lord, to whom
shall we go? You have the words of eternal life." (Jn 6:68)

If the words addressed by God through the prophets in
the Old Testament opened horizons of light and hope for
the Jews and made them feel the power of God and the loving
care that he had for them, the words of Jesus in the New
Testament communicate a light that is clearer and more exalted still. They give an even greater joy to those who believe and a much more striking feeling of the power and
presence of God. For now God himself speaks with human
voice and human words. And how is it possible that his power
not be felt through these words? Generally in a dialogue one
partner experiences the spirit of the other through the words
which the other speaks and so he is lifted up into the light
where the speaker moves. Through Christ's words, his Spirit
and his light are experienced at all times by those who believe in him.

If we look closely at Christ's teaching about the conditions
we must fulfill in order to reach his own state, we see that
this teaching is nothing other than a commentary on his own
way of life, a life which led to the resurrection. Yet he does
not leave us only to contemplate the conduct of his life; he

interprets it for us. His words are intended to achieve the fulfillment of his promise which has already been realized in him. His ministry as teacher is linked indissolubly with his ministry as prophet. The words of teaching are given in the present, but the fulfillment of the promise conditioned by them is given in the future.

In the Beatitudes the Saviour speaks in the present tense of the virtues which those who believe in him must also have in the future and of the goods which they will win through these virtues: "Blessed are the peacemakers, for they shall be called sons of God." (Mt 5:9)

The purpose of teaching cannot be separated from that of prophecy because the fulfillment of prophecy depends not only on the fact that it has been fulfilled in Christ but also on our own effort. Our hope can move between two points, one of which depends on us and leads us towards the second, that is, belief in the risen Christ together with our efforts to follow in our own lives his teaching and example. Christians know in their hope what it is they are moving towards and they also know the way which leads there. "I am the way and the truth, and the life . . . he who has my commandments and keeps them, he it is who loves me; and he who loves me will be loved by my Father, and I will love him and will manifest myself to him." (Jn 14:6,21)

The *types* of the New Testament revelation show this same function of present fulfillment and future promise.

We should first make clear that in the New Testament there has been a change from almost exclusively prophetic types to the real *image* in which God has revealed himself as man. In this image God has truly come to men in the closest intimacy and dialogue. God is now as close to us as we are to our fellow human beings. In our dialogue with him we are raised up to his level. We have now come to know that man is the real and most adequate image of God and that God is in the first place the model for man.[12] We know now what man is. But more especially we have entered into the most intimate relation with God as man, into a real interior communication with God who has come down from his transcendence and communicates himself as man. In accordance with this all the sacramental symbols of the New Testament have become real means of communicating the life of the incarnate Word, in contrast with the types of the Old Testament which were only shadows and heralds of the future. Baptism really gives us a share in the life of the Christ-God, something which circumcision did not give. Holy Communion in the sacrifice of the altar truly imparts Christ to us, something which the animal sacrifices of the Old Testament did not do.

On the other hand the human image of the divine Word and the sacramental symbols of the New Testament have a prophetic character. We progress towards a full sharing in the promised benefits of Revelation, but only inasmuch as we are helped by what we have received. We will all have a share in the resurrection of Christ and we will all grow up into his stature as perfect man and we will all be recapitulated in him in perfect love, inasmuch as we deepen the bond we now have with him by following his example, keeping his commandments, his "truth", and by loving him. "I would not seek you, Lord, if I did not already possess you", said Pascal. Our hope grows from what we have received and from what we now possess.

* * *

From the fact that Christ is not only the future goal towards which we gaze in our progress towards perfection, but also the one who perfects us (Heb 12:2), and from the fact that we have him both as "forerunner" in "the inner shrine behind the curtain" (Heb 6:19-20), and as the one who works our salvation within us (Phil 2:12-13; Gal 2:20), although not without our own cooperation, two conclusions result: a) we know what it is that we are moving towards at every moment; and b) our hope is active and at work in us through our own efforts aided by Christ who is present within us, and we do not need to await the final fulfillment passively, as though it were a purely eschatological fulfillment requiring no preparation on our part, something which Christ will bring with him when he comes.

A. It has been established in recent works dedicated to

THEOLOGY AND THE CHURCH

the theology of hope that the entire earthly life of Christians is a series of "exoduses" in hope according to the pattern of the Exodus of Israel from Egypt.[13] This would seem to imply that Christians do not enjoy a position which is better in any essential way than that of Israel, that is, they too would always have to be going out from their present condition to a better one, a state for which they strive in hope, although they receive nothing of the perfect fulfiillment of the last days prior to the conclusion of history.

The image of the "exodus" can indeed find application to the movement of the Christian life as well, but certain further explanations are also required. The various "exoduses" of the Hebrews in the Old Testament occurred, strictly speaking, with a view to some kind of return. The Israelites left Egypt, for example, in order to return to the land of their ancestors, and it should be added, to bring it subsequently under their complete control. Similarly they went out from Babylon in order to return to the land from which they had been forcibly removed. In an analogous way it can be said that there were no "new" covenants in the Old Testament, only the old covenants renewed time and time again.[14]

Consequently the "exoduses" of the Old Testament are not types of progress towards the ultimate fulfillment of the promises; they are types of conversion at various times from the fall into sin back to the condition of an earlier purity (we might almost say, to the primordial condition of man), and this has remained the constant interpretation of patristic spiritual literature. The exoduses of the Jews did not bring them to the fulfillment *par excellence* of the promises, because such a fulfillment was not to occur in the Old Testament. For Christians, however, the exoduses are types of their turning back from sin to a life with Christ, a life which they had once received and held as their own. Thus the Exodus is not just an abandonment of one's present condition for the sake of a condition that is totally new; it is also a return to normality, to an authenticity which has been lost. Baptism reestablishes man in his primordial state but it does so because at the same time it unites him with Christ. The "new man" is, up to a point, the original authentic man. Any repentance of

the Christian is also a return to this original man and a return
to Christ. It is true that the act of turning back is also an act
of progress, for the good condition which existed formerly
is never recovered exactly as it was; it is enriched by a new
experience. The return of the prodigal son is a return of a
son matured through experience, and the meeting of father
and son is marked by a much more profound manifestation of
parental love. On their return from Egypt to the land of their
fathers, the Jews subdued Canaan completely and made it
the home of the Tabernacle where they offered a more highly
developed worship to God and kept the Law he had given
them on Mt. Sinai. On their return from Babylon they built
a temple ultimately more beautiful than the earlier one and
began a life more faithful to God than their life before the
Exile. St. Maximus the Confessor says that we only find our
original condition by going forward. The movement that is
such a necessary part of our being accumulates new experiences even though it seeks to follow a path of return.[15]

In any case, both the Old Testament types which move
outside the region of the spiritual fulfillment of the Old
Testament promises, and the New Testament revelation
which represents a certain fulfillment of the Old Testament
promises, conceive the movement of man not only as
progress towards something that has not yet come to be in
any way, but also as a return. Progress is therefore also man's
return from estrangement to his own authenticity, which in the
Old Testament is a return to his former condition by a new
observance of the Law, and in the New Testament a return
to his primordial condition through grace or through Christ.

But there is no question of an "eternal return", for God
is God of what is new, not of what is repetitious. He has not
exhausted his generosity in his first act of creation. It is for
this reason that the idea of the eternal return has generally
been associated with a pantheist conception that does not
expect anything wholly new in comparison with what is given
from all eternity in the unique substance of an exclusively
immanent reality.[16]

Nor is there a question of eternal development, a continual actualization of infinite potentialities contained in the

dynamic substance of immanent realities. This too would be
no authentic newness. Nor can the future which has been
promised by revelation but which is now distant from Christians be conceived as something completely separate from what
man possessed at the beginning and what he has already received in Christ. This second and extreme alternative is generally accepted by Protestants who consider the divine image
in man to have been irremediably destroyed and who do not
in general believe that the Christian already receives Christ
in some measure in his life on earth.

Orthodoxy sees man's original authentic nature as combined with the original grace at work in that nature. Any
return to it means a return to the bond uniting that nature
with God. However such a return is possible only through
the grace of Christ or in Christ. Thus the return to man's
nature is simultaneously the return to man's original state and
the return to Christ.

On the other hand human nature is dynamic and has in
itself a certain *élan* towards perfection. But the process of
perfecting human nature is progress into God and into Christ.
Indeed the more human nature is dynamic, the less it is
weakened by sin. Its return to authenticity therefore is not a
return to its original undeveloped state as it existed at the
beginning, but to a condition that represents the term of the
development not only of the evil within it, but, in a certain
manner, of the divine image as well, provided that we acknowledge that the divine image was never completely obliter-
ated by sin and that it has not remained absolutely passive
and hence undeveloped.

Return is therefore simultaneously also progress forward,
and progress forward is return. It is a return of human nature
to itself, and a progress forward into itself, but at the same
time it is a return to and a progress forward into God and
Christ, for no development of human nature is possible except in God and Christ.

This return can also be explained in other ways if we keep
in mind the fact that from the time of Christ the world is
no longer an undifferentiated whole, but is made up of two
ages that are dialectically related and exist in a state of re-

ciprocal tension. The world is constituted by this age and the age to come, or by the old age and the new. The latter is identical with the Kingdom of Heaven already begun and developing secretly now within this world, but destined to achieve its full realization and revelation only at the end of history. These two ages are not without their corresponding links. The new or future age develops by promoting the dissolution or transformation of the present age, and conversely, the present age struggles to smother the future age hidden within it. Men can fall from the future age into this age, and if they are raised up once more into the future age it is therefore indeed a "return", but a "return to the future", or to that movement which is oriented towards the future. In fact it can even be called a return to a more advanced moment of the future age, because such a return is in itself an advance. Nevertheless although men belong to the future age or return once again to it, they do not cease to work in this age too, whether to transform it gradually to the extent that the age permits such a transformation, or to do away with it completely, to cast it into darkness and complete passivity, into that kind of condition which accepts no transformation.[17]

Because this return is an advance of spiritual nature into its own being, it has a spiral motion. But because it is a return and an advance into God its motion is that of a spiral moving around God and drawing ever closer to God as it moves higher and higher. God reveals himself to the human spirit ever more intimately; he discloses more and more of his spiritual riches as man climbs up in this spiral around God. But at the same time man discovers himself more and more, because God's light makes man ever more visible to himself. Man grows in awareness of himself as he grows in the light of God, the unique and infinite source of light.

This is the meaning of the spiral ascent of the angelic spirits around God described by Pseudo-Dionysius the Areopagite. Man's ascent is also pursued according to this same pattern of an "infinite column" (Brincusi), and it does not matter whether the course of a man's ascent includes numerous falls which have to be transcended, or whether he is preserved in a spiritual life less marked by the presence of sin.

Progress also means return even for the angels who commit no sin, or for men who have remained firm in a sinless life, and for this there are two reasons. The first is that neither angels nor men can contain the infinite dimensions of the divine reality all at once, and so when their gaze and joy have been attracted by one aspect of the divine reality they soon realize that they must not remain fixed forever on that one particular aspect of God but must move on to some other. Thus they are always returning to different sides of the divine reality, forgetting the things that have gone before but rediscovering them continually in other depths. The second reason is that God is, strictly speaking, beyond all knowledge, all expression and experience, and therefore every form which the knowledge or expression or experience of God assumes must itself be transcended, even though this act of transcending a particular form necessarily requires that we approach God by some other form of knowing, expressing or experiencing.

In this sense the Protestants are correct when they affirm that every "exodus" occurs in a kind of apophatic abyss which the spirit can perceive only when it has come to recognize its own particular and familiar forms of knowing, expressing and experiencing God as masks hiding the deeper reality. On the other hand, this experience of the apophatic abyss of divinity is itself the experience of a presence of God in man, and any new form of expressing and experiencing him represents some progress into God.

These are the spiritual "exits" and "entrances" described by St. Gregory of Nyssa and it is a blessing upon these that the Church seeks from God for the faithful even when these spiritual exits and entrances are overlaid by the external ones of this life. They are not opposed to a certain stability in the life lived in God or even in the benefits attached to this life. On the contrary they are the very condition of this stability. Whoever does not thus ascend, falls, says St. Gregory, for by remaining a long time in one state, gazing at one aspect only of the divine reality, or by confusing the apophatic in-

finity of God with some limited form of knowledge and expression — in effect, an idol — a man grows spiritually dull.
Whoever does not make his ascent in this path falls from the
living experience of God. An element of newness is necessary
for stability in an adequate understanding or living experience of God. Some element of freshness is necessary if the
spirit is to be maintained in the vigilant tension of continuous
self-transcendence, for without this there exists no life in the
Spirit. Purification is constantly necessary from that ignorance
into which the spirit falls if it confuses the living God with
the idol of some static and familiar form of understanding.

But the newness of that condition which is the goal to
which the soul "goes out" is not something completely unknown. It is discerned already in the present life of the spirit
both as a new consciousness of the divine apophatic reality
and also as a more adequate formulation of that reality or of
the higher experience of life which the soul has achieved. If
it did not see itself, the soul would rush into a new "exit" and
a new "entrance". The light of the "new" which appears on
the horizon causes the condition in which man finds himself
to pale, and he is attracted to this "new" thing, no longer
content with the condition he has already achieved. However,
because St. Gregory speaks of the "stability" of the one who
ascends, more precisely of his "moving stability" or "stable
movement", we see that the "exits" he describes are not dis-
continuous with the states already achieved but instead represent more profound realizations of these same states.

Thus progress is made within a perspective of newness
but this newness is the newness of a God who is himself already known to a certain degree. It is the newness of the same
God and the continual newness of the same human nature
which discovers, when it is authentic and free of paralyzing
sin, more and more of its own depths, aspirations and possibilities in the ever new divine light.

Thus, enthusiasm through hope in the future, together
with abandonment of the present condition, dialectically constitute an enthusiasm for what is unknown, yet an unknown
which we can only formulate as a good, and an unknown
which is identical with the God in whom we have believed all

along. In every instance man and society are both eager for
the future. They are driven on by their aspiration towards
something better, and seek, in part successfully, to find a
better individual and social expression of the condition which
they have achieved. In this sense the progress of man and
society in hope towards the future means a stability and a
deeper appreciation of the good which is already possessed,
or a return to this good with the desire to realize it at a higher
level and to do away with the evil which may be bound up
with it.

We must not then sleep on peacefully as though the state
in which we now find ourselves were a comfortable bed,
trusting in the conviction that this state suffices for our nature.
Nor should we think that we do not now have nor will ever
have in this life anything of what will be ours in the life to
come. How would we know what to strive for if we did not
already possess something of it? We would be wanderers in
the darkness, eternally anxious, strangers to any kind of fulfillment and always throwing ourselves headlong into some
dark gulf hoping that at the end of life or history we would
fall into the arms of God — these are the very words of some
of those theologians who are scornful of all that is given in
the Christian life through the Church, her teaching and the
sacraments she celebrates.

We must always move forward, but by deepening what
we have and with the aid of what we have. We must advance
on a path which rises up continually towards the sign, the
reward of the divine call from on high in Jesus Christ, yet
without ever thinking that we have finally arrived (Phil
3:13-14). We must always be running, but our running must
not be in some dark void with only the hope that we will find
salvation on the other side. Our course leads from a lesser to
a fuller knowledge and deeper experience of Christ, and our
aim is to become ever more like him in this life and therefore
also to attain his resurrection. (Phil 3:10-11)

We must not let ourselves be tempted on this path either
to the right or to the left, because on both sides there is the
gulf of perdition, to use the phrase of the spiritual fathers of
the East. It is in this sense that St. Gregory of Nyssa speaks

of exits and entrances. We must start out again from every plateau we had been eager to reach, and have in fact reached, to go on to another that is shown to us for the first time from that new height. We can always see the goal for which we have set out, and this new plateau forms a continuous path with the one from which we began. In this sense we can look at what lies behind us in an endless series of what St. Gregory of Nyssa calls *"epektaseis"* or strivings (strainings) forward.

The Church, like the individual believer, will neglect neither her concern to preserve what she has received from Christ, nor her intense and prophetic ministry that leads her on to an *approfondissement,* a deeper spiritual understanding and a more purified and heart-felt living of what she has received, in other words, to a closer approximation to the heavenly kingdom of perfect love among men and between men and God. In the same way theology must not mechanically rehearse formulae from earlier manuals written down and repeated without any of the life-breath of the Living Spirit, and without that spiritual depth which corresponds to new aspirations and needs. But on the other hand it should not abandon the essence of Christ's truth preserved in the Church at all times and throw itself into some unknown path out of sheer love for novelty.

All the realities communicated by Revelation have spiritual depths and endless degrees. Christ as man, or as the perfect union of the human with God the Word, has an infinite depth of meanings and of power to console, to love and to guide which must call us always forward and higher in our understanding and experience and in the discovery of ever greater horizons which, in time, we can offer to the world as modes of a higher life. The words through which Christ interprets himself or through which he is interpreted by his Apostles have this same inexhaustible potentiality.

The sacraments themselves do not give us graces of a static kind, virtues or benefits which are limited and kept carefully enclosed within their present borders so that we can show them to God on the day of judgement neatly preserved, like the unproductive talent in the Gospel parable. The sacraments have a prophetic character, a "sacramental prophetism"

178 THEOLOGY AND THE CHURCH

as the Reformed theologian von Allmen puts it, perhaps in a too exclusively eschatological sense. They give us powers which have to be developed and which are meant to lead us towards final perfection by ever more advanced spiritual stages.

It is not only by ourselves, by our own efforts to understand and experience, that we discover the infinite depths of the Person of Christ. Christ himself also reveals them to us and for this purpose he uses new aspects of the historical reality, emphasizing them at times by slow evolution and at other times by sudden historical change. Christ is not satisfied to point out to us, passively as prophet, that state of his which is the goal of all our striving. He is the permanent Prophet who actively leads us ever closer to himself and to the Kingdom of Heaven.

In the light of these dimensions, forms and aspirations of the spiritual life, Christ himself, together with his words and the graces that he bestows on us, discloses their new depths, or better, their new heights as so many new exigencies or stages through which we are to draw near to him and to his Kingdom.

The Church, and theology too, must be unceasing in their efforts to unfold in the light of Christ and his Gospel the meaning of this constant "exit" or going forth, these continual invitations to new understandings and new efforts on the road that leads towards intimacy with Christ and the fulfillment of his Gospel. They must likewise strive to illuminate the meaning of these calls to go forth from inferior ways of understanding and of realizing this intimacy in order to enter into the higher ways of understanding and experience, taking care only that these exits and entrances are not merely ventures out into some world of the unknown, but constitute real progress with Christ in the evangelical values already long familar to us.

Everything in the New Testament revelation is gift for the present time and perspective and power for a future unending progress. We are branches in Christ. As long as the branches remain alive and do not wither, they grow in Christ, absorbing power continually from him who is the vine of boundless life.

B. From the above it should be clear that however mistaken is the view that Christian life impels Christians to launch themselves out into a total unknown simply because this unknown is something new and as such conducive to their perfection, it would be equally as mistaken to imagine that Christian hope has a passive character, that it means waiting for the Kingdom of Heaven at the end of history as an exclusive gift of God which requires no effort on the part of Christians to prepare for it or to advance towards it. This is the conclusion drawn by certain Protestant theologians from the teaching that Christians receive no power from Christ in their earthly lives, no change for the better in their natures and that, consequently, any effort is vain which seeks either to change Christians themselves or to constrain mankind and history to change for the better.

But just as the first conclusion has been abandoned today by many Protestant theologians, so has the second. Professor Bassarak of the University of East Berlin said in a lecture at the Theological Institute of Bucharest in May of 1968: "We allow ourselves to take refuge neither in some enchanting eschatological fantasy, nor in a past which is no longer accessible. . . . The goal is not a utopian world but the Kingdom of God which comes by itself when no one expects it. The goal is the world of man for the sake of tomorrow's humanity, a world which must be programmed and ordered today so that tomorrow there may still be a world and a humanity which can exist and coexist."

The Protestant theologian Moltmann has expressed this same conviction that the Kingdom of God need not be awaited passively but must be prepared for by a general effort towards the improvement of relations between men — an effort which Christians must support because, according to their faith, it is Christ himself who uses such efforts to lead the world to the fulfillment of the final promise: [The Christian salvation we hope for] "does not merely mean salvation of the soul, individual rescue from the evil world, comfort for the troubled conscience (This is what existentialist theology provides: Author's note) but also the realization of the eschatological *hope of justice*, the *humanizing* of man, the *socializing* of humanity, *peace* for all creation. This 'other side' of reconciliation with God has always been given too little consideration in the history of Christianity because Christians no longer understood themselves eschatologically and left earthly eschatological anticipations to the fanatics and the sects." [18]

It is about this growth, achieved with the help of our own efforts, yet not apart from Christ and not wandering aimlessly about or running off now in one direction and now in another, that St. Paul speaks in Ephesians: "Rather, speaking the truth in love, we are to grow up in every way into him who is the head, into Christ, from whom the whole body, joined and knit together by every joint with which it is supplied, when each part is working properly, makes bodily growth and upbuilds itself in love." (Eph 4:15-16)

CHAPTER VI

The Orthodox Doctrine of Salvation and Its Implications for Christian Diakonia in the World*

The Orthodox Church has not generally used the term "reconciliation" as a title for the complete saving work of the Lord Jesus Christ and for the appropriation of this salvation by the individual believer. The term has been favoured by Protestant theology on the basis of four texts from the epistles of St. Paul: Rom 5:10, 2 Cor. 5:18-20, Col 1:19-23 and Eph 2:14-18.

Roman Catholic theology has also made use of the term "reconciliation" but only as a secondary expression after the word "redemption" (Gal 3:13; 4:5), and with the added explanation that this reconciliation or redemption is achieved by the "satisfaction" (*Genugtuung*) offered to God by Jesus Christ.[1] This satisfaction is distinguished in some measure from the "expiation" which underlies the Protestant understanding of reconciliation.

For some time past, Orthodox theological manuals, taking into account accepted Western usage, have also used the term "redemption".[2] Similarly the concept of reconciliation has also appeared in Orthodox theology in recent years as an expression which is shared with Protestant Churches in ecumenical contacts both inside and outside the World Council of Churches. It is a word which also reflects the common concern of Orthodox and Protestants to promote every effort made on

---

* Originally published in Romanian in *Ortodoxia* 24 (1972), 195-212.

behalf of peace. "Reconciliation" was accepted by Russian theologians in their dialogue with their Lutheran colleagues at the third Arnoldsheim meeting in March of 1967 as a term meant to express the whole content of Christ's saving work.[3]

But it can be said more generally that while Orthodox theology accepts the use of the terms "redemption" and "reconciliation" it gives them a broader meaning than that understood by Catholics and Protestants. This has been more especially true ever since Orthodox theology has returned to its patristic foundations and consequently to a closer conformity to the liturgical tradition of the Eastern Church. This broader, more many-sided meaning has always been expressed in the Orthodox Church by the term "salvation", and this remains the preferred usage of the Orthodox Church for many reasons. In the first place, it is the word found most frequently in the New Testament either as a name for the work accomplished by the Lord Jesus Christ (σωτηρία — about forty times), or as a title given to Christ because of the work he accomplished (σωτήρ — about twenty times). Secondly, and also following the New Testament example, "salvation" is the term most used by the Church in its tradition and worship. It is found, for example, both in the Nicene-Constantinopolitan Creed and in the prayers of the faithful. Finally, it expresses the deepest, most comprehensive and many-sided meaning of the work which Jesus Christ accomplished. In this last dimension, that is to say, understood as the destruction of man's death in all its forms and the assurance of full and eternal life, the word "salvation" produces in the Orthodox faithful a feeling of absolute gratitude towards Christ to whom they owe the deliverance of their existence and the prospect of eternal life and happiness. This is a fact which should not be overlooked.

It is the view of the Orthodox Church as it was the view of the early Church that the word "salvation" not only embraces the deep, complete and complex meaning of the activity of Christ better than these other words do, but that it also contains within itself the various partial meanings of salvation which these other terms express. It includes the idea of "life", "eternal life" and "the Spirit" who together with the multitude of his gifts is given to those who believe. It also includes what is expressed by the words "union with Christ", "life in Christ" (Jn 14:20-23; 15:1-9; Gal 2:19-20; Eph 3:17), "adoption" (Gal 4:5; Rom 8:15), the forming of man in the image of Christ (Gal 4:19), "membership in the same body with Christ" (Eph 3:6), "fellowship with the Father and his Son" (1 Jn 1:3; 1 Cor 1:9), the "fellowship of the Holy Spirit" (2 Cor 13:14; Phil 2:1), the condition of "righteousness", "holiness", "divine sonship" (Rom 8:14, 19; 9:26; Gal 4:6, 7; Heb 2:10 etc.), "participation in the divine nature" (2 Pet 1:4), rebirth in the Spirit, and an "inheritance which is imperishable, undefiled and unfading." (1 Pet 1:4)

The wealth of our salvation in Christ is so rich that it cannot be expressed completely in any one single formula, nor even in all of them taken together. It is a mystery which can never be completely understood or defined. St. Gregory Nazianzen, for example, after he has treated briefly of the work of salvation accomplished by Christ, declares: "Let us respect what remains by our silence" for "nothing can equal the miracle of my salvation".[4] The exclusive use of any term, especially if it becomes the key to interpret all other terms, will inevitably enclose us within a very limited understanding of this ineffable mystery. Lossky comments on the texts of St. Gregory Nazianen cited above: "After the constricted horizon of an exclusive juridical theology, we rediscover in the Fathers an extremely rich notion of redemption which includes the victory over death, the first fruits of the general resurrection, the liberation of captive nature from the devil, and not only the justification, but also the restoration of creation in Christ."[5]

Each of these terms is precious because it casts into relief some one aspect of the salvation which Christ has gained for us. We ought therefore to take account of all the biblical language in our understanding of this salvation, but at the same time we must avoid forcing everything within the confines of any one single word. If there is need of some more general expression, we must choose the word which is already the most comprehensive and then broaden its meaning still further in such a way as to include within it the meanings of all the others. In any case we must explain each term in harmony with all the others.

The special value of the term "reconciliation" is that it emphasizes the character of both man and God as "persons" in the economy of salvation, especially as the word "salvation" taken by itself might suggest an escape from certain evil powers or situations contrived either by impersonal forces or by man's own actions. The expression "reconciliation", on the other hand, makes it clear that salvation is brought about by the re-establishment of a normal personal relationship between man and God, by the re-establishment — through an act accomplished in Christ by the personal God — of a relationship of peace between God as person and man as person. It is probably for this reason that Luther preferred to speak of "reconciliation", although, as we have seen, the Orthodox faithful also experience their "salvation" as the most complete freeing of their personal existence from the powers of destruction and therefore as a profoundly personal everyday relationship with God.

Luther's choice of "reconciliation" as the most adequate and sensitive expression of the personal relationship between the individual man and his God came at a time when man was beginning to rise to an exceptionally acute consciousness of his own destiny as an individual person, and to an equally acute anxiety as to whether he, as a person, was at peace with God and whether, given the ethical imperfection of his life, he was considered righteous before God. If, at an earlier period, man was satisfied to know an objective redemption within a collective framework, and was content that this should be expressed by the earlier soteriological language of the universal destruction of sin and death with the prospect of the general resurrection to come, in Luther's time man awoke to the consciousness of his own individuality and began to seek above all else the assurance of an inner personal peace with God, the assurance that God had turned towards him lovingly as to a separate person in spite of the fact that man could not abandon his own sinful condition. In a paper entitled "Reconciliation through Christ and the Peace of the World", Professor E. Wolf of Göttingen has written: "Peace of conscience, and indeed a good conscience before God, is therefore the first fruit of the reconciliation. So it is that Christ makes us secure before God and at peace with our conscience." [6]

It is probably for the same reason that Luther brought the two terms "reconciliation" and "justification" so closely together in the conviction that they contained everything a man inherits as a result of that act whereby God reconciles man to himself. Renaissance man with his heightened self-awareness perceived that the cause of his lack of inner peace with God was the lack of his own righteousness before God's face. He realized that he could not achieve any intrinsic personal righteousness, and so he found his consolation or reassurance in the notion that he was counted righteous by God thanks to the expiatory sacrifice offered to God by Christ on man's behalf. In the idea of "justification", therefore, salvation as the restored personal relationship of man with God is once again thrown into relief.

While it recognizes the importance of Luther's emphasis on the condition of salvation which Christ has achieved for us, the Orthodox Church also believes that man can grow continually in the new life of Christ as it is described by the Scriptures and the Fathers, and that the foundation for this growth, the foundation of man's new and true life, is the relationship of peace between man and God now experienced consciously by man as a result of Christ's sacrifice. Obviously this spiritual growth does not take place in isolation within the self, but within the dialogue of peace re-established with God. For what man experiences within this dialogue is no exterior, formal peace but a power that grows within him, preserving him in this peace and producing more and more fruit. These fruits in turn represent a righteousness which increases until it becomes the expression of the sum of all the virtues. This is righteousness as it is understood in the Old and New Testaments. There Christ himself is named "righteous" (1 Pet 3:18) ; there we read of the active power of the prayer of the just man (Jas 5:16) ; there too it is demanded of the just man that he grow ever more perfect (Apoc

22:11), and yet that he not practise his justice before men
(Mt 6:1).

It seems to us that Protestant theology today is developing
more and more in the direction of this germ contained in the
very teaching of Luther, and therefore, that it is moving towards an encounter with Orthodox teaching. Orthodox theology on the other hand is stressing the fact that the new life
in man is not produced by man's own powers, but by the powers he receives in dialogue with God. This emphasis is clear
in the following lines taken from Professor Wolf's paper:
"Thanks to Christ's act of reconciliation, this peace is already
a hidden reality; it becomes effective in the Christian community, and through it for the world." [7] Once we perceive that
justification is conceived by Lutheran teaching as something
organically united to peace, then we can say that the righteousness which Christ gives as a gift to every man is just such
a hidden reality. In order to be effective among the members
of the ecclesial community and through that community to
be effective in the world, this peace and the righteousness
which it implies must have the nature of a power which, although it comes from God, is nevertheless manifested through
man and is assimilated like a divine reflex by the human subject in his dialogue with God. This reflex can and must be
activated by us believers; indeed ours is the responsibility for
seeing that it is active.

The Orthodox Doctrine Of Salvation In Christ

What follows will be a brief description of the new life
and power which the incarnate Son of God, crucified, resurrected and exalted, gives us, through the Holy Spirit, as the
content of "salvation" according to the Orthodox understanding of that word. The Son of God communicates this
life and power in their eschatological fullness to the humanity
which he assumed, but he communicates them to us by degrees through his own humanity, and we receive them as a
principle of growth, as a gift and a promise implying eschatological development and therefore hope. For as long as

Jesus Christ is "full of grace and truth" and as long as he is the "perfect man", then we have only the first fruits of his fullness (2 Cor 1:22; Eph 1:14), and we must grow in him into the perfect man according to the measure of the stature of the fullness of Christ (Eph 4:13). The life and power communicated by Christ to his humanity are manifested in three directions: towards God, towards human nature as such, and towards his fellow human beings. This new life and power which the Son of God, through the humanity he assumed, communicates to those who believe in him, are also manifested in the same three directions. And just as the Son of God communicated them to his assumed humanity through his incarnation, crucifixion, resurrection and ascension, he communicates them in the same way to those who believe in him, that is, through the acts which he accomplished and the states which he reached as man.

We should make mention of the fact that in the last three or four centuries Orthodox theology also suffered from a certain scholastic influence on its soteriological teaching, and came to present salvation therefore as something achieved almost exclusively by means of the cross of Christ and to understand salvation in general as a vicarious satisfaction offered to God by Christ. Beginning however with the Russian theology of the last century, Orthodox theology has returned almost completely to the broader understanding of salvation proper to the Greek Fathers, and, under the influence of the ministry or *"diakonia"* to the world which the Church has assumed, Orthodox theology in recent years has been developing in a contemporary form those pan-human and cosmic dimensions of salvation which also form part of the patristic heritage.

We will now consider the new life and power which Christ has brought us, and the ways in which it is manifested through his incarnation, crucifixion, resurrection and ascension.

A. Even through his incarnation the Son of God brings man a new life and power in his dealings with God, with himself and with his neighbour. Christ unites humanity with God through the incarnation in a manner which is most intimate and at the same time indissoluble, inseparable and definitive. The Son of God made man becomes, even in his quality as man, the Son of God. His eternal and perfect filial love for the Father fills his humanity also, and therefore as St. John Damascene says, "the incarnation is a modality of the second personal subsistence (τρόπος δευτέρας ὑπάρξεως) accommodated solely to the Only Begotten Son in such a manner that its personal individual attribute might remain unchanged."[8] Only the Son was able to fill the humanity he assumed with filial love for the Father, and through his humanity to fill every man who unites himself to Christ through faith with that same filial love. The human will becomes the will of the Son of God who directs it toward the Father with his filial love. According to St. Maximus the Confessor, Christ possessed a natural human will, but because the subject or hypostasis which bore the natures was the Logos himself, he could not have had a gnomic will. Those who attribute a gnomic will to Christ think that, like us, he had a will which was "ignorant, hesitant, and at conflict with himself. . . . In the humanity of the Lord which had no simple human hypostasis but a divine hypostasis . . . there cannot be said to be a gnomic will",[9] which is to say, a will moving independently of the divine hypostasis and able to make decisions contrary to his divine will. This implies a perfect obedience to the Father on the part of the incarnate Christ. His human will is moved by its divine hypostasis in conformity with his own divine will, and hence in accordance with the will of the Father. In this way Christ gives the Father perfect glory on earth as man too. In all the movements of his human will, in all his acts — and therefore in all his thoughts too — Christ is devoted completely to the Father.

This implies the complete sanctification of the humanity he assumed. All the holiness of his divinity becomes proper to his humanity and takes on human form. He is holy in his thoughts, in the movements of his will, in his feelings and therefore also in his flesh. Christ thus became a second Adam but surpassing the first Adam in purity even in the state in which Adam existed before the Fall. Although Christ carries in his assumed nature the effects and the burdensome necessities of the condition Adam entered into after the Fall, nevertheless he falls no more. Rather, he exercises the mastery of the spirit upon these weaknesses; he frees nature from the burden they impose and gives us also the power to do the same.

He is the second root of the human race according to St. Cyril of Alexandria, a new root keeping itself permanently new and whence any son of the first Adam can continually be renewed, being born of the Spirit of the second Adam and remaining ever united to him, or returning to union with him after every lapse as to a fountain of renewal. "Although man has turned away from God and grieved him on account of his disobedience and numberless sins, Christ has once again placed him before the face of the Father in himself as in the first (man)." [10] In Christ man has been brought back into the Father's sight. "In Adam the root of the human race, like a mother, has died; but those who came forth from it — that is, we ourselves — have blossomed anew in Christ and we exist and are saved if we have him as our life and our second root." [11] He is, as St. Gregory Palamas says, "the new Adam who grows old no longer but is the source from which the world is continually renewed." [12]

Because of Christ's filial love for the Father and because of his perfect holiness, the Father looks upon the human face of Christ with the same love with which he regards his Only Begotten Son. [13] In this way, by having his Son become man, God has renewed the human race; he has reconciled it truly and radically with himself and has justified it in the most real way. Borne by the divine hypostasis of the Son, human nature has indeed become holy and righteous in its very root. Its peace with God lies in the filial love which Christ as man has for the Father, and this means that human nature has been re-established with the consent of its own will. Righteousness and peace have not been imposed upon it unwillingly nor do they remain external to it; rather they are inwardly assimilated just as dry soil assimilates the moisture of the rain even though the rain must necessarily always come down from above. Christ "re-established human nature in conformity with itself", writes St. Maximus the Confessor, [14] and by becoming

man Christ has preserved free will delivering it from the passions and setting it at peace with nature. It is precisely through
this harmonizing of the will with nature that the reconciliation of man with God is achieved. "As the inclination of the
will unites itself in this way with the *logos* of nature, there
is brought about the reconciliation of God with nature." [15]
But this could only have been achieved in men after it had
been realized in Christ in whom the human will was the will
of the divine hypostasis. It is only because the divine hypostasis has taken on human nature that it has harmonized the
human will with human nature and brought the will at the
same time into harmony with God who desires only what is
in conformity with human nature, and who is alone in truly
desiring this.[16] Through the incarnation the Son of God re-
stores in men "the greatness of the divine image", because
he possesses a reason which is not enslaved to those lower
affections and impulses which are opposed to God.[17] "The
Word of God", says St. Athanasius, "came in his own Person,
because it was he alone, the Image of the Father, who could
recreate man made after the Image." [18]

The real peace and righteousness which Christ through his
incarnation as man shares with God also becomes for those
who believe in him a real peace and righteousness through
their union with Christ. For the relationship between the
Father and the man Jesus includes within itself, potentially
at first but increasingly also in act, all those who believe in
Christ. The holiness of Christ as man is available to all, and
is directed actively towards all. If it is true in general that
the saint is the man *for* men, the man who is a stranger to
every kind of selfishness, so much more is this true of Christ,
inasmuch as his humanity, which is not borne by a human but
a divine hypostasis, cannot be enclosed within itself in a kind
of individualism, but thanks to the divine hypostasis which
is the God of all, communicates itself to all together with his
holiness and his perfect generosity. "And for their sake I con-
secrate myself, that they also may be consecrated in truth."
(Jn 17:19) In a relationship of union with Christ whose human
will is the pure will of the divine hypostasis the rest of men
too can become saints. The human will has cut the bond of

unity between men by its own arbitrary and selfish choice. In Christ the human will has abandoned this choice and become conformed not only to the will of God but also to human nature, to that which truly promotes the life of all men. For this reason those who are united with Christ no longer work for the dismembering of humanity but for brotherhood among all men.[19]

Through his human and divine wills, both guided by love, Christ himself exercised and still exercises even more at the present time a unifying influence upon mankind. "The Word was not hedged in by his body", says St. Athanasius. "Present in every part of it (the universe) yet outside the whole, he is revealed both through the works of his body, and through his activity in the world." [20]

That the East sees the incarnation of the Lord as so important for the unification of mankind is due on the one hand to the divine hypostasis in which Christ's human nature has been assumed, and on the other hand to the doctrine of the uncreated energies. The divine hypostasis is actively opened out by the humanity because the latter is not enclosed within a human hypostasis and so subjected to the limitations of created nature. The humanity of the Word, enhypostatized in him and penetrated by his energy, is the leaven working secretly within the whole body of mankind, the foundation of the doctrine of man's deification, a teaching so dear to the Greek Fathers.[21] "It is within the framework of this Cyrillian thought that one understands what Leontius of Jerusalem meant when he spoke of the common hypostasis of Christ: a hypostasis that, instead of being another isolated and individualized hypostasis among all the hypostases that constitute the human nature, is the hypostatic archetype of the whole of mankind; in whom 'recapitulated' mankind, and not merely an individual, recovers union with God. This is possible only if Christ's manhood is not the human nature of a mere man (ἀνθρώπου ψιλοῦ or γυμνοῦ) but that of a hypostasis independent of the limitations of created nature." [22] It could be said that Christ is the central hypostasis which connects all human hypostases to one another because he first connects them to himself.

The incarnation is an astonishing *kenosis* of the Son of God whereby he becomes the hypostasis both of those affections which enslave human nature and also of the limitations which confine it, in order to free human nature from the former and to throw open the latter. But the incarnation is also a *kenosis* of the humanity in Christ which has its existence, not autonomously in its own hypostasis, but in the divine hypostasis, a *kenosis* which is wholly dedicated to God. The emptying out of self is so much the sign of love that without it love cannot be manifested. For in love a person forgets himself and gives himself to the other in a total self-surrender; yet it is precisely through this love that he reveals himself in his own fullness. "And as man does not exist except to the extent to which he abandons himself, the incarnation of God thus appears as the supreme and unique example of the essential fulfillment of the human reality." [23] From this supreme focus of divine love which has also raised up human love to the highest degree and laid itself open to all men by taking its place among them, love shines forth among us and takes us up into its own inner movement.

The importance of the incarnation for understanding our salvation in Christ is clear from what has been written above, but there are also other dimensions of the incarnation. If we had seen only the cross of Christ and not his earthly life as God in the flesh as well, we should be without the teaching of Christ and the example of his life. Not only do these reveal to us the meaning of the cross, they also teach us and give us the strength to live a life of obedience to God, a life of purity and of active love in the service of our fellow men. St. Athanasius insisted on this fact: "Men had turned from the contemplation of God above, and were looking for him in the opposite direction, down among created things and things of sense. The Saviour of us all, the Word of God, in his great love took to himself a body. . . ." [24] God seeing men wander in error did not wish to lose those who had once participated in his image but desired that his image be renewed in them that through it men might come to know him again. "Therefore the Word of God came in his own Person because it was he alone, the Image of the Father, who could recreate men made after that Image." [25]

Through his life on earth in the body the Son of God made clear in a general way the value of our earthly life for the achievement of salvation. He showed us how we must strive while still on earth to gain a profound reconciliation with God and with our neighbour, a reconciliation full of love. The fact that God is thus open, personally and hypostatically, to created earthly existence and agrees to live it on our behalf, proves that this existence is a reality which has value even for him.[26] St. Athanasius says that in the beginning man was created by a decree of God's will. "But once man was in existence, and things that were, not things that were not, demanded to be healed, it followed as a matter of course that the healer and Saviour should align himself with those things that existed already, in order to heal the existing evil. For that reason therefore he was made man, and used the body as his human instrument . . . and by that means unfolded himself to all." [27] It was not his wish to take us up into eternal life without any consideration for our earthly life. This life had to be sanctified too as a condition for life eternal. Taking St. Paul's prompting as his starting point, namely that we are to grow in love in order to "comprehend what is the breadth and length and height and depth and to know the love of Christ which surpasses all knowledge" (Eph 3:17-19), St. Athanasius says: "The self-revealing of the Word is in every dimension — above, in creation; below, in the incarnation; in the depth, in Hades; in the breadth, throughout the world. All things have been filled with the knowledge of God. For this reason he did not offer the sacrifice on behalf of all immediately he came, for if he had surrendered his body to death and then raised it again at once he would have ceased to be an object of our senses. Instead of that, he stayed in his body and let himself be seen in it, doing acts and giving signs which showed him to be not only man, but also God the Word." ". . . the Word submitted to appear in a body, in order that he, as man, might centre their senses on himself, and convince them through his human acts that he himself is not man only but also God. . . ." [28] The Son of God does not scorn

man's earthly life as worthless and meaningless; instead he
adopts it as his own so that in the course of this very life the
healing and sanctification of man may have its beginning.

B. But of the three ways in which the new life and power
of Christ are manifested it is much more by his death on the
cross that Christ has effected the restoration of human nature.
The cross of Christ represents a new step in the work of our
salvation. Without the cross of Christ salvation would not
have been achieved. In his death Christ gives himself to the
Father not merely by an exemplary life but also by the very
renunciation of life itself. As man he gives the Father everything and holds nothing back for himself. In his death the
loving *kenosis* reaches its climax. St. Cyril of Alexandria has
developed St. Paul's idea that man can only come before the
Father in the condition of a spotless victim, but that we ourselves are not in a position to bring the Father such an offering.
Therefore Christ as man offered the spotless sacrifice to the
Father, not intending to bring the Father some juridical
equivalent but to endow us through our union with him with
the power of becoming ourselves a spotless sacrifice, so that
we too might be able to enter with him into the Father's presence. Thus we have access to the Father through the Cross
of Christ, through his body crucified on the cross. "For through
him we have access in one spirit to the Father." (Eph 2:18,
3:12) Only if Christ is in us as a spotless sacrifice, or if we
are in him who alone is in the condition of a pure victim, do
we also have access to the Father. And together with this
access, according to St. Paul, we also have reconciliation or
peace among ourselves and between ourselves and God. For
through the cross of Christ, the supreme surrender of himself
as man, that hostility which resides within us is truly brought
to an end (Eph 2:16). But at the same time, in his body
sacrificed on the cross and thus in a condition of supreme self-
surrender or loving *kenosis* before God on our behalf, we,
his most beloved creatures, are reconciled among ourselves
and with God as well. It is remarkable how St. Paul links
reconciliation and mankind's peace with God together with
access to the Father, and how for him this reconciliation also
implies that those who were once estranged and at enmity

with one another are to be built up into a new man. The power to accomplish this is found in the cross of Christ, in his totally pure sacrifice, his complete giving of self. This clean sacrifice, like a holocaust offered to the Father with the fragrance of a sweet odour, is nothing other than his total surrender to the Father. St. Cyril says that wherever sin exists, there no pure sacrifice may be found. Sacrifice is the rejection of all selfishness as the very form of sin. It is total surrender to the Father, and Christ alone was able to offer such a sacrifice. This he did in order to create in himself as man the condition of complete surrender to the Father and thus, like a magnet, to attract us also into the same condition as his own, to form his image in us, the image of himself in this state of sacrifice (Gal 4:19). "It is certain that the sin which exists in us is a sad thing and evil smelling ... But in Christ this life of sadness and foul odour is transformed into joy. Faith imparts to it a sweet fragrance. Through Christ we offer ourselves to God. For it is he who purifies sinners and effects a spiritual cleansing of those who are unclean ... Through Christ we offer ourselves, through him we who are impure dare to draw near. But we draw near through faith and we offer ourselves to the Father with a sweet fragrance only when we cease to exist for ourselves alone, when we have in ourselves only Christ as the sweet savour of the Spirit." [29] But this sweet savour is the death of Christ.[30]

In this sense we too die in baptism in the likeness of the death of Christ, or better, we are rooted in the likeness of his death, and have been buried into his death (Rom 6:3-5). Thus we become righteous in Christ before the Father. This is not a righteousness of vainglory but of our surrender to God. For true union in love or in the dialogue of love comes about only in total surrender. It is only in this surrender in Christ that we are reconciled with God, only in this sacrificial condition that we receive holiness from God, a holiness which is one with the transcending of all egotism as the root of sin. It is in this holiness that our righteousness before the Father consists, the righteousness which we have won through Christ. We gain this holiness or righteousness from the Father, for when we enter through Christ into the Father's presence in

a state of pure sacrifice, we are raised to a condition in which
full communication with God is possible. Because it is only
in this state of total surrender in Christ that we are reconciled
with God, we can say that reconciliation demands sacrifice,
the sacrifice of our own existence, that very existence which
we want to hold on to and keep as a good for ourselves alone
when we are in a condition of sin and selfishness. Now the
foundation of our own sacrifice and the source of its power,
the source of our love for the Father in which is our true life,
is the sacrifice of Christ, his spotless self-surrender to the
Father accomplished out of love for the Father and for us,
and out of the love for the Father which he has on our behalf
as a man. Communicating in the death of Christ, "we communicate in a death which brings life." [31]

It is clear that this conception of sacrifice implies the
ascetic vision of St. Paul and the Fathers according to which
after the Fall of Adam the flesh has become the seat of sin
through the appetites at work in it. This flesh must die so that
sin may die together with it. It is also clear however that the
flesh of Christ was not the seat of these kinds of appetites,
and therefore neither was it the seat of sin. He put to death
even the sinless affections that he had assumed together with
the body.[32] Nevertheless he crucified the flesh on the cross so
that his crucified body might be a source of mortification for
our own bodies. As Nicholas Cabasilas says: "That death,
inasmuch as it was a death, did away with the life of evil.
Inasmuch as it is a punishment, it removes the guilt for sin
which each of us bears on account of his evil deeds." [33] This
is the state of justice which Christ won for us on the cross, the
reconciliation of the two parts of man — spirit and flesh —
through reconciliation with the Father, and the ending of all
hostility (Eph 2:16-18). This view of the crucifixion means
that the body of Christ must contain potentially all bodies,
and that all men must be drawn into Christ's sacrificial state.
"And he died for all, so that those who live might live no more
for themselves but for him who for their sake died and was
raised. . . . Therefore if any one is in Christ he is a new creation." (2 Cor 5:15, 17)

In this sense although Christ dies no more as he did once

on earth, he nevertheless permanently retains his sacrificial disposition of total surrender to the Father in order to draw all men into this same disposition. "Christ thought to preserve in his body the witness of his sacrifice and to bear in his own person the scars of the wounds he received in his crucifixion. In this way he wished to show that when he comes again in dazzling light he will remain for his servants the same Lord, crucified and pierced, and these wounds will serve as his kingly adornments." [34]

Since death entered into the world through sin and Christ committed no sin, it was on account of our sins that he suffered death. And through his death sin and selfishness are destroyed in their very roots together with the fruit which they produce, death. All men can escape these if they in turn are rooted in the death and sacrifice of Christ. Offering his humanity in sacrifice to the Father, the Son has raised it up to a state of supreme perfection so that from this state of perfect fulfillment all men can derive their own perfection together with freedom from the power of sin and eternal death. We see therefore that this understanding of sacrifice as the spotless gift of self to the Father presupposes the incarnation of the Son of God, for it was only in the divine hypostasis that mankind was able to present itself as a perfect offering to the Father.

C. If St. Cyril of Alexandria emphasizes the God-ward direction of Christ's sacrifice and death — as will both Anselm and Luther after him — St. Athanasius, St. Maximus the Confessor and other Fathers emphasize its man-ward direction, its power to heal and strengthen human nature, to overcome death and sin. We have in these authors a kind of anthropocentrism of grace (*gnadenhafter Anthropozentrismus*). God in his great love for us is not concerned with himself in even the slightest degree, but only with us.

In between these two explanations of the death of the Lord, the one theocentric and the other anthropocentric, we might situate the explanation of St. Gregory Nazianzen which serves as a kind of bridge between the two. Rejecting the theory of a ransom whether from the devil or from God, he says: "Is it not plain that the Father receives the sacrifice not because he has need of it, but because in his plan it was necessary for man to be sanctified through the humanity of Christ, and for God to call us to himself through his Son the Mediator who fulfilled everything for the sake of the Father's glory?" [35]

According to St. Athanasius, St. Maximus and other Fathers, the immortal subject accepts death in his body in order to overcome death. The death of Christ was the occasion of the victorious struggle of human nature, strengthened by the divine hypostasis, in its battle with its most powerful foe. It was the occasion for the supreme strengthening of human nature and of the spirit within it. "Thus it happened that two opposite marvels took place at once: the death of all was consummated in the Lord's body; yet, because the Word was in it, death and corruption were in the same act utterly abolished." [36] The cross of Christ was the occasion of the revelation of God's power and his love for man who had been made subject to death because of sin, as it was also the occasion of the destruction of death.

The majority of the Greek Fathers have stressed this understanding of the death of Christ in order to link his death closely to his resurrection, and to his incarnation as well. In fact they never speak of the death of Christ without bringing it into connexion with the resurrection and without presenting this victory as an act of the incarnate Word. Christ accepts death in order to destroy it in the resurrection, but this happens only because he is the Word of God. The Fathers do not make the death of Christ into a saving event independent of the resurrection and incarnation. Thus if the incarnation is the fruit of God's love for mankind with whom he unites himself definitively and indissolubly, and if in the passion this love goes further still, then its purpose and result are seen in the resurrection which brings to perfection God's union with us for all eternity. Christ does not become incarnate and die simply for the sake of an external reconciliation with us and in order to make us righteous before him. The purpose of the incarnation was our deliverance from eternal death, our complete and eternal union with him in that condition of peace which is constituted precisely by the most complete loving union between himself and us, a condition in which we live his entire righteousness and holiness in union with him. If the Father loves the face of all men when he gazes on the face of his incarnate Son, then on the face of the crucified and risen Christ the face of mankind appears to the Father as even more worthy of love because through the cross humanity has become one with God in an act of supreme love for him. We ourselves consent to this supreme surrender, and in the resurrected state the penetration of humanity by the Spirit of God is perfected and assured for all eternity. The whole economy that God has devised for us through his Son has as its purpose this eschatological perfection of the union of God with the whole of mankind.

In his resurrection Christ raises up his entire humanity — soul and body — to a state of righteousness, of union with God, of perfect and eternal holiness. This is the state of complete surrender to the Father. In the ascension the righteousness of God, the very glory of the Father, is communicated to man. This glory is revealed perfectly through the incarnate Christ in the very moment when, as man, he offers perfect praise to the Father.

All who believe in him will have part in this peace, righteousness, holiness and glory, and through the Spirit of Christ they participate in the first fruits of these gifts even in the course of this earthly life. For from the risen and exalted Christ the Holy Spirit shines forth immediately and superabundantly, exactly as heat radiates from an incandescent body. The risen and exalted state of Christ is his humanity perfectly filled and penetrated by the Holy Spirit, the unobstructed irradiation of the Spirit from within him. His body no longer represents in any way an obstacle separating him from those who believe in him. On the contrary it has received the power to impart most perfectly the Godhead with which it is united.

On the cross Christ has taken us all into his embrace, for his love has gone out to us all, drawing us all into his condition of self-surrender to God and to man, the condition in which he empties himself for the sake of both God and man.

And in his love he gives us too the power to overcome ourselves with all our selfish impulses.

Through the resurrection Christ combines within himself the condition of victim and the state of resurrection, the full revelation of the divine life in his humanity. And to those who believe in him he imparts this same combined nature. St. Paul says, "We always carry in the body the death of Jesus that the life of Jesus may also be manifested in our bodies. For while we live we are always being given up to death for Jesus' sake, so that the life of Jesus may be manifested in our mortal flesh." (2 Cor 4:10-11) And St. Athanasius says in turn: "Christ, to whom these all bear witness, himself gives the victory to each, making death completely powerless for those who hold his faith and bear the sign of the cross." [37] Through Christ we have the power to die to selfish passions and appetites and to die to ourselves; but we also have the power to live a new life, a life triumphant in us, born in our spirit but revealed in our body as well. It is a power which we know does not come from ourselves but has its objective source beyond ourselves. From the risen Christ his Spirit shines forth most powerfully, giving us a foretaste of the likeness of his death and resurrection and leading us at the same time towards perfect likeness to him.

Through his incarnation, death and resurrection the incarnate Word of God ascends by degrees to a state in which the Holy Spirit increasingly shines forth from him. It is through this same Holy Spirit that the Word unites to himself, after they were separated from him and scattered abroad, all creatures that will ever come to be (Eph 1:10; Col 1:16). Salvation in its final stage, according to St. Paul, is the reunion of all things in Christ. As sin consists in the selfishness which separates men from God and from one another, so salvation consists in going beyond selfishness, in mutual love of all men, and in union with God. Between the resurrection of Christ and our own resurrection stretches the interval in which Christ works to unite us all completely in himself, and in which we strive towards the same end, stimulated and sustained by his activity. This activity of Christ is directed towards all men and is at work in all men in ways which are tangible and visible to a greater or lesser degree. It struggles against the selfishness found in all men but does not deliver them from it without their own consent, and indeed its striving is to win man's consent and collaboration towards this goal of union with Christ.

Christ has laid in himself the foundation and supplied the power for this reunion of all mankind in himself by means of his incarnation, passion, resurrection and ascension, and by sending out his Holy Spirit who is at work secretly in the world and visibly in the Church. Henceforth the Spirit of Christ is imparted to us continually as the unifying power of Christ. On his part the Word, through whom and in whom all things in the beginning were created, gives a new orientation and integration to the whole of creation by the act of assuming it into himself, the same creation which had formerly abandoned the original direction God had intended for it. Christ overcomes the enmities which first appeared among creatures when those elements which had been intended to constitute a single and unified creation first disintegrated and drew apart from one another. Thus it happens that the power which flows out from the unity achieved in Christ exercises its unifying influence over the whole of creation. Through his virgin birth Christ has overcome the opposition of the sexes. In Christ "there is neither male nor female." (Gal 3:28) Through his death and resurrection he has done away with the separation between Paradise and the universe which appeared after the Fall. He has opened for mankind the forbidden entrance into Paradise, and he even came himself to earth after his resurrection to show that in him Paradise and the universe are made one. Through his ascension he unites heaven and earth, raising up the human body which he had assumed, a body of the same nature and substance as our own. Exalted body and soul above the hosts of angels, he restored the unity of the sensible and intelligible worlds and secured the harmony of the entire creation.[38]

It is therefore through his incarnation, passion, resurrection and ascension and through the mission and activity of his Holy Spirit that he unites all things. Through his incarnation the mode of union is, so to speak, ontological. Through his death he purifies the whole cosmos, and in a special way he purifies all men as the conscious agents of the cosmos making it possible for them too to exercise a unifying activity. Through the resurrection he fills all things with the ultimate meaning of all this striving after unity by filling them with light.

But the most essential union which Christ pursues and which is his decisive contribution in effecting the unity of all mankind, is the union of ourselves and God and the union of ourselves with one another. This is the goal for which we were created in the beginning. In order to effect the union of all men Christ first unites all created things at the deepest levels of their existence, and it is through this union that he brings about the union of all men. St. Athanasius says: "But the Lord came to overthrow the devil and to purify the air and to make 'a way' for us up to heaven, as the Apostle says, 'through the veil, that is to say, his flesh' (Heb 10:20) . . . and thus he re-opened the road to heaven, saying again, 'Lift up your gates, O ye princes, and be ye lifted up, ye everlasting doors.' (Ps 23:7 LXX) For it was not the Word himself who needed an opening of the gates, he being Lord of all, nor was any of his works closed to their maker. No, it was we who needed it, we whom he himself upbore in his own body — that body which he first offered to death on behalf of all, and then made through it a path to heaven." [39] We see here once again how closely St. Athanasius connects the death of Christ with his resurrection. His body had to die in order to rise again and in order that through his risen and transfigured body all of us with our own bodies might reach heaven and the transfiguration. St. Athanasius says therefore: "Moreover, as it was the death of all mankind that the Saviour came to accomplish, not his own, he did not lay aside his body by an individual act of dying, for to him, as life, this simply did not belong; but he accepted death at the hands of men, thereby completely to destroy it in his own body." [40]

Once drawn into union with God by the sacrificed and risen body of the Lord we, the works of his hands, are also drawn into union among ourselves. Our own *logoi* and the *logoi* of our existences are attracted to union with the divine

Logos, the Word in whom we find our eternal archetypes and for whom our natures yearn as for the fathomless depths of life and the secret source of that knowledge we crave of the essence of all things. When our wills have returned to their conformity with their own being and their own inner rational purposes and structures (*logoi*), and have rejected the arbitrary dispositions of their irrational and unnatural selfishness, then they are called to be united to the human will of Christ and through it to his divine will which is one with his human will.

The force of attraction in Christ is his love. This love is revealed in the act of the incarnation and in the manner of his earthly life. It is revealed with greater effect in the manner of his sacrifice, and most efficaciously of all in his risen and exalted state from which love shines forth as the Holy Spirit. All these modes of being, concentrated in the risen state of Christ, attract us towards resurrection as to the climactic union with him and with one another, making use at the same time both of our natural longings and of our sacrifice which is nourished by his. Although Christ has ascended he nevertheless also remains in contact with us and with the deepest levels of the world through the force of attraction exercised by his love. "Behold I am with you always to the close of the age." (Mt 28:20) These words were spoken by the Lord to those who were sent to call the world to him, showing that he himself would draw all men to himself through them.

It is a general truth that love attracts and binds together. It is a unifying force arising from the divine reason and the divine will in which all other reasons and wills have their origin, and in and through which all things are able to find a common harmony. The divine reason is the basis of the harmony of our reasons and wills which are united so intimately together, and this union is realized through love just as the union of God with all men and of men with one another is extended through love.

The final union of all in God, the goal towards which Christ wishes to lead men according to St. Paul (Eph 1:10, Col 1:16-20), is equivalent to the Kingdom of God, the King-

dom of Love. This is the purpose of the entire saving work
of Christ, a work which is inconceivable apart from this
eschatological goal and our straining towards it.

*Christian Obligations To The World Today In The Light Of
Orthodox Soteriology*

Christ did not bring us salvation so that we might continue to live in isolation, but that we might strive towards a
greater and ever more profound unity which has as its culmination the eternal Kingdom of God.

We see this reflected in the fact that we cannot gain salvation if we remain in isolation, caring only for ourselves.
There is no doubt that each man must personally accept salvation and make it his own, but he cannot do so nor can he
persevere and progress in the way of salvation unless he is
helped by others and helps them himself in return, that is,
unless the manner of our salvation is communal. To be saved
means to be pulled out of our isolation and to be united with
Christ and the rest of men. "Let us commend ourselves and
each other and our whole life to Christ our God", sing the
faithful at the Orthodox liturgy. Salvation is communion in
Christ (κοινωνία) and therefore the obligation of Christians to strive to maintain and develop their ecclesial unity
through love is plain: "For the love of Christ gathers us together." (2 Cor 5:14)

Inasmuch however as Christ has accomplished the work
of salvation and continuously offers its fruits in order to
bring all men together into the Kingdom of God, Christians,
as servants of Christ obliged to strive for the union of all
men in that Kingdom of perfect love, also have certain obligations towards those who are not Christians. In what follows
a brief attempt will be made to set forth these obligations,
or, more precisely, the motives which lie behind them.

1. Christ offered his sacrifice and rose from the dead outside Jerusalem, and it was mainly outside Jerusalem that he
appeared after his resurrection. This was to sanctify those
peoples who had no kind of connexion with the God of the

Law. We read in the Epistle to the Hebrews: "Let us go
forth to him outside the camp, bearing abuse for him. For
here we have no lasting city, but we seek the city which is to
come." (Heb 13:13-14) The reference is clearly to the constant necessity of leaving the world behind, of rising above
the world in order that the world might be led in turn to transcend itself. To be confined, however, within any condition
which is made static by the limitations of existence means to
be confined within the world, and Christians must not be
confined even within their own churches as if these were
lasting cities, for then their mobile character is forgotten and
they lose their very *raison d'être* as ways toward heaven.
Christians and Christian Churches must always work among
those men who remain outside them in the world in order
to transcend the world as a static order, to raise it to a condition higher than its own. Christ became man in the world;
he taught and ministered in the world. It was in the world
that he offered himself in sacrifice and was buried. He rose
again from the dead in the world; he sent his disciples into
the world teaching them foreign languages through the Holy
Spirit, and it is in the world that he still works, even if his
work there is principally carried out now through his disciples,
that is, through the Church. According to our teaching Christ
is in the world but he is also in heaven, sending his disciples
out into the world with the promise he made at his ascension
that he would be with them. Again he said at the close of his
earthly ministry, "I do not pray that you should take them out
of the world." (Jn 17-15)

Christ is in the world but he is also in heaven. We ascend
to the heavenly Christ through the earthly Christ within a
world which, even more than the Church, is always seeking
to progress beyond whatever happens to be its present condition, always yearning for something better, always convinced
that the *status quo* need not be definitive. Today perhaps more
than ever before, Christ draws the world towards himself in
a state of continuous change. He reveals himself to the world
at every new step of the way in some new perspective even
though for the world he may remain someone *incognito*. We
Christians must move forward along this road together with

the world, and tell the world who this person is who is attracting it. We must help the world to remember what true progress means, and this is a special obligation for Christians today at a time when the progress of the world has become so rapid and it becomes more and more evident to all that the world is no "lasting city", but that, in fact, the constant aspiration of men everywhere is for improved relations among themselves.

2. If "the love of God has been poured into our hearts" (Rom 5:5), and as a consequence we can and therefore must see the faces of our fellow men in the human face of Christ, just as in beholding his incarnate Son the Father sees and loves us all as sons and adopts us through the incarnation of his Son, then it is plain that in the face of every man we must see and love some aspect of the face of Christ, indeed the very face of Christ himself. Or to state the matter more precisely, every face is potentially a face of Christ; that it is able to become a real face of Christ is due to the fact that Christ has placed his image there, and it has become transparent of him. But we too have a part to play in the passage of each human face from this potential state to one in which it is truly the face of Christ.

If the humanity of Christ does not belong to an individual human hypostasis but rather to the Son of God, then it belongs to all men much more truly than the humanity of each individual human person belongs to all. It belongs to all and is for the sake of all. It is destined for each of us, destined to become the possession of each man and to form him inwardly as it was itself formed inwardly in Christ by the divine hypostasis. As the humanity of God and of ourselves it is destined to be reflected in all men, and similarly we are, all of us, called in turn to be reflected in the humanity of Christ and to take our image from him. St. Symeon the New Theologian says that the man who does not meet the needs of his fellow man, "despises him who said: 'as you did it to one of the least of these my brethren, you did it to me' (Mt 25:40). . . . Thus he has accepted to take on the face of every poor man. He has made himself one with every man in such manner that none of those who believe in him may despise his brother, but must treat the brother or neighbour he sees as if he were his God, and he must consider himself just as insignificant before his brother as he himself would be before God his Creator. And let him receive and honour his brother as he would God, and let him strip himself of his own belongings in his brother's service just as Christ poured out his own blood for our salvation." [41] We must therefore come to live out our union with Christ who fills us with his own consciousness of self-sacrifice, and so come to sacrifice ourselves too for the rest of men. At the same time we must treat all other men as we would treat Christ himself, and seek union with them as we do with Christ through the service we offer them.

3. Everything which Christ did — his incarnation, his teaching, his life of obedience to the Father and loving service of us in the trials of our earthly lives, his sacrifice in the world — all these things emphasize, as we have already seen, the value of human life on earth. No path towards eschatological perfection exists which bypasses life on earth and the struggles which accompany that life. Every single aspect of eternal happiness is promised by the Lord as the result of certain ways of living and acting in this life, as the fruit of certain seeds sown and nurtured in the fields of this world. "Blessed are the peacemakers (on earth, of course, for there will be no more peacemaking in heaven), for they shall be called Sons of God." (Mt 5:9) Work "while it is day" said the Lord (Jn 9:4), and even St. Anthony asked that his life might be prolonged so that he could do penance. [42]

It is Christ we serve in the person of those who need our help in this world; Christ has identified himself with them. The Fathers speak of this world as a fair where we make purchase of the Kingdom of Heaven. Anyone who does not take part in the fair by trading with other men, anyone who produces no fruit by his labour, who develops no talent by his activity, will leave this life with an empty soul. We purchase the Kingdom of heaven from our fellow men both with the return we have won from our labours and also with the capabilities which our faith in Christ has conferred upon us. "Life and death come to us from our neighbour for if we win our brothers we win God, and contrariwise, if we destroy our brother we sin against Christ." [43] It is not however only from the other faithful that we purchase the Kingdom. The fair is universal and we must deal with every man. The fair is made up of everyone and everyone has his part. We can even acquire the Kingdom more readily from other men than we can from our fellow believers, because our service and generosity in their case demand of us greater effort and disinterestedness. Yet, strictly speaking, it is not men who give us the Kingdom of Heaven in exchange. It is Christ who gives it through them, and not immediately in this life but in the life to come. Let us not expect therefore to bring in a harvest as if ours were a visible crop. It is only when we expect no immediate return but believe that we will receive it in heaven, that we are truly sowing in the belief of a reward from on high. Of those who look for an immediate return, who want to receive something right away in exchange for what they give, who do not believe that from the moment they have given something they have already received the Kingdom of Heaven in exchange — although this will not be visible until the life to come — of such as these the Saviour has said: "If you love those who love you, what credit is that to you? For even sinners love those who love them. And if you do good to those who do good to you, what credit is that to you? For even sinners do the same." (Lk 6:32-33) Such men as these are trapped within a vicious circle; they contribute nothing to the spiritual progress of relations between men and nothing to the spiritual progress of the world.

4. We quoted above the remarks of St. Symeon the New Theologian who likened the stripping of ourselves of goods and power in the service of the needy to the power of Christ's act in shedding his blood for us, but here we will allow ourselves to go a step further and say that any sacrifice one man makes for another in this world comes from the sacrificial consciousness and power of Christ, from the power of his loving *kenosis*. Moreover any appeal, whether silent or voiced, addressed by one man to another on this earth, is also an appeal made in word or in silence by Christ himself. Any sacrifice, any act of service or love for others is a response prompted by the power of Christ's sacrifice to an appeal which also

comes through us from Christ himself. The call and response of mutual service among men is the way in which the love of Christ binds us together and helps us to progress in love. Conversely, all our appeals and responses of service come together in Christ and become his own, adding new depths to his sacrifice and to his own cry for help. In him all our cries for help and all our responses have their echo. Men are beings who do cry out and who do respond, and because of this they are bound together. Man is inwardly obliged to respond but he does so only because he has been appealed to, because a cry has gone up and he has been called. The unconditional and binding force of this call has its ultimate source in God, and from the nature of the call there flows an unconditional obligation and power to respond. Thus God has taken up his position among men and within men through the power of this absolute call and of its perfect response in Christ. In his sacrifice Christ made and continually makes the supreme response to the call of the Father and to man's cry for help. He also gives us the power to make this same response. By his identification with those who stand in need of help he addresses to us a call which obliges us to love and to minister unconditionally to all men.

5. If the Christian must see Christ in every man and hear Christ's cry for help in every human cry, then he cannot accept with patience the fact that his brother exists in a condition inferior to his own. It is of the nature of love, moreover, that it cannot tolerate inequality, for inequality creates distance. One who loves does not consider himself superior to the beloved. Instead love prompts us to strive for the achievement of equality and justice among men. St. Symeon the New Theologian goes on to say in the passage already referred to above: "The man who treats his neighbour as himself is not content to have more than his neighbour. But if he does have more and does not give with abundance so that he himself becomes poor and so resembles his neighbours, that man has not fulfilled the Master's command." Even should he serve and give to as many of his fellow men as he can, "yet if he despises or ignores even a single one it will be

counted as though he had ignored the divine Christ in his hunger and thirst." [44]

Obviously we need not interpret St. Symeon as pleading for a universal equality in poverty. He does affirm however the necessity for every man to seek to become the equal of the rest so that all may be able to serve, and that all may come to realize that they have need of the others and that in this equality of need they ought not to feel that any distance separates them from one another. All must come to the realization that they are poor in themselves, which is to say that each man needs the help of the others in order to live and grow in their unity in God.

6. Reconciliation therefore does not consist of a purely formal peace, a mere coexistence and lack of aggression covering over profound disagreements. Lasting reconciliation is inseparable from the kind of love which strives to secure equality and justice among men and nations, and to promote continuous mutual exchange animated by love. It is the result of a true understanding of the meaning of reconciliation with God who unites himself to man and causes him to partake of all good things in Christ. Through such a reconciliation God adopts us as his sons and divinizes us according to his grace.

7. Christians can make no fruitful contribution to this profound reconciliation between men and nations if they are concerned solely with service to individual men and therefore neglect to promote just and equitable relations on a broader social and international scale. If Christians in the past often limited their acts of service to needy individuals because social structures tended to remain static, today, when social structures are more elastic because of the powerful influence of those who are aware of their own solidarity as victims of injustice and who confidently believe that they can produce more satisfactory forms of social life, Christians must make the kind of contribution which will favour the continuous adaptation of these structures to meet contemporary aspirations for greater justice, equality, and fraternity in man's relation to man. It has become more obvious today that the whole world is being moved to seek more just and fraternal

human relations, and it is our belief as Christians that we can see in this movement the effect of Christ's activity guiding the world towards the Kingdom of Heaven, in spite of the fact that this is a goal which in its final form cannot be reached in this world, given the corruptible nature of matter and all its attendant ills.

Any reconciliation not founded on true universal justice and equality among men will always be threatened with collapse, and the absence of a lasting peace will threaten the life of every human being. Christians therefore must labour on behalf of such a lasting peace in order to assure to every man the chance to prepare for his own resurrection. Seen in this light, war presents as many risks to those who are killed as it does to those who do the killing. Though it may seem that the same risk sometimes attaches to a premature natural death, we can be sure that this happens according to the will of God and that God has his reasons. The Christian has a duty, therefore, to fight on behalf of justice because the presence of injustice can appear to provide a justification for eternal death, while the removal of injustice deprives eternal death of any such justification. One who struggles to end injustice follows in the path of Christ who was the first to use justice as a means to deprive death of its justification. Moreover Christ gives us the power to do the same because our own struggle for justice depends on his power.[45]

8. Justice, equality, brotherhood and lasting peace cannot be realized if we have no interest in the material universe. The material universe, like mankind itself, is destined for transfiguration through the power of the risen body of Christ, and through the spiritual power of his love which urges us to restore the material universe to its original role of manifesting our mutual love, not, as is now the case, of serving as a means of separation and strife. We must demonstrate increasingly in practice the meaning of material goods as gifts, as the means of mutual exchange between men. The universe belongs to Christ; it is mysteriously attached to his crucified and risen body. Yet it also belongs to men, to Christians and non-Christians alike who suffer and advance towards salvation. Nicholas Cabasilas says: "That blood flowing

from his wounds has extinguished the light of the sun and
caused the earth to quake. It has made holy the air and
cleansed the whole cosmos from the stain of sin." [46]

Only if all men are united can they transform the world
and respond to the call to treat the world as a gift, as the
means of mutual exchange. When we share in the material
goods of the universe we must be conscious that we are moving
in the sphere of Christ, and that it is by making use of these
material things as gifts for the benefit of one another that we
progress in our union with Christ and with our neighbour.
We must also be aware that when the material world becomes the means whereby we communicate in love, then we
are communicating in Christ. Thus the universe is called to
become the eschatological paradise through the agency of
fraternal love. It is our duty to free the universe from the van-
ity of the blind and selfish use we make of it as sinners, and
to see that it shares in the glory of the sons of God (Rom
8:21), the glory which is an inseparable part of our union as
brothers.

CHAPTER VII

The Problems and Perspectives of Orthodox Theology*

The respect which Orthodoxy has always had for the mysterious character of God and of God's work in the world and among men imposes an obligation on Orthodox theology both now and in the future. Orthodoxy respects and will continue to respect the mysterious character of the Christian faith. But this obligation does not restrict the possibility for theology to meditate on the faith. On the contrary, it is precisely the mystical character of the faith which makes possible a fruitful theological meditation like that which marked the patristic period. For the mystery implies a richness and an infinite complexity of meanings which can never be reduced to any one-sided explanation. The Eastern Fathers thought that God transcended any understanding of him which might find expression in a given formula, and it was apophatic theology that they esteemed most highly. These are the attitudes which made possible a continuous progress into the inexhaustible wealth of meaning of the divine or theandric mystery. Contemporary Orthodox thought has discovered anew the theology of mystery, a knowledge spoken of by both St. Gregory of Nyssa and St. Gregory Palamas, a knowledge which does not claim to exhaust fully either the content of the divine reality of God and Christ, or the divine-human realities expressed by other areas of theology. Instead it recognizes that

* Originally published in the present English translation in the *Altar Almanach*, a publication of the Romanian parish in London, England, vol. 2 (1971-1972), 40-50.

this knowledge moves in the ocean of mystery. It recognizes that the formula in which the divine or theandric reality is expressed is a window through which the light from the ineffable infinity of the mystery can be sensed or perceived.

Contemporary Orthodox theology has escaped from the influence of the scholasticism of the last few centuries. This scholastic current, by claiming to give a complete definition of God and his saving work and to supply rigid and supposedly comprehensive formulae, was able to inhibit the progress of theological thought, at least until theology was compelled by the force of the current revolution in human thinking to abandon these formulae.

While Western theology, which has only now abandoned the rationalist formulae of scholasticism under the pressure of the present intellectual revolution, seeks to explain the doctrines of the faith just as exhaustively by means of rationalist formulae of another kind, especially those based on the results of the natural sciences, Orthodox theology considers that these same scientific results have thrown even greater light upon the infinite mystery of the divine interpersonal life and upon the ineffable mystery of the human subject, as well as upon the personal relations which obtain among these human subjects and between them and the God who transcends reason.

In these two theologies we have today two paths along which human thought can progress.

Nevertheless, by claiming today as it did in the past that it can fully grasp the divine reality and its saving relationship to men by means of reason, Western theology runs the risk of soon having to replace the rational explanation of today with other explanations, for today's explanations will soon prove insufficient for the minds of tomorrow — a fact which we have continuously observed, especially in Protestant theology. On the other hand, because it allows the light of the inexhaustible mystery to appear through any of its formulae in any age, Orthodox theology does not make earlier formulations obsolete when it moves forward to new ones, but remains in continuity with them, the former being in fact a new explanation of the latter, a new step forward in the perception of the divine mystery which had also been correctly perceived by the previous formulae. For Orthodox theology this same mystery remains transparent in every new theological expression, even though each new expression is a step forward in making the mystery manifest and in rendering the inexhaustible richness of its meanings visible. Each expression makes explicit something of the manifold *logoi* contained in the mystery, while at the same time it implies the presence of the mystery. Thus Orthodox theology still remains faithful to the dogmatic formulations of the first centuries of the Church, while nevertheless making continuous progress in their interpretation and in the revelation of that ineffable mystery which they only suggest.

The door of the infinite riches of the personal or interpersonal divine being has opened up before the reflections of Orthodox theology, and with it the prospects of an endless progress of the human spirit within the divine. The time has passed when everyone thought that nothing more could be said in dogmatics, that theology was condemned to repeat and systematize the old formulae in different and merely external ways, or that the old dogmatic terminologies were a kind of shell, opaque and impenetrable. Orthodox theology today understands that every dogmatic term and every combination of dogmatic terms indicates the boundaries and safeguards the depths of the mystery in the face of a one-sided and rationalist superficiality that seeks to dissolve it. Every dogmatic formulation, under theological reflection, allows the light of the mystery lying beyond it to shine through. Today we think that the terms of every dogmatic formulation indicate — as though they were signposts — the entrance where we are admitted to the depths of the abyss, but we do not think that they assign limits to these depths. Through each doctrinal definition we come into contact with certain realities and ultimate meanings which become ever more profound before our minds to the extent that the human spirit experiences them and becomes absorbed in them, and thus is capable of still deeper and more subtle experiences and intuitions. The concepts of "person", the union of the divine with the human in a person, the incarnation of the divine

Logos, the sacrifice assumed by God himself for the sake
of mankind, that interpersonal communion which ascends
even to the supreme degree of divinization, the divinization
of man — all these ideas indicate the sources, perspectives,
and infinite perfections of the divine mystery, and they open
the paths of an unending progress into that mystery.

However, because any progress in understanding the
realities of the abyss to which dogma points depends on the
progress of the human spirit, which is itself conditioned by
the whole of its experience — an experience always growing
richer in the various contexts of world, history, and society —
it follows that any progress in understanding dogma depends
in part on the progressive understanding that science has of
the world. It is also true however that theological thinking
cannot be separated from spirituality.

In its estimation of the role of scientific progress in the
understanding of dogma Orthodox theology is in agreement
with Western theology. What distinguishes it from the latter
is the fact that it takes scientific progress into account only in
so far as science makes a contribution to the progress of the
human spirit, and only in so far as it deepens in man the
experience of his own spiritual reality and of the supreme
spiritual reality, neither of which can be reduced to the phys-
ical and chemical level of nature. Orthodox theology gives
us the possibility of understanding the mystery of the relationship between God and man. Yet it is also our belief that
scientific progress *does* produce, generally speaking, an over-
all progress of the human spirit. We look upon the man of
today with this kind of confidence because Orthodoxy has
had confidence in the man of every age, believing that he can
neither be reduced by any fall to a condition of "pure nature"
(*natura pura*) enclosed within the limits of exclusively
worldly concerns, nor become, by reason of the fall, such a
totally corrupt human nature that his every thought and action
and his whole being are completely sinful. We do not agree
even today with Western theology when it says that contemporary man is progressing only in the areas of science and
technology and is being stripped more and more of a spiritual
life. This is why we do not think it necessary to give up our

stress upon the spiritual content of dogma when we are faced with the argument that such content can say nothing to the man of today, and therefore we must insist only on the conformity of dogmas with the results of the natural sciences. We believe that dogmas can only be preserved by emphasizing the spiritual meanings they contain.

And yet, we must also recognize that by its rational criticism of those older formulae of Christian teaching which lent a mythical prestige to certain equally rationalist concepts, Western theology often leads toward the same spiritual and mystical core of Revelation, and so by this path comes to merge with Orthodox theology.

The spiritual progress of man as a force to be reckoned with is evident today in man's aspirations for deeper relationships between himself and his fellow man, and for a content to his life more meaningful than the sad monotony of life in a consumer society. Man today is not content to be just a consumer of the products and distractions provided by technology; he demands to be a man of ever closer relationships with his fellow men, and consequently a man who, in a manner much more acute now than ever before, lives out his obligation to find those ways and means which will assure that these relationships do not become painful and inimical, but instead remain friendly and responsible. These ways and means can only be discovered however by experience, by coming into contact with those higher realities that man thirsts for in order to escape the deadly monotony of purely material distractions.

This is why Orthodox theology, by experiencing once again the impulse to be a theology of mystery, experiences at the same time the impulse to be a theology of spirituality. In both respects it remains in continuity with the teaching of the Gospels and of the first Christian centuries.

2. From what has been said so far we can see that in the spiritual theology required by the need to promote better human relations there is also implied a theology of communion and of the Church. True spirituality implies communion and true communion implies spirituality. True communion cannot be fostered or achieved by external measures of dis-

cipline or worldly interest. True spirituality is not individualist in character nor is it realized by taking refuge in the self,
and that is certainly not true spirituality which is found wanting in love for the rest of men. Spirituality does not mean
the accumulation of the experiences of a refined spirit, an
undisturbed enjoyment of certain insights which can be cherished without reference to the community. True spirituality
grows with the experience of the communion of many persons, with the understanding of the many complex situations
born in the life of communion. It is fed from the richness of
the nature of concrete realities and from the limitless variety
of relationships with more and more persons, and it shows
its power by overcoming contradictions and by establishing
a harmony among these relations. True spirituality is seen in
the efforts of all men to achieve a common unity, but a unity
which respects the specific contribution which each individual
can bring to this growth of understanding and to the content
of mankind's common experiences and values.

In the future, therefore, Orthodox theology will also be
a theology of the Church. For the Church is the communion
of the faithful realized in Christ and sustained by the Holy
Spirit. It is communion and profound spirituality at one and
the same time. And because of this it is life. It is communion
in the Holy Spirit. The very existence of the Church is an
effect, continually renewed, of the action of the Holy Spirit
in creating communion.

Orthodox theology is a theology of spirituality and of
communion, and inasmuch as it is the theology of the Church
it is at the same time a theology of the mystery of God's activity in men and of the growth of men into God. The Church
maintains the unity of faith so that the object of faith is
not just a passive object of individual intellectual analysis, nor
merely an object of a certain will to believe which seeks to
remain obedient to the decisions of an exterior authority. The
object of faith is the God who works in the Church through
the Holy Spirit. It is the divine-human relationship lived out
in the sacramental and spiritual communion of the Church
which is filled with the Holy Spirit. The subject of the faith
can be the individual believer only in so far as he is the sub-

ject of faith together with the Church. The Church is the subject of the faith in so far as she is made to be such by God
himself, who works in the Church through the Holy Spirit.
The Orthodox theologian therefore has no other task in his
work than that of interpreting the experience of God as lived
by the community of the Church, an experience in which he
himself participates. Only in this way will his theology be
more than merely his own theology, and become a theology
illuminated by the Holy Spirit who is at work in the Church
guiding her teaching ministry. Thus the Orthodox theologian
strives to show that his theology is only an expression of the
mind of the believing community, that is to say, an expression of the mind of the Church.

Individual intellectual effort is by no means to be neg-
lected, but it consists in merging the individual mind with the
mind of the community of the Church, in which the Holy
Spirit is working, in order to give expression in new terms
to what is consonant with the Church's mind. It is the duty
of the Orthodox theologian to remain in the context of the
Church quickened and guided by the Holy Spirit, and to let
himself be carried where the Spirit himself is directing the
Church. For the Holy Spirit guides the Church "into all truth"
(Jn 16:13), that is, from the truth of the present to the truth
of the future. He guides the Church in the light of this truth
to find answers to what new questions may arise, urging it by
way of anticipation toward the future truth and, in this
sense, "declaring the things which are to come" (Jn 16:13).
He does this however without leading the Church away from
the path of the whole truth which is contained implicitly in
Christ, and therefore without ever taking her out of continuity with those answers which the Church has given to
problems of an earlier age; for from those things which are
Christ's "he will take and declare it to you" (Jn 16:14).
Theology thus fulfils the function of a prophetic midwife,
interpreting the prophetic orientation given the Church by
the Spirit, renewing the Church's continual striving towards
those things which are to come, and ultimately making her
eschatological tension present again within her.

But because it is a theology of the Church which from the

very beginning has the whole Christ as our final goal, and because therefore the whole of Revelation is to be found in Christ, this theology is at the same time a theology of Tradition, a Tradition which the Church has handed on from her very beginnings in her sacramental, doctrinal, and pastoral activity, not as if it were a mass of theoretical propositions, but as a living Tradition of sanctifying power and spiritual activity.

Orthodoxy is convinced that only the community is able to preserve such a living Tradition of spiritual activity, an experience of doctrine lived within a spirituality handed down from generation to generation, a Tradition in which the hierarchy certainly has a role to play, but not the only role.

Western theology on the other hand — and I refer here especially to Protestant theology — has moved from considering the Scripture as an absolute norm in itself to understanding the Tradition of the primitive Church as the living basis of Scripture and the fundamental and permanent context in which the meaning of Scripture is to be discovered. In following this direction Western theology is moving along the path towards a fuller understanding of the Church, even though Protestant theology is still relatively far away from any understanding of the apostolic tradition as the unified tradition of a unified Church.

We have said that Orthodox theology is a theology of communion inasmuch as it is a theology of the Church. We emphasize this because in a special way the Orthodox Church is the Church of communion, for according to the Orthodox conception the Church and communion in the Holy Spirit are one and the same, the Church herself is communion, and where there is no communion there is no Church.

In the future Orthodox theology will study more profoundly all that is contained in the concept of communion, and through this special concern will encourage the life of communion which is the object of man's deepest yearning both now and in the future.

The concept of communion is one in its most profound meaning with the concept of "sobornicity" (catholicity). Accordingly, Orthodox theology will seek to develop the richness contained in the concept of sobornicity, a reality to be distinguished as much from individualism as from unity understood as uniformity, as much from isolation among the individual members of the faithful as from their mere external unity. Sobornicity, like the unity of a living organism, is a unity in which the parts condition and complement one another within a single life; it is a continuous giving and receiving, a kind of symphonic unity in which "there are varieties of gifts, but the Spirit is the same" (1 Cor. 12:4), in which the wide variety of members makes up a single Body of Christ (1 Cor. 12:12).

3. Thanks to the stress it lays on the symphonic character of the Church, Orthodox theology will be able to make an important contribution to the present movement towards the union of the Churches. Great ecumenical possibilities are contained in the idea of the catholicity of the Church, and by bringing these into the light and giving them their rightful place, Orthodox theology can become a truly ecumenical theology and so contribute greatly to the ecumenical cause.

Orthodox sobornicity, as a true organic unity in plurality, can serve as a model — even as a final goal — for the different Churches in the progress of their ecumenical relations, showing them the possibility of combining a many-sided and real unity together with a mutual recognition of their diversities in other areas and a mutual respect for their freedom in a shared unity.

Prompted by this common desire for Christian unity, Orthodox theology has begun to study the doctrine of the other Churches in an irenic spirit, and to help along the progress of dialogue between the Orthodox Church and the other Churches, a dialogue which is already moving towards the official level.

Orthodox theology can be of great help in bringing the Churches together because of the close connection it makes between doctrine and spirituality, and because of the living spiritual core it looks for in every doctrinal formulation. In this process the doctrinal formulae of one Church cease to be rigid and opaque expressions opposed to equally rigid and opaque expressions used by the other Churches. Instead, they are seen to suggest the meanings of a living reality which shines through the formulations of one Church and encounters the living meanings of the doctrines of the other Churches. The different teachings of the Churches, if they take into account the spiritual effects which they themselves produce in the lives of men, can find a common interpretation corresponding to the spiritual purposes and necessities which are a matter of concrete concern to the Churches in the lives of their faithful.

This Orthodox contribution to the *rapprochement* of the Churches, which is, as we have seen, represented by the spiritual interpretation of doctrine, joins with the contribution of Western theology in its efforts to understand doctrinal formulations more flexibly and in conformity with the nature of human reason. This Western approach presents no fundamental contradictions to an understanding of the same doctrines that grows out of a spirituality penetrated by grace.

4. Orthodox theology, however, by emphasizing the sobornic or communitarian aspect of any true Christian life, can open up vast perspectives similar to those we have seen, not only on the level of Christian ecumenism, but also on the level of relations between Christians and mankind in general. Only in Christ do we see revealed the universal unity of mankind and the design of mankind's "recapitulation" and resurrection to eternal life in God. For the Son did not become an individual human hypostasis, but the hypostasis of human nature in general, and so a kind of "hypostasis-head" of the whole of humanity, destined to become a theandric subject together with all human subjects and thus a subject in whom all human subjects converge, yet without the loss or confusion of their own identities.

Christians are able to introduce Christ into the lives of the rest of men by entering into communion with them, because Christ is a joint subject with the faithful in their own thought, feelings, and actions. For in a dialogue which is the expression of a sincere and profound communion, one partner always introduces something of his own life into the life of the other.

Orthodox theology will be increasingly characterized, therefore, not only as an ecumenical theology but as a theology concerned with the aspirations and the problems of mankind as a whole, a theology which is concerned to provide ever deeper foundations for human cooperation and for the service of all mankind. Orthodox theology today is tending to become not only a theology of the ultimate meanings implied in individual human existence, an interpretation of human aspirations and human destiny in the light of the Gospel, but also a theology of history understood as the process by which mankind develops and moves forward towards the fulfillment of its destiny.

Christian theology in the past, although it asserted strongly that Christ had come for the salvation of men, was concerned mainly with the spiritual progress of individual believers and had no interpretation of the progress of humanity as a whole. It preserved the outlook of primitive Christianity which had spread originally from individual to individual. Once the believer had been drawn out of the pagan milieu of society by his faith he continued to be preoccupied largely with his own individual spiritual life. Today, under the influence of those tremendous problems which are confronting the whole of mankind at the very moment when men are appreciating more and more that they share a common destiny, Orthodox and Western theologies are both discovering the historical dimension of the work of Christ in the world. Orthodox theology has risen to this historical vision of the divine activity attested in the Old Testament, in the eschatological prophecies of the Saviour, the Epistles of St. Paul, and the Revelation of St. John. Obviously, the historical vision of contemporary Orthodox theology is able to embrace the whole world in an explicit way which was impossible in the Old Testament period. For Orthodox theology it is the historical and cosmic vision of St. Paul which begins to provide a content and a meaning that become more and more concrete. The God who works in history is Christ, the Son of God, who has entered into history in the incarnation and has placed himself in a personal relationship with all of humanity. Thus Christ is understood more and more today as the cosmic Christ, and his act of recapitulating all things in himself is no longer a mere general affirmation, but has become instead a crucial object of theological

attention. Theology always seeks a clearer understanding of
the ways in which Christ is leading humanity towards its recapitulation in himself. In this way it wishes to provide the
Church with a foundation for its desire to serve humanity and,
therefore, to serve Christ who leads mankind towards the
final goal he has willed for it. Among the many desires of
mankind theology wishes to recognize and identify those
which Christ is using to draw men towards this final goal,
because it is to these desires that theology must lend its
support.

5. But a theology which is concerned to emphasize the
destiny of mankind and the meaning of history cannot avoid
facing the world in which men actually live out their lives.
Orthodox theology has therefore become — together with
Western theology — a theology of the world, returning
through this aspect to the tradition of the Eastern Fathers
themselves who had a vision of the cosmos recapitulated
in God.

From this point of view the most important problem for
the Orthodox theology of tomorrow will be to reconcile the
cosmic vision of the Fathers with a vision which grows out
of the results of the natural sciences. The universal technology born of the progress of the natural sciences shows us
that man through his science is not merely the passive specta-
tor of the causal processes of the cosmos, but can give shape
to these processes actively. At every stage man is able to
choose among numberless ways of combining natural forces
and substances and managing their causality. The human
spirit has wide possibilities of giving form to nature. For nature has shown itself to be extremely plastic and contingent
in its relations with the human spirit. It is a field in which
human liberty has limitless possibilities for a complex and
varied activity. The world is presented to man not as a closed
and determined system, but as a constant and infinitely varied
appeal to human freedom. The rational character of the
cosmos or, in other words, the causality of nature, can be used
to serve any number of ends conceived and chosen by the
human spirit. Still more, we can say that nature cries out to be
used in the service of certain ends which man chooses. The

meaning of nature is fulfilled by the use which man makes of it in pursuing the ends he has chosen. We might say that God who created both man and nature proposes certain ends to man through nature, certain rational goals of a higher kind, so that from among the many possible ends open to his choice he may choose to fulfill and to develop these higher ones.

The theology of the world must make clear the positive meaning of the world which God created for the use of man and for his spiritual growth into God. It is called upon to discern the true prophetic sense of the world, and of man's activity in the world. It is called upon to give to the man of today the consciousness of his own real superiority in the face of technology, just as the Gospel and the Fathers once gave man this consciousness of his own superiority in the face of nature. It is called upon to deliver man from the feeling that he is crushed by technology, just as the Gospel and the teaching of the Fathers delivered him from the feeling that he was at the discretion of certain capricious spiritual beings who made use of nature in an arbitrary way. The theology of the world must help man affirm his sovereignty even in the face of technology, just as the Gospel and the teaching of the Fathers helped him to affirm himself before nature, thus, in fact, giving birth to the sciences and to technology. Man must follow his higher ends even in his use of technology, for technology exists for the sake of man, not man for the sake of technology. Moreover it is a fact that the danger of his being enslaved, dehumanized, or even destroyed by technology is much more serious than the former danger of his being enslaved and destroyed by nature. In the face of modern technology mankind experiences more acutely than ever before the alternative in which he has been placed by his Creator: "I have set before you life and death, blessing and curse; therefore choose life, that you and your descendants may live." (Deut. 30:19)

This demonstrates that we cannot understand nature and the meaning of science and technology without recognizing a higher human destiny, the calling of man to find his fulfillment in God.

The theology of today and tomorrow can no longer remain

an individualist or psychologist theology preoccupied exclusively with the inner motives and needs of the soul, nor
can it be a strictly confessional theology, nor one which sees
the Church as something hermetically sealed off from the
world. It must be a theology which perceives the cosmic dimension and the complexities of the whole of humanity; in this
way it will keep the Church herself open to such a vision.
Theology today must remain open to embrace both humanity
and the cosmos; it must take into account both the aspirations
of all mankind and the results of modern science and technology. Nevertheless, it must not substitute for its own proper
task any of the particular pursuits of contemporary man,
whether science, technology, production, or any political
system or social organization.

The task of theology is to fill all these activities and institutions with the consciousness of certain ultimate meanings
now manifest at the spiritual, scientific, technical, and social
level peculiar to the man of today. The role of theology in our
day is to give men a supreme light for all aspects of their lives,
a final consolation, a firm trust that their activities do have an
ultimate sense; its purpose is to urge men to engage themselves wholeheartedly in these activities convinced that they
are working to fulfill the plan of God who calls the whole of
creation towards its final goal. The theology of tomorrow must
be open to the whole historical and cosmic reality, but at the
same time it must be spiritual. It must help all Christians to
achieve a new spirituality, a spirituality proportional both
to the cosmic dimensions of science and technology, and to
the universal human community, a spirituality which has
already begun to spring up before our eyes.

Notes

NOTES TO CHAPTER I

[1] "The Ecumenical Situation," a paper read at the Fourth World Conference of the Faith and Order Commission in Montreal on 12 July 1963, and published in *Ecumenical Review* 16 (1963-1964) 1-13. The citation is found on page 9. In the report of the Second Section of the same Conference dealing with "Scripture, Tradition and the Traditions," we read: "It is clear that many of our problems of communication have arisen from the inadequate understanding of the life and history of the Eastern Churches to be found even among scholars in the West, and vice-versa. Here again is an area in which we would recommend further study, e.g. of the problem of the Filioque, its origin and consequences." *The Fourth World Conference on Faith and Order. Montreal 1963. Faith and Order Paper No. 42,* London 1964, p. 56. Moreover, Dr. Lukas Vischer at the meeting of the Faith and Order Commission held at Aarhus in August 1964 in a paper entitled "The Faith and Order Movement at the Beginning of a New Period," asks: "How are we to conceive the relationship between christology and pneumatology? What are the consequences of our doctrine of the Holy Spirit for our doctrine of the Church? What must we say about the activity of the Holy Spirit in the Church?"

[2] N. Nissiotis in *Le Monde*, 6 Oct. 1964, p. 10, said among other criticisms of the schema *De Ecclesia* and of the debates which surrounded it, that "it betrays a weakness with respect to the place of the Holy Spirit in the conciliar theology. It seems to me that the Holy Spirit as Paraclete completes the work of Christ who founded the Church on the day of Pentecost." Olivier Clément derives the exaggerated Catholic institutionalism from the *filioque* in an article "Ecclésiologie orthodoxe et dialogue oecuménique," *Contacts* 15(1963) nr. 42, pp. 92, 103-106. Elsewhere, "Vers un dialogue avec le catholicisme," *Contacts* 16(1964) nr. 45, pp. 17-34, Clément gives as a sign of the spirit of renewal the fact that "the best Catholic theologians have begun to be aware of problems of trinitarian and pneumatological theology which can lead them to a 'liturgical renewal'." He quotes in this context these words of L. Bouyer: "... the East, always preferring to emphasize the Persons of the Trinity rather than the abstract nature in their view of the Trinity, tended to look upon the *filioque* as an indication of the Latins' imperfect appreciation of the personal role of the Spirit. The answer of many a mediaeval theologian in the West, which was designed to mollify their scruples, namely, that the Spirit proceeds from the Father and the Son as from one sole principle (*tamquam ab uno principio*), seems rather to have aggravated them by appearing to be a supplementary indication of an imperfect personal distinction between the Father and the Son himself. Therefore, it would be

better to say, according to the ancient and beautiful formula of Pope Dionysius (in his letter to his namesake of Alexandria, in the 3rd century) that the Spirit proceeds from the Father in the Son, and returns with Him to the Father." (*Dictionary of Theology*, NY 1965, p. 211).

[3] "Is the Vatican Council Really Ecumenical?" *Ecumenical Review* 16(1964) 365.

[4] Published in *Russie et Chrétienté*, 4th series, 2nd year, 1950 nr. 3-4, pp. 123-244.

[5] In the study "How to Solve the Problem of the *Filioque?*" (in Russian) *Messager de l'Exarcat du Patriarche Russe en Europe*, 1955 nr. 24, pp. 259-291.

[6] Georgius Cyprius, *Expositio Fidei Contra Veccum* 3, *PG* 142, 239D-240A.

[7] *De Fide Orthodoxa*, 1, 12 *PG* 94, 849A-B.

[8] *Expositio* 3, *PG* 142, 240A-B.

[9] *Expositio* 4, *PG* 142, 240B-C.

[10] *Confessio, PG* 142, 250C.

[11] *Expositio* 9, *PG* 142, 242B: οὐδὲ πάλιν ὅτι προβολεὺς τοῦ Πνεύματος δι' αὐτοῦ Υἱοῦ ἐστιν ὁ Πατήρ, ἤδη καὶ δι' αὐτοῦ αἴτιός ἐστι τοῦ Πνεύματος.

[12] *Expositio* 9, *PG* 142, 242B-C.

[13] *Epistula ad imperatorem, PG* 142, 245D-246C.

[14] *Apologia, PG* 142, 262D.

[15] *Confessio, PG* 142, 251A-B.

[16] V. Rodzianko, *op. cit.*, p. 262, believes that the shining forth of the Spirit through the Son is an essential relation. Hence Gregory of Cyprus did not succeed in disproving the charge brought against the Orthodox by Catholics that the East knows of no personal relation between Spirit and Son, nor did he succeed in his attempt to throw out a solid bridge to join Orthodox and Catholic doctrine.

[17] *Apologia, PG* 142, 266D.

[18] *Apologia, PG* 142, 266D-267A.

[19] *Apud* Gregory of Cyprus, *Apologia, PG* 142, 266D.

[20] *De Processione Spiritus Sancti, PG* 142, 286A.

[21] *Cf.* the reference in *PG* 150, 833 to a work entitled *Two Apodictic Treatises Proving that the Holy Spirit Does Not Proceed from the Son but Only from the Father*. This exists in a Romanian translation, *Two Demonstrations of the Procession of the Holy Spirit, of St. Gregory Palamas, Translated by Gregory, Metropolitan of Ungrovalachia*, Buzau 1832. The citation is found on pp. 80-81.

[22] *Oratio* 23, (*De Pace* 3) 8, *PG* 35,1160C-D.

[23] "Any attempt in this direction is doomed to fail should we try to draw near and capture the Dove as a reality independent from that of the Lamb. When the Spirit is examined apart from the Beloved Son, he flees and disappears; nothing as it were remains in our hands. We do not attain to the Dove except by uniting ourselves with his flight towards the Lamb and by accepting from the Dove the presence of the Lamb." "La Colombe et l'Agneau," *Contacts* 15(1963) nr. 41, p. 13. T. F. Torrance writes in his paper *"Spiritus Creator"* presented to the Patristic Study Group at Aarhus in August 1964 and published in *Verbum Caro* 23 (1969) No. 89, pp. 63-85: "It is not the Spirit which is expressed but the Word, and the Spirit is known only because he illumines us and makes us capable of understanding the Word. The Son is the only *Logos*, only *eidos* of God. [*Cf*. Athanasius, *Contra Arianos*

3.15, *PG* 26,329C-332B; *Ad Serapionem* 1.19, *PG* 26,573C-576D.]....
It is through the Son that the Spirit shines forth (*eklampei*) [*Ad Serapionem*
1.18, *PG* 26,572D-573B.] and it is in the Spirit (*en pneumati*) that God is
known." (Page 69) "The difficulty of the doctrine of the Spirit comes from
the fact that he hides himself as Spirit behind the face of the Father in the
Son and behind the heart of the Son in the Father...." (Page 82) St. Basil
also compares the relation between Son and Spirit as we know it with the
relation between the light which cannot be separated from visible objects and
these objects themselves: *De Spiritu Sancto* 26.64, *PG* 32,185A-C. "But because he is the Spirit and neither the Father nor the Son, we must keep ourselves from thinking of him according to the mode of being of the Father
or of the Son, but come to know him according to his own mode as one who
pronounces the Word and illumines the Son of the Father, creating in us
the capacity of hearing and seeing him. In his very nature the Spirit hides,
as it were, his own hypostasis from our eyes and reveals himself to us in
revealing the Father and the Son; pouring out his light on us and illuminating
our spirits so that we may know the triune God, he places us in front of
[the ultimate reality of God.]" Torrance, *"Spiritus Creator,"* p. 82.

[24] "La Colombe et l'Agneau," p. 12: "It might be said — without pressing
these philosophical terms too hard — that because the Spirit identifies with
us, though without any confusion of natures, he thereby makes himself the
subject of our life as Christians, a subject filled with yearning and aspirations,
while Jesus is the *object*, the model, the immediate goal of our striving; the
Spirit is the consciousness of prayer while Christ is its content." (1 Cor
14:14-15).

[25] *Ibid.*, p. 14: "The Spirit is not the final goal of our prayer. He is 'what
is between' us and the goal of our prayer. He is an *élan* which moves towards
the Son. He is also an *élan* moving us towards the Father but towards the
Father as found in the Son."

[26] *Ibid.*

[27] Acts 2:33; 1 Cor 12:3.

[28] *Hymns of the Divine Love* 24, 261-265.

[29] *Hymns of the Divine Love* 39, 61-63.

[30] Translated into Russian by Archimandrite Cyprian Kern, *The Anthropology of St. Gregory Palamas*, Paris 1950, p. 356: "The Spirit of the Word
is like a kind of ineffable love of the Begetter for the Word ineffably begotten. The beloved Word and Son of God, moreover, himself returns to the
Father through the Holy Spirit as love, and possesses (within himself)
the Spirit who has come forth from the Father and abides together with him
(the Son)."

[31] *Capita Physica, Theologica etc.* 36, *PG* 150,1145-A-B.

[32] *De Adoratione in Spiritu et Veritate* 9, *PG* 68,620D.

[33] *De Adoratione in Spiritu et Veritate* 9, *PG* 68,593A.

[34] I have deliberately changed the place of the word "because" and have
put it after the word "and", inasmuch as our sonship in the Spirit is not a
cause but rather a consequence of the sending of the Spirit, as St. Paul says in
Rom 8:14 and as can also be seen in Gal 4:7.

[35] These addresses of Joseph Bryennios exist in a Romanian translation
published by Metropolitan Gregory of Ungrovalachia, *Twenty-Two Lectures
on the Procession of the Holy Spirit*, Buzau 1832. The text is followed by

three graphs which Bryennios himself provided to illustrate the scheme of Hierotheos.

[36] Bryennios, *op. cit.*, p. 344.
[37] *Ibid.*
[38] *Ibid.*
[39] *Ibid.*, p. 345.
[40] *Ibid.*, pp. 345-346.
[41] *Selecta in Psalmos* 23,1 *PG* 12,1265B.
[42] *Ambigua, PG* 91,1193C-1196C.
[43] Approved report of the Third Section dealing with "The Redemptive Work of Christ and the Ministry of His Church," *The Fourth World Conference on Faith and Order. Montreal 1963. Faith and Order Paper No. 42,* London 1964, p. 64.
[44] *Ibid.*, pp. 64-65.
[45] Torrance, "*Spiritus Creator*," pp. 82-83.
[46] Torrance, "*Spiritus Creator*," pp. 83-84.

NOTES TO CHAPTER II

[1] "Report on the Second Vatican Council," *Ecumenical Review* 18(1966) 190-206.
[2] Nissiotis, *op. cit.*, pp. 199-201.
[3] *Ibid.*, p. 201.
[4] *Ibid.*, pp. 201-202.
[5] *Ibid.*, p. 203.
[6] *Ibid.*, pp. 204-205.
[7] *Ibid.*, pp. 203-204.
[8] *Ibid.*, p. 204.
[9] *Ibid.*, p. 191.
[10] *Ibid.*, p. 192.
[11] Nissiotis' statement that the principal role assigned to the Holy Spirit in the Roman Catholic Church is that of keeping order and equilibrium in the Church is confirmed by Benvenuto Matteucci, "Novità o integrazioni," *L'Osservatore Romano*, 23 March 1966.
[12] Nissiotis, *op. cit.*, pp. 193-194.
[13] *Ibid.*, p. 194. The thesis that the Church in fact came into being through the cross before the descent of the Holy Spirit suggests the western spirit of christomonism together with an exclusive understanding of salvation as the satisfaction or atonement achieved by Christ through his sacrifice on the cross. But in the biblical and patristic conception, salvation is the ontological reestablishment of creation through the cross, resurrection and union of the risen and exalted Christ with the rest of men, and through the sending of the Holy Spirit from himself to them. In this teaching the Church is more than just a visible or invisible society standing on the legal foundation of a redressed balance between the offence man committed against God and the satisfaction or expiation offered for it.
[14] *Ibid.*, pp. 194-195.
[15] *Ibid.*, p. 195.

[16] *Ibid.*

[17] In the Romanian text of the Nicene-Constantinopolitan Creed the phrase "one, holy, catholic and apostolic Church" reads: "una, sfinta, *soborniceasca* si apostoleasca Biserica". [Tr. note.]

[18] "The Doctrine of Infallibility at the First and Second Vatican Councils," *Ortodoxia* 17(1965) 459-492 [in Romanian].

[19] *In Pentecosten Oratio* 41,16 *PG* 36,449C.

[20] *Encomium in S. Stephanum, PG* 46,704D-705A.

[21] *Sancti Hermae Pastor, Sim.* 9, *PG* 2,979-1010. Ed. K. Lake, *Apostolic Fathers,* vol. 2, London 1924, pp. 216-296.

[22] *In Pentecosten Oratio* 41,16 *PG* 36,449C.

[23] *De Spiritu Sancto* 16, *PG* 32,140D-141A.

[24] *Ibid.,* 9, *PG* 32,108C.

[25] *Ibid.,* 26, *PG* 32,181A-B.

[26] *Ibid.,* 26, *PG* 32,181B-C.

[27] *De Sancta Pentecoste Homilia* 2, *PG* 50,467-468.

[28] *In Epist. I ad Corinthios Homilia* 30,3 *PG* 61,253.

[29] *Ibid.*

[30] *Ibid.*

[31] *Ibid.*

[32] *In Epist. I ad Corinthios Homilia* 31,3 *PG* 61,260.

[33] *In Epist. I ad Corinthios Homilia* 30,3 *PG* 61,253-254.

[34] *In Epist. I ad Corinthios Homilia* 30,4 *PG* 61,254.

[35] *In Epist. I ad Corinthios Homilia* 31,3 *PG* 61,261.

[36] *Ibid.*

[37] *De Spiritu Sancto* 26, *PG* 32,181C.

[38] M. Buber, "Das Problem des Menschen," *Werke.* Erster Band. Schriften zur Philosophie. Heidelberg 1962, pp. 405-406.

[39] V. Lossky, "Concerning the Third Mark of the Church: Catholicity," *One Church* 19(1965) 181-187.

[40] Lossky, *op. cit.,* p. 185.

[41] *Ibid.,* p. 186.

[42] *Ibid.,* pp. 185-186.

NOTES TO CHAPTER III

[1] "Disregarded Causes of Disunity," *The Orthodox Observer* 36(1970) nr. 599, p. 40.

[2] "The Continuity of the Church and Orthodoxy," *Sobornost* Series 5, 5(1965) p. 18.

[3] Romanian has richer resources than English in trinitarian discussion because the verb "to proceed" (a purcede) can be used both transitively and intransitively. In this particular case the juxtaposition is both elegant and very striking: *Duhul purcede, dar si Tatal il purcede.* [Tr.]

[4] P. Florensky, "Der Pfeiler und die Grundfeste der Wahrheit," in *Ostliches Christentum II. Philosophie,* Munich 1925, p. 47. Florensky here follows Pseudo-Dionysius who defines the divine being as goodness.

[5] P. Florensky, *op. cit.,* p. 35.

[6] In the formula of Chalcedon it is said of Christ that he is "of one substance with us as regards his manhood". We too therefore are of one substance among ourselves.

[7] M. Buber, "Ich werde am Du," in *Ich und Du*, Heidelberg 1977,[9] p. 18.

[8] P. Florensky, *op. cit.*, p. 62.

[9] Dionysius the Pseudo-Areopagite and Maximus the Confessor have demonstrated this unity between all things in a most extensive manner. The latter writes: "For, conformable to true reason, all things which exist after God and which have their existence from God through creation coincide in some way among themselves, though not completely. Not one existing thing, however lofty or greatly esteemed, is detached by its nature from this general relation to the one who is himself wholly free of relation, nor is any of the least honoured of existing things isolated from or outside the compass of this general and natural relation with those things of creation which are more highly esteemed. For all things which are distinguished among themselves by their own proper differences are united as *genera* by identities which are universal and common, and are together impelled towards a unity and a common identity for a certain general reason of nature." *Ambigua*, explaining the words: "Natures are renewed and God is made man." *PG* 91,1312B-C. Florensky even says that theoretical knowledge also has an ontological character: "Knowledge is a real going forth from self on the part of the one who knows, or — what amounts to the same thing — a real entering into the knower by the known, a real union between knower and known." (*Op. cit.*, p. 49).

[10] *Adversus Eunomium* 5, *PG* 29,756A.

[11] E. Kovalevsky, "Sainte Trinité," in *Cahiers de Saint Irénée*, Jan.-Feb. 1964, nr. 44, p. 3. Metropolitan Philaret has said: "When the three Persons of the Trinity contemplate themselves, we see that each rejoices in the glory of the others without turning back to his own glory. The Father in me, I in the Father, I in the Spirit, the Spirit in me, each for the other." In E. Kovalevsky, "Les nombres dans la Génèse," *Cahiers de Saint Irénée*, June-July 1961, nr. 29, pp. 10-11.

[12] *Epistola I ad Serapionem*, *PG* 26,576A.

[13] *Contra Eunomium* 2,*PG* 45,493B. Ed. W. Jaeger, *Gregorii Nysseni Opera. II*, Leiden 1960, p. 337.

[14] Gregory of Nyssa, *Contra Eunomium* 8, *PG* 45,789C. Cf Basil, *Adversus Eunomium* 2, *PG* 29,593A-B. Jaeger II.205.

[15] P. Verghese, *Ecumenical Review* 15 (1962-1963) 16.

[16] Another analogy: "The object which is substance precedes the trajectory which is motion. Their dynamic circulation reveals in a specific way the encompassing space." (P. Faideau, *Cahiers de Saint Irénée*, June-July 1961, nr. 29).

[17] E. Kovalevsky, "Les nombres dans la Génèse": "Medieval philosophy — if we can appeal to the great schools of Chartres and Poitiers — often analyses the problem of the Triune. Hugh of St. Victor proposes an admirable definition of the One: the One, he says, is, from the moral point of view, a satisfaction, an egotism, a thing enclosed, while God on the other hand is open in some manner to love, to the mutual penetration of the one and the other and the renunciation of the one on behalf of the other. The two is already the love of a pair. It still contains imperfections because when one loves the other at bottom he is loving himself. The other is a reflection of himself. One does not love himself, two love each other. But true, ecstatic, sacrificial,

radiant and open charity, charity which is without restriction and which is
fruitful through love, only appears in fact where there are three." (p. 10).
"As long as we remain in the One we are on the metaphysical beach, in the
spiritual initiation — mystical or mystagogical — which precedes revelation.
The progress which we make ourselves cannot achieve revelation which is a
free gift, a grace." (p. 11).

[18] In *Little Eyolf* Henrik Ibsen has portrayed this selfish, unhealthy and
uncertain love of a wife for her husband, a love jealous even of the husband's
love for their own chilld.

[19] P. Florensky, *op. cit.*, p. 36.

[20] *Quaestiones ad Thalassium* 13, *PG* 90,296B-C.

[21] *Ibid.*, 28, *PG* 90,361C.

[22] John Damascene calls the Father "the abyss of Being", and he calls the
"Mind" "the abyss of Reason". *De Fide Orthodoxa* 1,12, *PG* 94,848C-D.

[23] *Twenty-Two Lectures on the Procession of the Holy Spirit*, Buzau 1832,
p. 344.

[24] M. Lot-Borodine, "La doctrine de la déification dans l'Eglise Grecque
jusqu'au XIᵉ siècle," *Revue de l'histoire des religions* 107(1933) p. 46.
Maximus the Confessor, *Capitum de Charitate Centuria* I.10, 12, 24, 31, 32,
47 *PG* 90,964A-969B.

[25] T. F. Torrance in his paper *"Spiritus Creator"* presented to the Patristic
Study Group at Aarhus in August 1964 and published in *Verbum Caro* 23
(1969) No. 89, pp. 63-85 gives the patristic thought in the following way:
"It is not the Spirit which is expressed but the Word, and the Spirit is known
only because he illumines us and makes us capable of understanding the Word.
The Son is the only *Logos*, only *eidos* of God. [*Cf.* Athanasius, *Contra Arianos* 3.15, *PG* 26,329C-332B; *Ad Serapionem* 1.19, *PG* 26,573C-576D.]....
It is through the Son that the Spirit shines forth (*eklampei*) [*Ad Serapionem*
1,18, *PG* 26,572D-573B.] and it is in the Spirit (*en pneumati*) that God is
known." (Page 69) St. Basil also compares the relation between Son and
Spirit as we know it with the relation between the light which cannot be
separated from visible objects and these objects themselves (*De Spiritu Sancto*
26, 64, *PG* 32,185A-C). Elsewhere we read: "Any attempt in this direction
is doomed to fail should we try to draw near and capture the Dove as a
reality independent from that of the Lamb. When the Spirit is examined apart
from the Beloved Son, he flees and disappears... We do not attain to the
Dove except by uniting ourselves with his flight towards the Lamb and by
accepting from the Dove the presence of the Lamb." ("La Colombe et l'Agneau," *Contacts*, 15(1963) nr. 41, p. 13).

[26] E. Kovalevsky, "Sainte Trinité," p. 3: "The Spirit cannot be the love
of the Father and of the Son: if the Spirit is the love of the Father and of the
Son he is no longer a Person but a nature. Nevertheless it can be confessed
that the Spirit is the bearer of the reciprocal love between Father and Son."

[27] *Twenty-Two Lectures on the Procession of the Holy Spirit*, pp. 80-81.

[28] *De Fide Orthodoxa* 1,13, *PG* 94,856B.

[29] *Oratio* 23, (*De Pace* 3) 8, *PG* 35,1160C.

[30] In the Russian translation of Archimandrite Cyprian Kern, *The Anthropology of St. Gregory Palamas*, Paris 1950, p. 356 the sentence is as
follows: "The beloved Word and Son of God, moreover, himself returns to
the Father through the Holy Spirit as love, and possesses (within himself)

the Spirit who has come forth from the Father and abides together with him
(the Son)."

[31] *Capita Physica, Theologica etc.* 36, *PG* 150,1145A-B.

[32] *Twenty-Two Lectures on the Procession of the Holy Spirit*, p. 346.

[33] P. Sherrard, *The Greek East and the Latin West*, London 1959, pp. 85-86
cited by D. W. Allen and A. M. Allchin, "Primacy and Collegiality: An
Anglican View," *Journal of Ecumenical Studies* 2(1965) p. 67.

NOTES TO CHAPTER IV

[1] A. Malet provides a sound exposition of Bultmann's theology in *The
Thought of Rudolph Bultmann*, Shannon 1969. For critical interpretations
see: J. Moltmann, "The Theology of the Transcendental Subjectivity," in
Theology of Hope, London 1967, pp. 58-69 and A. Richardson, "The Existentialist Theology," in *The Bible in the Age of Science*, Philadelphia 1961,
pp. 100-121.

[2] J. A. T. Robinson, *Honest to God*, London 1963, pp. 45-63. We should
also mention here the American Lutheran theologians (Altizer, van Buren,
Hamilton, Vahanian) grouped in the "Death of God" movement which
proposes a Christianity without God. These theologians have all studied in
Germany and reflect the influence of the Bultmannian school.

[3] *Cf.* reports in the *Ecumenical Review* 19(1967) 461-469 and 18(1966)
150-189 especially pp. 154-157.

[4] The Protestant theologian Reinhard Slenczka has demonstrated the in-
consistency of the various theories which deny the divinity or even the
historicity of Christ in *Geschichtlichkeit und Personsein Jesu Christi*, Göttingen
1967.

[5] *Cf.* Richardson, *op. cit.*, pp. 122-141, "The Heilsgeschichte Theology".
Richardson mentions among the Anglican leaders of this line of thought
especially G. E. Wright of Harvard, *God Who Acts*. Studies in Biblical Theology No. 8, London/Chicago 1952. Another representative of this same
school is Oscar Cullmann.

[6] The work *Adversus Macedonianos* of Gregory of Nyssa, PG 45,1301-
1333, presents the three divine Persons as a single energy/activity which
begins from the Father, passes through the Son and is fulfilled in the Holy
Spirit. *Cf.* especially 13, PG 45,1316D-1317B.

[7] J. Moltmann, *op. cit.*, p. 67.

[8] *Ibid.*

[9] These theologians speak consequently of a "theology of images". *Cf.*
Richardson, *op. cit.*, pp. 142-163.

[10] *Antirrheticus Liber Adversus Eusebium et Epiphaniden, Spicilegium
Solesmense IV*, ed. J. B. Pitra, Paris 1858, pp. 292-380, *cf.* especially p. 314.

[11] Richardson, *op. cit.*, p. 163: "The chief question in this field, with which
theologians must occupy themselves in the immediate future, is that of the
relation of the images to the biblical conception of the Word. Scripture says
that the *Logos*, not the *eikon* became flesh, and that the Word of the Lord,
not the image, came to the prophets; Christian theology is a theology of the
Word. When we understand the priority of the Word over the images, we

shall see the matter in its right perspective. The work of clarification here is likely to occupy us for a long time to come."

[12] *A Rebirth of Images. The Making of St. John's Apocalypse*, Glasgow 1941, p. 20. It would be interesting to make a comparison between this recognition of the revelatory function of images and the questioning of any revelatory value in them which characterizes the thought of the Romanian writer Lucian Blaga, especially in his *Genesis of Metaphor.*

[13] St. Nicephorus the Confessor declares that the icon can convey the Son of God because it conveys the "human image" which has become proper to his hypostasis. But this means that the Son of God who has his own divine image and takes on the "image of a slave" is himself reflected in the latter. "Just as, therefore, he has made the passions of the body his own through economy, and just as the body is called the body of God the Word, so the image and likeness of the most holy body are referred to him as something proper." (*Contra Constantinum Copronymum Antirrheticus* 1,47 *PG* 100,324A) Or: "If, therefore, they accept that incorporeal things such as an angel or the soul which do not have bodies can nevertheless be pictured, how is it that they do not wish to think that the incarnate Christ who took on the image and the form of man ... can be pictured, that is, in paintings and icons?" (*Antirrheticus* 2,17 *PG* 100,365A-B). And even more clearly: "Form (μορφὴν) and being are according to the Fathers the same thing, and both have the same meaning. ... Thus it is the Fathers' view that through the image the Son truly assumed human nature as well and became a complete man, body and soul. Just as through the image of God he is God completely, so through the 'form of a slave' he is man completely." (*Contra Eunomium* 16, Pitra I.398, Paris 1852).

But there does exist a relation between the "image of God" in which the Son of God was found and the "form of a slave" which he took upon himself. His divine image is a model for the form of a slave. Christ assumed what was in accordance with his divine image, that is, the image of the divine type (τὸ κατ᾽ εἰκόνα) as the Fathers say.

All men in fact are "in the divine image". But this image which has been weakened through sin is re-established in the first instance and most perfectly in Christ, because it is filled with the Godhead both by reason of its origin and also because the Son of God himself has become the bearer of this image.

A Russian theologian wants to correct the Fathers and say that the "image" in Christ does not refer to the nature but to the Person. Thus there are not two "images" in Christ, only one. But the one, because it is one, is the hypostasis. But whose image then is the total Christ? He cannot be the image of the Godhead, if the image is also divine. Or, if the human element in Christ is itself the divine pattern, is there not introduced here a monophysitism *sui generis*? More precisely, he says that God has no image at all in his quality as infinite, and that his proper image is humanity. But even if this were the case, the humanity of Christ is an image of the Godhead. (Икона и Иконопочитание, S. Bulgakov, Paris 1931, pp. 95-96).

[14] Farrer says: "The seer (Daniel) sees himself in, as it were, the fifth 'day' of the world's history, the day of the monsters which 'come up out of the great sea', always, to the Semitic mind, the symbols of chaotic and godless violence. But he knows that their time is appointed, and the day will come when the Ancient of Days will establish the everlasting dominion of the Son of Man 'over the fishes of the sea and the birds of the heaven and all

cattle, over all the earth and all that crawl the earth' (Gen 1:28). Of this
dominion there can be no end, for the Son of Man is the last work of God.
He is not spawned either out of the sea or out of the land, but is especially
the creature of heavenly God, made in his image and likeness: so whereas the
beasts come up out of the sea, the Son of Man comes with the clouds of
heaven. Daniel applies his parable to the history of mankind. There is the
age in which the image of Leviathan reigns; the age is coming when the image
of Adam will reign, and Adam is the image of God.... For the Christian,
Christ is primarily the image of Adam, and Christians derivatively his members." (Op. cit., p. 52).

[15] Farrer, op. cit., pp. 18-22.

[16] In Defence of the Holy Hesychasts. Third Treatise of the Second Series.
Codex Coislinianus 100, ff.187v and 188r. The text is printed in J. Meyendorff, Grégoire Palamas. Défense des saints hésychasts. Spicilegium Sacrum
Lovaniense. Etudes et Documents 31. Louvain 1959, vol. 2, pp. 501 and 503.
Cf. also ff.190v and 191r, Meyendorff, p. 519: "When Scripture says therefore
that the prophet was initiated through contemplation or that an angel raised
him up from contemplation to initiation, it does not say that he took him
away from contemplation, but that from contemplation the prophet learned
what he had not known before as from a cause and source of knowledge, and
that the angel, being an angel and therefore understanding better what was
contained in contemplation, explained it to the prophet and raised him up
from ignorance to understanding. The ignorance from which he was removed
is inferior to the understanding to which he was raised. But how is this vision
itself, which gave the seer knowledge, and which in imitation of God possesses this knowledge implicitly in itself, not better than the knowledge which
it offers?"

[17] F.188v; Meyendorff, 2.503. Cf. De Mystica Theologia 1,1 PG 3,997A-B.

[18] Ibid. Cf. Gregory of Nyssa, De Vita Moysis 1,58 PG 44,321A.

[19] F.189v; Meyendorff, 2.511 Cf. In Isaiam. Prooemium, PG 30,124C,
125C.

[20] F.190r; Meyendorff, 2.513, 515. Cf. De Coelesti Hierarchia 8,1 PG
3,237C.

[21] F.190r; Meyendorff, 2.515. Cf. Maximus the Confessor, Cent. Gnost.
2,82 PG 90,1164A reproducing Mark the Hermit, De Temperantia 24, PG
65,1064B.

[22] F.190v; Meyendorff, 2.517.

[23] Ibid. Cf. Ps 33:15.

[24] F.182v; Meyendorff, 2.469.

[25] M. Sora, "On Poetic Meaning: A Song for Two Violins," Familia Dec.
1967, pp. 12-13 [in Romanian].

[26] Dogmatics. Vol. III. The Christian Doctrine of the Church, Faith and
the Consummation. London 1962, pp. 404-406.

NOTES TO CHAPTER V

[1] Revelation Through Acts, Words and Images," Ortodoxia 20 (1968)
347-377 [in Romanian; =Chapter 4, above].

[2] V. Zimmerli, "Verheissung und Erfüllung," in *Probleme der alttestamentlichen Hermeneutik*, Kaiser-Verlag 1960², p. 92.

[3] In this context see the valuable study of I. V. Georgescu, "My Covenant Is A Covenant Of Life And Peace," *Biserica Ortodoxa Romana* 82(1964) 456-495 [in Romanian].

[4] Georgescu, *op. cit.*, p. 494.

[5] Maximus the Confessor, *Capita Gnostica* 2,28 *PG* 90,1137B-C.

[6] *Ibid.*, 1,89.93 *PG* 90,1120C; 1121A-B.

[7] Georgescu, *op. cit. passim*.

[8] J. B. Metz, "L'Eglise et le monde," in *Théologie d'aujourd'hui et de demain*, Paris 1967, p. 146.

[9] *Ibid.*

[10] J. Moltmann, *Theology of Hope*, London 1967: "The divine word in Christ is new, it not only reveals anew the one eschatological salvation, but in addition also guarantees the realizing of that salvation." (p. 148).

[11] At the ecumenical meeting between professors of the Orthodox and Protestant theological institutes in Romania which took place at Cluj in May of 1969 on the theme "The Active Meaning of Hope", the Protestant theologians Binder and Lengyel themselves stressed the fact that we must also speak of a "present" of God in the Church and in history for otherwise hope itself would become an act of man and not of God. It was established that Moltmann's position which lays a well-nigh exclusive emphasis on the "past" of Christ as the one who rose from the dead and on the "future" of Christ as the one who will raise us up also, is now considered more or less out of date. Another Protestant theologian writes: "Hope does not stand in itself. The action of God is in an excellent sense its pre-supposition (Voraussetzung)." Hence its foundations are laid by the very achievement of this action, or by speaking the word which promises. G. Sauter, *Zukunft und Verheissung: Das Problem der Zukunft in der gegenwärtigen theologischen und philosophischen Discussion*, Zurich 1965, p. 53. Or again: "In his promise God directs our gaze towards the fullness of the fulfillment which is always seen in anticipation where he deals with us." *Ibid.*, p. 367.

[12] K. R. Dunstan-Jones, "Creation and Fall," in *Mirfield Essays in Christian Belief*, London 1963², p. 130.

[13] K. Rahner, "Zur Theologie der Hoffnung," in *Internationale Dialog Zeitschrift* 1(1968) 75. There seems to be a certain difference in the way in which Rahner understands these "exoduses" when he writes: "For precisely this radical departure from self (von-sich-Weg) towards God, the one whom no man has at his disposition, founds our future absolutely in that grace of God which had its unique appearance in the crucified Christ who gave himself up so radically to the disposition of God." (*Op. cit.*, p. 79) We know the way in which we can win God — the Kingdom of Heaven is taken by force: Matt 11:12. Abraham and Jacob did not let go of God until he fulfilled their requests. We cannot say absolutely of God that he cannot be won, but he is won by other methods.

[14] Georgescu, *op. cit.*, p. 492.

[15] *Quaestiones ad Thalassium* 59, *PG* 90,613C: "At the very moment when he began his existence man cast his own origin behind him through disobedience, and since that time he can no longer seek what lies behind him. And inasmuch as origin naturally circumscribes the movement of what begins

from it, it has also rightly been called the final goal in which, as though in a cause, the motion of that which moves finds its end."

[16] G. Sauter, op. cit., cf. pp. 165-177.

[17] The notion of two "ages" (aeons) which make up the world beginning from the time of Christ is underlined by N. Afanassieff in his article " 'Le monde' dans L'Ecriture Sainte," Irénikon 42(1969) 6-32. Although the idea is true in principle, we think that Afanassieff has not brought out all the complexity of the relations between the two "ages" but has remained content with a too-rigid presentation of the contradiction between them. He sees no influence of the new age upon the old, of Christ and Christianity upon the world. Yet such an influence surely exists, even if it is not always in the moral and religious order. And the world influenced by Christianity exerts its own influence in turn upon Christianity. In the conception of Afanassieff Christians are in the world only to convert men directly, totally and personally to Christ. Otherwise their presence in the world would have no effect upon it and therefore no purpose. According to this conception history has no meaning. But it is our view that the world, even when considered as a whole, is being led towards Christ and that men — if not all of them at least some of them — are won for Christ and for an activity on behalf of men in the historical and social order. Here is in part what Afanassieff says: "But in the sense given it by the Church 'aeon' indicates *a new state of the world.* This new age/aeon to which the Church belongs remains hidden. *In the same way the changes which have been produced in the world and which are connected with the permanence of the new aeon in the world also remain hidden.* The Church awaits the revelation of the glory of Christ which will be the full realization of the new aeon. This aeon is anticipated by the Church. But at the same time it will entail the destruction of the former aeon." (p. 16).

If the new age is wholly hidden, we may wonder how it can be represented by the Church which is a reality visible in history and having an activity with repercussions upon history. The Saviour likened the Kingdom of Heaven to yeast hidden in a quantity of meal and meant to leaven the whole batch (Matt 13:33). However hidden in the world the Kingdom of Heaven may be, it makes its effects known. In another place Christ compared the Kingdom to the seed which, though hidden in the ground, yields a visible fruit; even while its fruit is still growing in the field, it activates the powers of the earth (Mk 4:26-29). And even the sowing of the tares and the crop they produced were provoked by the sowing of the good seed (Matt 13:24-30).

[18] J. Moltmann, op. cit., p. 329.

NOTES TO CHAPTER VI

[1] Cf. Ludwig Ott, *Fundamentals of Catholic Dogma*, St. Louis 1964, pp. 186-190.

[2] Cf. *Teologia Dogmatica si Simbolica*, II, Bucharest 1958, pp. 616-657. The present study represents a new handling of the same subject matter.

[3] *Versöhnung, das deutsch-russische Gespräch über das christliche Verständnis der Versöhnung*, Wittenburg 1967.

⁴ *Oratio* 45,22 *PG* 36,653B and *Oratio* 45,29 *PG* 36,664A.

⁵ Vladimir Lossky, "Rédemption et déification," in *A l'image et à la ressemblance de Dieu*, Paris 1967, p. 100.

⁶ *Versöhnung*, p. 135 citing Luther *WA* 26,37: "Der Friede des Gewissens ist so die erste Frucht der Versöhnung, und zwar das gute Gewissen vor Gott. Darauf kommt es an, dass Christus 'uns gegen Gott sicher und unser Gewissen zufrieden macht.' "

⁷ *Versöhnung*, p.131: "Dieser Friede kraft der Versöhnungstat Christi schon im Verborgenen Wirklichkeit ist und sich in der Gemeinde Christi und durch sie für die Welt auswirkt."

⁸ *Contra Jacobitas* 52, *PG* 94,1464A.

⁹ *Disputatio cum Pyrrho*, *PG* 91,308C-310A. See also Jean Meyendorff, *Christ in Eastern Christian Thought*, Washington/Cleveland 1969, pp. 113-114.

¹⁰ *De Adoratione in Spiritu et Veritate* 9, *PG* 68,620D.

¹¹ *De Adoratione in Spiritu et Veritate* 10, *PG* 68,704C.

¹² *Homilia 16 de Dispensatione Incarnationis*, *PG* 151,193A.

¹³ Nicholas Cabasilas speaks of the Father finding the image of the Son in our faces and recognizing in us the members of the Only Begotten One. *De Vita in Christo* 4, *PG* 150,600B.

¹⁴ *Expositio in Orationis Dominicae*, *PG* 90,877D.

¹⁵ *Ibid.*, *PG* 90,901C.

¹⁶ *Opuscula Theologica et Polemica*, *PG* 91,77A-80A.

¹⁷ *Expositio in Orationis Dominicae*, *PG* 90,889B.

¹⁸ *De Incarnatione* 13, *PG* 25,120B. ET: A Religious of C.S.M.V., *St. Athanasius On The Incarnation*, London 1953², p. 41.

¹⁹ Maximus the Confessor, *Opuscula Theologica et Polemica*, *PG* 91,77A-80A.

²⁰ Athanasius, *De Incarnatione* 17, *PG* 25,125A-B. ET 45.

²¹ Meyendorff, *op. cit.*, p. 64 and *cf.* pp. 97-98.

²² *Ibid.*, p. 55.

²³ Karl Rahner, "Considérations générales sur la christologie," in *Problèmes actuels de christologie*, H. Bouëssé ed., Bruges 1965, p. 21.

²⁴ *De Incarnatione* 15, *PG* 25,121C-D. ET 43.

²⁵ *Ibid.*, 13, *PG* 25,120B. ET 41.

²⁶ Meyendorff, *op. cit.*, pp. 163-166.

²⁷ Athanasius, *De Incarnatione* 44, *PG* 25,173B-C. ET 80.

²⁸ *Ibid.*, 16, *PG* 25,124B-D. ET 44.

²⁹ Cyril of Alexandria, *De Adoratione in Spiritu et Veritate* 15, *PG* 68, 972D-973A.

³⁰ *Ibid.*, *PG* 68,973A-B.

³¹ *De Vita in Christo* 2, *PG* 150,541B.

³² Maximus the Confessor, *Ad Thalassium* 21, *PG* 90,312B-316D.

³³ *De Vita in Christo* 2, *PG* 150,537B.

³⁴ *De Viata in Hristos*, Sibiu 1946, p. 138.

³⁵ *Oratio* 45, 22, *PG* 36,653B.

³⁶ Athanasius, *De Incarnatione* 20, *PG* 25,132B. ET 49.

³⁷ *Ibid.*, 29, *PG* 25,145D. ET 60.

³⁸ Meyendorff, *op. cit.*, pp. 105-106.

³⁹ *De Incarnatione* 25, *PG* 25,140B-C. ET 55-56.

⁴⁰ *Ibid.*, 22 *PG* 25,136A. ET 52.

[41] Symeon the New Theologian, *Capita Practica et Theologica* 113-114, *PG* 120,664C-665A.

[42] *Paterikon*. Cf. *Apophthegmata Patrum*, Sisoes 14, *PG* 65,396B-C.

[43] *Apophthegmata Patrum*, Anthony, *PG* 65,77B.

[44] *Capita Practica et Theologica* 116, *PG* 120,665A-B.

[45] I have taken this idea from a work found in the Athanasian corpus, *Sermo in Sanctum Pascha, PG* 28,1077A-C.

[46] *De Vita in Christo* 4, *PG* 150,592A.